D1288898

THE WITHERED BRANCH

D. S. SAVAGE

THE
WITHERED BRANCH

Six Studies in the Modern Novel

LONDON
Eyre & Spottiswoode

This book, first published in 1950, is printed in Great Britain for Eyre & Spottiswoode (Publishers) Ltd., 15 Bedford Street, London, W.C.2, by The Stanhope Press, Ltd., Rochester, Kent

Contents

	Page
Preface	9
ERNEST HEMINGWAY	23
E. M. FORSTER	44
VIRGINIA WOOLF	70
MARGIAD EVANS	106
ALDOUS HUXLEY	129
JAMES JOYCE	156
Notes	201
Index	205

Acknowledgment

All but the last of the studies in this book, which were written over the period from 1944 to 1948, have appeared severally – in some cases in a shortened form – in the following publications: *Now, Focus, Humanitas, The New Spirit,* and *Writers of To-day.* Especially am I indebted to Mr. George Woodcock and to Dr. B. Rajan for their consistent editorial encouragement of work of a critical temper which, in the present constitution of the world of letters, could not expect wide agreement or acceptance.

D. S. S.

THE WITHERED BRANCH

Wisdom is common to all things. Those who speak with intelligence must hold fast to the common as a city holds fast to its law, and even more strongly. For all human laws are fed by one thing, the divine. It prevails as much as it will, and suffices for all things with something to spare.   HERAKLEITOS

PREFACE

TRUTH AND THE ART OF THE NOVEL

'In the beginning was the Word . . .'

TOLSTOY, who has been well described as the most truth-loving writer in Russian literature, wrote in later life a pamphlet entitled *Bethink Yourselves!* in which he called on all his readers to halt in whatever they were doing, to detach themselves from whatever functional position they held in society, and seriously and radically to ask themselves *who* they were, *what* they were doing, and whether what they were doing was in conformity with their ultimate destiny as human beings. The call was to change a sleeping for a waking state. Now, it is not only the general life of society which is subject to a perpetual condition of habitual automatism; this condition affects even the production and the consumption of literature, so that in this field also the necessity arises from time to time for someone to rise up and issue a similar call to *Bethink Yourselves!* and in so doing to let loose the unpredictable dynamic of *the idea* in the midst of a mass of unquestioned assumptions, fixed opinions and established reputations. Why do we read novels and what are we really doing when we indulge in that habitual recreation? What *is* a novel, and – more largely – what is *art*? I begin with these awkward questions so that the reader to whom they are unwelcome can put this book back on the shelf before he gets involved in any unpleasantness. This is a book of criticism, not a collection of literary appreciations: behind it the idea is already at its incalculable work.

THE attempt to formulate a theory of the nature of a work of art resembles the attempt to formulate a theory of the nature of a man. Everyone knows what a man is, and likewise everyone knows what a work of art is – until he comes to think about it and to investigate what others have thought, when it transpires that there are endless theories, both of the nature of man and of

9

the nature, purpose and meaning of artistic activity. These are not idle questions. Misconceptions of the nature of man may have disastrous consequences in human life, and it is the same with art. The two questions are quite closely related, and as it helps an argument to rest in the first place upon an axiom, I begin with the assertion of the close and organic dependence of art upon life: that is, upon human experience. Art is personal, being rooted in the existence of a concrete and particular individual, the artist. An artist, more particularly a literary artist, and specifically a novelist, must create out of the particular situation in which he finds himself, and to which he has been brought by the interaction of his character (and all that goes to form it) with the circumstances of his time and place. His work will bear the stamp of all these factors. Every novel has a pattern which is imposed upon it by its author's essential being – and this applies no less when the work has the quality of universality. Of all art forms the novel is the most patently personal: it is always autobiographical in its origins. Autobiography itself is merely the simplest form of fiction; the autobiographical novel, so called, is in turn the simplest form of the novel proper; but the more complex forms are no less personal in their foundations. In the simple autobiographical narrative the author presents himself to himself as the central character, in whom the action meets and has its meaning. Complexity enters first of all with dramatization, which reflects an advance in objectivity consequent upon an apprehension of the inter-personal mutuality of living. Implicit in the dramatic form is the avowal of the interdependence of all human destinies, where the meaning of the action is centred not in one character but in each severally, according to his capacity.

To begin with, the general problem which confronts the novelist is that of transmuting the chaos of experience into the order of significant form. Experience in its raw state is incommunicable: that which is communicated is never experience but a mental construct which stands in a symbolic relation to it, mediating between writer and reader, and the craft of fiction consists in discovering and presenting such a construct. Writer and reader must meet on a ground which is objective in its presence to both, and it is the novelist's technical task to prepare it. Somehow he must translate his intrinsically incommunicable experience of reality into a reversed mirror-writing which will be reflected back again, right side up, in the mind of the reader, and first of all in his own mind as his own reader. The novel, that is to say, grounded in subjectivity, aspires towards objecti-vization – not in the sense of alienation from the subjective, but of its embodiment in apprehensible form. It is objectivization of this kind which alone can set the novelist free from a helpless and inartistic inentification with his experiencing self, making possible a form of self-transcension.

What is the operative factor in this interchange, which trans-forms the raw material of human experience into art? The American critic Mark Schorer follows a familiar course, which stands in need of examination, in calling it 'technique'. In an essay entitled 'Technique as Discovery', he writes forthrightly: 'The difference between content, or experience, and achieved content, or art, is technique.' This he elaborates as follows: 'When we speak of technique . . . we speak of nearly everything. For technique is the means by which the writer's experience, which is his subject-matter, compels him to attend to it: tech-nique is the only means he has of discovering, exploring, develop-ing his subject, of conveying its meaning, and, finally, of evalu-ating it. And surely it follows that certain techniques are sharper tools than others, and will discover more: that the writer capable of the most exacting technical scrutiny of his subject-matter will produce works with the most satisfying content, works with maximum meaning.' This writer goes on to define technique as 'any selection, structure, or distortion, any form or rhythm imposed upon the world of action; by means of which . . . our apprehension of the world of action is enriched or renewed'. In accordance with this definition, he speaks of Defoe's failure, in *Moll Flanders*, to distinguish his own values from those of the heroine, as a *technical* defect: 'Because he had no adequate resources of technique to separate himself from his material, thereby to discover and define the meanings of his material, his contribution is not to fiction but to the history of fiction, and to social history.' Discussing *Sons and Lovers*, he points to D. H. Lawrence's inability to separate himself as a writer from his experiential material – to sufficiently objectify his situation for

the purposes of art; and this again he describes as a technical
failure. 'All this, and the character of a whole career, would
have been altered if Lawrence had allowed his technique to
discover the fullest meaning of his subject.'

Clearly, in this dizzy elevation of 'technique', something has
been left out of account. Misgiving is roused in the first place by
the very inclusiveness of 'technique' as the word is here used;
for something which means nearly everything may come
frighteningly close to meaning almost nothing. The error, however, is so common that it indicates the importance of making a
clear distinction between technique and a much more primary
and fundamental activity, which I propose to call *vision*. In
order to create the artistic entity which shall adequately objectify his subjectivity, the novelist must, of course, employ a
technique, but his job will be not to make use of some impersonal instrument lying indifferently to hand, but to discover the
method which is exactly suited to himself and to his subject, and
this means in practice that he must *create* a technique for his
always unique and particular purpose. As his vision penetrates
the substance of his experience and subjects it to itself, it projects the *idea* of the form of the finished work, and the rest is a
matter of experimental verification, of discovery and elimination in the chosen medium. No writer can possess himself of a
technique for a creative purpose except through an act of
imagination, and this applies even when a technique is apparently borrowed from another writer. Seen in this light, it would
appear that Lawrence's difficulty lay on a far profounder level
than that of technique; it was an interior, personal one – as
common sense readily perceives. *Sons and Lovers* is an imperfect
work of art not, at bottom, because of a defect of technique, but
because of a failure of artistic imagination. Undoubtedly this
deep defect is manifested in the structure and texture of the
work, but to nominate it a technical fault is implicitly to deny
depth to the novel and to misunderstand its nature.

So far we have two terms of the artistic synthesis, the subjective and the objective. It is in the simple opposition of these
factors that two paths to artistic failure reveal themselves: the
loss of balance which follows when subjectivity is regarded as all
but self-sufficient and the corresponding deflection when the

structure of objectivity is sought for its own sake. The first, which is the romantic error, leads to a formless expansiveness; the second, which is the classical, to an empty constructivism. But an integrated work of art contains within itself a resolution and equilibrium of the personal with the impersonal, the subjective with the objective, the particular with the universal. The subjective and the objective meet and fuse to illuminate and to concretize each other, forming a third entity, a diamond of compressed carbon. There has been a qualitative transformation. In order, therefore, to understand the nature of the artistic synthesis we must put our finger on the third term in which these disparate parts may be drawn together and resolved into unity. That term is Truth. I use the capital initial to emphasize that truth is an absolute.

ALL art arises from the creative need to raise content into its proper form. Form is that which orders content into significance; the 'significant' is that which has meaning, and meaning consists in a relation to truth. The artist – not the craftsman, the entertainer or the dilettante, but the authentic creator – is one who confronts his experience with a passionate and inflexible question as to its meaning, its inherent value, and who, working in his chosen medium, utilizes a particular technique to present the meaning he discovers, in symbolic form, to himself and to others. The discovery of meaning and its embodiment in the concrete artistic work is his justification and his triumph. To uncover the pattern in the formless flux, that which is meaningful in the midst of the sordid and the banal: to lay hold on this and to give it corporal, symbolic expression is the creative mission of the artist.

Truth, the absolute, forms in every integrated work of art the invisible centre around which everything in it coheres and in relation to which it becomes a communicator of value. Truthfulness is accordingly the first and absolutely indispensable prerequisite of all authentic art. There are degrees of truthfulness, and of authenticity: a novel may be constructed out of a secondary or a tertiary or even a negative relation to truth, but a great novel can be brought into being only as the outcome of a primary act of apprehension of truth. The apprehension of truth is *imaginative vision*. Imaginative vision is not a mere extension into nothingness, it is a vision of experience informed by meaning – in other words, it is a concrete perception of truth. For it is *truth* which performs the liberating act that lifts the novelist from immersion in his subjective states and enables him so to objectify his experience that it is communicable: to others, indeed, but first of all to himself. Art humanizes. Human life is that of personal movement and response, of communion, of communication, and thus of speech. Relationship is only possible through a mutual relationship to truth; speech is only possible through an avowal of and an aspiration towards truth. Art is speech.

The artist and the thinker are thus akin. 'Literature,' as John Peale Bishop acutely remarked, 'is the criticism of ideas by life.' While the novelist may well be devoid of the capacity for systematic abstract thought, there is no good novel which does not demonstrate in a highly concrete and complex state, a process of thought. The common factor between the thinker and the novelist is precisely their orientation to truth.

Truth being an absolute, a resolute personal orientation is an act of transcendence. The pursuit of meaning presupposes a vow, an act of dedication, and the acceptance of a vocation. It is here that life and art are most intimately drawn together. Before the novelist can embody meaning in his work, he must have discovered the pattern of meaning in experience. At its highest and most complete, his artistic task is secondary to and dependent upon a prior personal devotion to truth.

In the transcendent relation to absolute truth, the relative is imbued with meaning, the particular becomes fraught with universality, the temporal wears an aspect of the eternal. From this arises the permanence of great art and the perishability of the inferior work. Art draws its *autotelic* quality from its relation to the eternal. Great art is a vision of eternity, and the lesson it teaches is that life, in so far as it, too, embodies truth, is itself autotelic. Great art declares the inherent structure of the universe.

ORIENTATION to truth is essentially a religious act. It implies an act of faith in the truth and of constancy in devotion to it.

Accordingly, the interdependence of art and life is most clearly shown, in conditions of cultural unity and compactness, in religion, which is the very heart of culture. Religious dogma, cult and ritual are the communal concretion and consolidation of man's transcendent apprehension of truth. Religion in its primitive unity is both art-in-life and life-in-art. The elevation which it effects of men's experience into a unified archetypal pattern results socially in a drawing of the multiplicity of particular lives into symbolic or typical relation with the eternal, the universal and the absolute. In a condition of cultural unity truth is thus represented in however imperfect a form in the beliefs and practices which are held and performed in common and which hold society together in relation to a single centre in relation to which, in turn, each social function has a non-utilitarian meaning. In a condition of comparative disintegration, on the other hand, truth ceases to be represented in this unified and unifying way. This means that not only is the self-questioning modern man deprived of the inwardly and outwardly sustaining power of an established symbol of truth, but he lives in a world of manners similarly deprived of accepted significant patterns. Because the life of western man stands inescapably in a relationship to the Christian faith which has provided the foundation for his culture and his civilization, so his art is, willy-nilly, positively or negatively, in a similar relationship. The disintegration in which the modern novelist lives and moves is that of a *Christian* culture; what meaning it has is, inevitably, a religious meaning.

In such a state of radical disorder and confusion the conscious individual must turn ever more inwards to seek out the foundations of his life. It happens that there is no more satisfactory way of presenting his own situation to himself in all its diversity and complexity than that provided by the art of the novel, and it is suggestive that the part played by this literary form in human life has increased in importance commensurably with the decay of religion and the subsequent disintegration of cultural unity, while simultaneously the novel itself, in its higher forms, has increased proportionately in scope and depth, accompanying, in its progress towards artistic self-consciousness, the increasing self-questioning of modern man. In order to substantiate this statement one has only to compare the seventeenth-century prose romance, still close to poetry, with the realistic narratives of the eighteenth-century writers, and those in turn with the increasingly rich and subtle novels of the nineteenth century, which gave us not only Scott, Dickens and Balzac, but Stendhal, Dostoevsky, and Henry James. No longer a running commentary upon contemporary manners, the novel increasingly centres upon itself, accentuating its inherently autotelic quality. At the same time it compensates by greater richness, subtlety and elaboration for the essential impoverishment of the modern man's life consequent upon his alienation from the larger world.

In the latter part of the nineteenth century the novel would appear to have reached its apogee. Although since then the writing of fiction has expanded almost into a branch of industry, the effect of yet further cultural disintegration has been to isolate the artist from his milieu, with the consequence that 'creative' fiction has ceased directly to portray the social scene and has come increasingly to concern itself with the inner predicament of the individual. Since, as a man, the alienated novelist cannot in practice live in a state of pure flux, and since the very act of composition does in itself presume a search for intelligible form and thus for personal meaning, a situation arises in which the novel comes ultimately to be shaped by the novelist's human predicament, which, in a disintegrating culture, unavoidably takes the quite primitive and fundamental form of an absence of and a need for faith. It would be vain, and a misunderstanding of the novelist's role, to look to him for positive leadership in this matter. But by reason of the indirect relation to truth which obtains in the practice of his art, we may with assurance look to him for articulation of the condition in which he is enmeshed. It is here that the critical function finds its justification. As the novelist presents life to itself as art, so it falls to the critic to present art to itself as thought, drawing out its concealed meanings and tracing them to a common centre, and relating his findings to the general cultural situation.

LIKE the arts of thought and of fiction, that of criticism presupposes a disciplinary orientation to truth on the part of its practitioner, and like them its power is immeasurably reinforced when this orientation is not only artistic but first of all existential. The creative critic must have at command an uncommon admixture of faculties. Standing midway between the novelist and the philosopher, he must have something of the former's sensitiveness to the particularity and multifariousness of human experience, together with not a little of the latter's capacity for abstraction and generalization.

And here, once again, it is necessary to distinguish between an inadequate subjective or objective critical attitude and an approach which is an integral combination of both. To suppose that there can be a form of criticism which is entirely personal and subjective is as fallacious as to suppose that there can be brought into being a foolproof critical discipline which is impersonal, objective and automatic; and yet we do find critical theory to oscillate in great part between these two misconceived extremes. As with every other art, that of criticism is fundamentally personal, but the critic's purely subjective perceptions, responses and insights are endowed with objective quality, through the rigour of his relation to truth. It is out of such strict and inflexible orientation that critical theory establishes its principles and formulates its disciplines, which, once more, cannot be mechanically appropriated, but have to be possessed from within. Granted such a rigorous personal self-orientation on the part of the ideal critic, it follows that there can be no essential discontinuity between the mind he brings to his critical work and that which he takes to the rest of his human concerns. The same difference is effective here between the creative and the merely academic or popular critic as between that artist whose relation to truth is circumscribed by the specific discipline of his art, and that other whose orientation to truth is both artistic and existential – or, in other words, *religious*. It follows that the work of the creative critic will be powerfully affected by the *ideas* resulting from a relation to truth; it cannot be either impressionistically 'personal' or studiously unbiassed and colourless, like the popular forms of criticism which are encouraged and exalted by reason of the fear of ideas which animates the general mind.

In the six studies of modern novelists which compose this book an attempt has been made in every case at a sympathetic

B

penetration to the heart of the work, and a consequent intuitive discovery of the underlying pattern which has shaped the sequence of the writer's novels. It will perhaps seem strange that I should use the word 'sympathetic' in connection with studies which will appear severe and even harsh, but that word nevertheless expresses my primary approach, and I use it to indicate that, doubtless with many failures, I stand not in an exterior but in an interior relation to the writers with whose work I deal. In the greater number of cases I had submitted myself more or less passively and at random to their influence over a long period of time before finding it necessary to my own development to separate myself from them in order to relate their work with increasing strictness to my own apprehension of truth. To the charge of a destructive negativeness, therefore, which may be brought against my treatment of them, I would reply that the severity towards a particular attitude or idea expressed must be considered in some degree as severity towards that part of myself which inclines or has inclined to the same direction. But in a time of general laxness, severity is its own justification. In the words of Blake, Establishment of Truth depends on Destruction of Falshood continually. I have little doubt that these novelists reveal in their work several distinguishable varieties of Falshood which, taken together, indicate an acute stage of spiritual malaise, as well as of cultural disintegration.

Just here another objection must be met. It will be charged that in concerning myself with the underlying formative forces which determine the novelist's work, I am overstepping the rightful terrain of criticism and raising issues which have little or nothing to do with literary values. The critic, runs this type of argument, should concern himself only with the purely literary qualities of the work before him, leaving the novelist to enjoy his personal vagaries as he pleases. The fact is, of course, that there are no such purely literary qualities which are not deeply connected with the inner movements of the novelist's personality. Flaws in the surface of a work are the outcome of a disrelation to truth, and disrelation to truth is a part of a more general disorientation of being. As, being an independent writer, I am not compelled to observe that rigid departmentalization of 'subjects' which is enforced by educational institutions, I see no reason why I should accept a widespread critical convention and draw an arbitrary line at the point where literature passes over into life. I can therefore state candidly that the typical modern novelists considered in this book reveal in their work several varieties of disorientation of being (or dehumanization) parallel with the deflection from truth which determines the structure of their work as a whole.

The varieties of slavery inherent in the human disposition which wait upon any such disorientation of being have been distinguished with great insight by Nicolas Berdyaev in his book *Slavery and Freedom*. Without in any way attempting to imitate Berdyaev's analysis, or to 'apply' his findings to the modern novel – a procedure which would in my view show critical insufficiency and bad faith – I am bound to say that my penetrations into the work of the writers dealt with in the ensuing pages confirm just such an insight into the conditions of inner subjection. Thus in the writings of Ernest Hemingway there is displayed a clear form of the slavery to war and to violence, in those of E. M. Forster there is marked slavery to the bourgeois spirit and to society, in Margiad Evans can be distinguished a pronounced form of slavery to passion and to nature, in Aldous Huxley the erotic lure is prominent, and in Joyce the aesthetic lure dominates everything, while in Virginia Woolf we see the elementary bewilderment of a mind incapable of formulating a clear view of her world of experience consequent upon inability to establish foundations in belief of whatever order. The lesson of the modern novel, as displayed in these figures, is that of the disintegration of the consciousness of modern man, resulting from his divided and depolarized being, sundered from its absolute centre. But while as a thinker I am interested in the organic manner in which, in these examples, one form of disorientation is connected with another, as a critic I note above all that each path here traced leads to a condition which may fitly be described as *the impossibility of speech*.

I BEGAN with a declaration of the dependence of art upon life. In order to understand this relationship in its larger sense it is necessary to make a formal distinction between two levels of life.

Life and art, in the context of culture, are engaged in a continuous cyclic interchange, to comprehend which we must
discriminate between the 'lower' level of the primary experiential flux and the 'higher', i.e. the distinctively human life of
values, of meaningful action and significant relationship.
Between the two stand those transforming agents of which art
is not the least important, which perform their function by
reason of their specialized relation to truth: in a state of cultural
unity it is religion which performs this office. The lower life is
transformed into the higher by means of the aspiration towards
and the embodiment of truth. Thus art is born out of life, and
the values it reveals again drawn into the current of social
living, to fertilize and once more give birth. Culture is the
result of this process, or rather, it is the process itself. It has two
faces, being at once a triumph – of form over the chaos of raw,
undifferentiated 'life' – and a failure – the failure to achieve
and to *incarnate* truth in existence, and thus to effect the real,
and not merely the symbolic, transfiguration of life. Yet without this transcendent endeavour towards the transfiguration of
life in the truth, culture itself would be emptied of meaning,
would shrivel and cease to exist.

Art is speech, and speech is ultimately impossible when there
is no absolute existential relation to truth. The relation to truth
which is implicit in the practice of art cannot be permanently
sustained when truth is withdrawn from existence. Not only will
life disorientated completely from truth succumb to chaos, but
art which originates from a life which is chaotic will eventually
also crumble from within. The instruments of technique will
perish, the structure of the artistic work will collapse, drama
will give place to a monologue which will end in the disintegration of language, of the sentence, even of the unitary word. The
word has meaning only in relation to the Word.

In its cultural aspect, indifference to truth has the effect of
upsetting the cyclic interchange of art and life, so that they
become confused, merge and lead to a common debasement.
The tendency towards this appears in artistic theory beforehand
in the forms of *vitalism* and *aestheticism* – the broken halves of an
entity formerly united by the aspiration towards truth. I consider them here first of all in their theoretical form. As a theory

of art in its relation to life, then, vitalism is a despair of art which demands its subordination to the service of some utilitarian aim on the level of society and nature; while aestheticism is a despair of life which exalts art into a sterile and vacuous self-sufficiency. The vitalistic heresy may be either directly naturalistic and 'pagan', as with D. H. Lawrence, or may take a sociological form, as in the varieties of Marxism. Poetry and the novel must lead to *more life* – either to a heightened sense of biological vitality, or to an intensified social activism. In any case its goal is no longer transcendent, but is displaced to the level of the primary experiential flux. The aesthetic theory is the converse of this, in its elevation of art at the expense of life. Life it sees as intrinsically meaningless and degraded; the revulsion it evokes can be alleviated only by retirement into a compensatory realm where all is refined, elegant and unsullied. Life is a deplorable reality, art a desirable dream. Both are linked with hedonism – truth being replaced by the pleasure-principle; and in each case there is a Utopian tendency in the final conclusion of art and life, the one being linked to notions of an idyllic state of nature, while the other inclines towards the aristocratic or plutocratic luxury of an artificial paradise. The vitalistic debasement of art to a functional purpose clearly leads to its extinction in a condition of sensational immediacy. The aesthetic denial of life progressively deprives art of content, forcing it ever further into insubstantiality.

To pass beyond the abstract theory to its emotional foundations, we find in E. M. Forster and in Margiad Evans a very plain substitution of ethical vitalism for spirituality, vitalism in this form being the quantitative valuation of life without regard to the qualitative distinctions which would be introduced by a relation to truth. On the other hand, the aesthetic attitude has profoundly conditioned the work of James Joyce and Virginia Woolf. It is of the greatest interest to see how in these cases an artistic sentimentalism is forced to give place at the last to a particularly gross vitalistic animality – a reduplication of the course of an earlier aesthete, W. B. Yeats. Thus art and life descend together to the level of undifferentiated 'lower' life, where the human image is dissipated in the phenomenal stream.

In these essays, then, I have endeavoured not merely to point out artistic failure but to some extent to uncover the existential roots of disintegration. It would be mistaken to condemn these novelists for their failures, not simply because their condition is also ours, but because of the real contribution which is made by the mere articulation of their situations, in their contributions to speech, which are contributions to our understanding of ourselves – even when it can be clearly shown that the course they have taken terminates in speechlessness. That man is inconceivable whose life stands in no relation to truth; every human thought, word and action stands in such a relation, but it may be at a multiple remove, to the furthest degree of automatism, or it may be wavering and negative and infirm, or contradictory of preceding and succeeding movements. These novelists, in the works which have grown from their searching of experience, have declared themselves and spoken their meaning, and it behoves their readers not to submit passively to the spell, but to examine that which is spoken and to relate it to their own understanding of life. So I have understood my critical task, and what follows, taken as a whole, is my critical contribution to our common understanding of our human predicament.

ERNEST HEMINGWAY

I

ERNEST HEMINGWAY is known as the author of a number of miscellaneous novels and short stories, as well as two books on blood sports. His best-known works, however, are two 'novels of love and war', *A Farewell to Arms* and *For Whom the Bell Tolls*, and his significant development, such as it is (for only in a very special sense can he be said to develop at all), may best be seen by a comparison of those two works. In the second section of this essay such a comparison will be made, but to begin with I propose to examine the essential or typical qualities of the Hemingway presented to us in the general body of his work.

Hemingway first received attention, when he was publishing his earlier stories, as a *stylist*. And this is interesting, for the content of his stories is in great part crude violent action, not essentially dissimilar from the subject-matter of the stories found in the cheap 'pulp' magazines of a primarily masculine appeal. It may reasonably be assumed that Hemingway satisfies, on a somewhat higher level of culture or of sophistication, the same imaginative cravings fed among the semi-literate proletarian masses of England and America by such productions as *War Aces* and *Action Stories*. The difference is that where the writer of 'pulp' stories is writing deliberately to a known consumer-demand, and where his products are, consequently, mechanical and lacking in psychological content, Hemingway is consciously an artist, writing to achieve an aesthetic effect, and is himself, therefore, emotionally involved in his own work. It follows that in his stories the emphasis is not, as in the 'pulp' magazines, entirely on the crude, mechanical action, taking place in a complete psychic vacuum. The psychological implications of the violence of the 'pulp' mentality are made explicit. In reading Hemingway we are made aware that the violent action itself, of so many of his stories, arises from the need for the alleviation of a prior and underlying psychic vacuity – an emotional state which is sometimes in his work suggested with great skill.

Hemingway is, within very narrow limits, a stylist who has brought to something like perfection a curt, unemotional, factual style which is an attempt at the objective presentation of experience. A bare, dispassionate reporting of external actions is all that Hemingway as a rule attempts in presenting his characters and incidents. His typical central character, his 'I', may be described generally as a bare consciousness stripped to the human minimum, impassively recording the objective data of experience. He has no contact with ideas, no visible emotions, no hopes for the future, and no memory. He is, as far as it is possible to be so, a *de-personalized* being.

A brief glance at Hemingway's first book, a collection of tales entitled *In Our Time* (1925), will give us some notion of the essentials of his attitude and his equipment as a writer. These tales are really a series of brief, laconic sketches from the life of a man, together forming a fragmentary novel. The settings of the sketches alternate between the American countryside of Nick's boyhood, the scenes of war on the Italian Front, and post-war America and Europe. The action, however, is slight and subordinated to the predominant mood, conveyed with admirable honesty and artistic scrupulousness, which is one of utter and complete negation, almost of nihilism. 'Nick', wrote D. H. Lawrence, reviewing the book on its appearance in England, 'is a type one meets in the more wild and woolly regions of the United States. He is the remains of the lone trapper and cowboy. Nowadays, he is educated, and through with everything. It is a state of conscious, accepted indifference to everything except freedom from work and the moment's interest. Nothing matters. Everything happens. Avoid one thing only: getting connected up. If you get held by anything, break it. Don't get away with the idea of getting somewhere else. Just get away, for the sake of getting away. Beat it! . . . His young love-affair ends as one throws a cigarette-end away. "It isn't fun any more." "Everything's gone to hell inside me. . . ." He doesn't love anybody, and it nauseates him to have to pretend he does. He doesn't even *want* to love anybody; he doesn't want to go anywhere; he doesn't want to do anything. He wants just to lounge around and maintain a healthy state of nothingness inside himself, and an attitude of negation to everything outside himself. And why shouldn't he, since that is exactly and sincerely what he feels?'

In Our Time, like much other of Hemingway's work, is fairly transparently autobiographical; it reads for the most part like a literal, though of course uncommonly discriminating, transcription of bare experience. A simple stylist like Hemingway, in search of a material upon which to exercise and develop his skill, would naturally turn first of all to the material nearest to hand – i.e. the material of simple personal experience. But a mind of Hemingway's negative and static quality will, it is evident, be unable to furnish sufficient material of a straightforward autobiographical kind for the simple craftsman to work on. Unlike a novelist of more complex and active mentality, gifted with psychological insight and the power to project, through the creation of character, a personal vision of experience – for whom, consequently, there would be no abrupt transition from 'autobiography' to 'fiction' – Hemingway is forced to turn for material to the plane, as I have said, of the 'pulp' magazine. His peculiarly negative view of human life quite naturally leads him to project his vision, when he leaves straight autobiography, into figures drawn from the lowest stratum of human existence, where life is lived as near as possible on an animal, mechanical level.

Here is a passage, from a work which is evidently of an autobiographical character rather than not, which has the advantage of representing Hemingway's characteristic factual style while at the same time presenting a fragment of typical subject-matter, which has its own implications on the human, moral plane. It is an incident in a military retreat from the novel *A Farewell to Arms*.

'I order you to cut brush,' I said. They turned and started down the road.

'Halt,' I said. They kept on down the muddy road, the hedge on either side. 'I order you to halt,' I called. They went a little faster. I opened up my holster, took the pistol, aimed at the one who had talked the most, and fired. I missed and they both started to run; I shot three times and dropped one. The other went through the hedge and was out of sight. I fired at him through the hedge as he ran across the field. The pistol clicked empty and I put in another clip. I saw it was too far to shoot at the second sergeant. He was far across the field, running, his head held low. I commenced to reload the empty clip. Bonello came up.

'Let me go finish him,' he said. I handed him the pistol and he walked down to where the sergeant of engineers lay face down across the road. Bonello leaned over, put the pistol against the man's head and pulled the trigger. The pistol did not fire.

'You have to cock it,' I said. He cocked and fired twice. He took hold of the sergeant's legs and pulled him to the side of the road so he lay beside the hedge. He came back and handed me the pistol.

'The son of a bitch,' he said.

The transition from writing on this level to the subsequent and alternative level of the human underworld involves no very considerable descent, it is clear. The following is from a sketch entitled 'The Killers'.

'What are you going to kill Ole Andreson for? What did he ever do to you?

'He never had a chance to do anything to us. He never even seen us.'

'And he's only going to see us once,' Al said from the kitchen.

'What are you going to kill him for, then?' George asked.

'We're killing him for a friend. Just to oblige a friend, bright boy.'

'Shut up,' said Al from the kitchen. 'You talk too goddam much.'

'Well, I got to keep bright boy amused. Don't I, bright boy.'

'You talk too damn much,' Al said. 'The nigger and my bright boy are amusing themselves. I got them tied up like a couple of girl friends in the convent.'*

The wider implications of the above examples of Hemingway's manner and matter are, of course, related to the almost complete extrusion of his vision of life upon the plane of the external – the plane of extreme objectivization where experience is alienated from its subject. To deprive life of its inwardness, and to see men, not as personalities, but as objects, as things, is to open the door, not for a morally condemnable cruelty or

* *Men Without Women* (1928).

brutality so much as for an even more devastating, because cold and spiritless, contempt of human values and of human life, which puts killing a man on the same level of actuality as cooking an egg or blacking one's boots. For good measure, I give a further, and incidentally later, example of Hemingway's objective eye for violence.

The other fellow pulled the one who was hit back by the legs to behind the wagon, and I saw the nigger getting his face down on the paving to give them another burst. Then I saw old Pancho come around the corner of the wagon and step into the lee of the horse that was still up. He stepped clear of the horse, his face white as a dirty sheet, and got the chauffeur with the big Luger he had; holding it in both hands to keep it steady. He shot twice over the nigger's head, coming on, and once low.

He hit a tyre on the car because I saw dust blowing in a spurt on the street as the air came out, and at ten feet the nigger shot him in the belly with the Tommy gun, with what must have been the last shot in it because I saw him throw it down, and old Pancho sat down hard and went over forwards. He was trying to come up, still holding on to the Luger, only he couldn't get his head up, when the nigger took the shot gun that was lying against the wheel of the car by the chauffeur and blew the side of his head off. Some nigger.*

Hemingway's de-personalized style, it appears, is the result of no detached, arbitrary choice. It is a style actually perfectly expressive of his outlook on life. In the flat, chaotic, elementary world into which we are introduced by Hemingway's fiction, everything is objectivized: inwardness, subjectivity, is eliminated, and man himself is made into an object, a thing. This entire extrusion of personality into the outward sensational world makes his characters the inwardly-passive victims of a meaningless determinism. They inhabit a world which, because it has been voided of inwardness, is entirely without significance. The Hemingway character is a creature without religion, morality, politics, culture or history – without any of those aspects, that is to say, of the distinctively human existence.

Such an outlook is a peculiar one in a writer because it

* *To Have and Have Not* (1937).

precludes the possibility of organic and interesting development. The Hemingway world is one of mechanical repetition, and in the series of Hemingway's nine or ten books there is no inward continuity to keep pace with the chronological sequence. It is therefore impossible to consider Hemingway as if there were some coherently developing pattern running through his progress as a writer. That there is a development of some kind, a *static* development, so to speak, I shall presently try to show. But the critic, I think, need feel no special obligation to consider Hemingway's works as a sequence. The pattern is essentially a fixed one, made by the running of the mind in a deterministic groove. Apart from the two 'war and love' novels which must be examined separately, there is only one book which throws any special light on Hemingway's mind, and that is the book on the Spanish bullfight entitled *Death in the Afternoon*, which serves the purpose of showing in a simple and explicit form Hemingway's fascinated preoccupation, which up to now I have refrained from commenting on, with the fact of death.

The profound spiritual inertia, the inner vacancy and impotence, which is a mark of all Hemingway's projected characters, issues in a deadening sense of boredom and negation which can only be relieved by violent, though still essentially meaningless, activity. The more violent the activity, the greater the relief from the sickening vertigo of boredom. But activity of this kind is in fact a drug, and like most other kinds of drug, for its effect to be maintained it must be taken in constantly increasing quantities. Ultimately, however, the state of boredom, certainly one of the most horrible of human experiences, reduces itself not merely to the absence of meaning, but to the total absence of a sense of life. Indeed, it is a feature of violent action that while it cannot produce a convincing sense of meaningfulness, it can at any rate produce an illusory sense of *life*. Violent action itself, however, is almost always destructive action. Its end is in death. And, ultimately, when the sense of life itself vanishes, there is only one way in which it may be recaptured, and that is by the violent, absolute contrast of life with death. Life regains its 'reality' in such cases – becomes, that is, aesthetically sensational and vivid in itself – only when it is brought up against the stark, black negation of the void.

Writing, in *Death in the Afternoon*, of his early interest in the bullfight, Hemingway says:

I was trying to write then and I found the greatest difficulty, aside from knowing truly what you really felt, rather than what you were supposed to feel, and had been taught to feel, was to put down what really happened in action; what the actual things were which produced the emotion you experienced.

. . . The only place where you could see life and death, i.e. violent death now that the wars were over, was in the bull ring and I wanted very much to go to Spain where I could study it. I was trying to learn to write, commencing with the simplest things, and one of the simplest things of all and the most funda- mental is violent death. . . .

So far, about morals, I know only that what is moral is what you feel good after and what is immoral is what you feel bad after and judged by these moral standards, which I do not defend, the bullfight is very moral to me because I feel very fine while it is going on and have a feeling of life and death and mortality and immortality, and after it is over I feel very sad but very fine.

Death in the Afternoon, which partakes of the nature of an esoteric introduction to a blood-cult, is written throughout in a tone of alternating naïve solemnity and cynical jocularity. But here, he seems to imply, in a senseless, mechanical and phoney world, is something which seems to be real and meaningful, and which may somehow be approached in a way which will impart a sense of significance and reality to living.

. . . Someone with English blood has written: 'Life is real; life is earnest; and the grave is not its goal.' And where did they bury him? and what became of the reality and the earnestness? The people of Castilla have great common sense. They could not produce a poet who would write a line like that. They know death is the unescapable reality, the one thing any man may be sure of; the only security; that it transcends all modern comforts and that with it you do not need a bath-tub in every American home, nor, when you have it, do you need the radio. They think a great deal about death, and when they have a religion they have one which believes that life is much shorter than death. Having this feeling they take an intelligent interest in death. . . .

Such passages as this do at least reveal the nature, whatever one may think of its value, of the chief preservative of Heming- way's significance as a writer, that kind of desperate honesty which, once the bottom has been knocked out of things by painful and horrifying experience, cannot rest content with the pusillanimous compromises with which most people afterwards patch up their lives, and which one detects in the revulsion from the 'bath-tub in every American home', and in the manifest dread of any kind of 'faking' (in writing as in bullfighting) which is displayed throughout the book. A glance at one further facet of Hemingway's personal outlook, and we can pass on from this brief survey of his typical work. In *Green Hills of Africa* (1936), a tedious description of a hunting trip, there are two passages which are of interest for the light they throw on Hemingway as a writer. The first concerns *subject*.

I thought about Tolstoy and about what a great advantage an experience of war was to a writer. It was one of the major subjects and certainly one of the hardest to write truly of, and those writers who had not seen it were always very jealous and tried to make it seem unimportant, or abnormal, or a disease as a subject, while, really, it was just something quite irreplaceable that they had missed.

The second concerns, not subject, and not technique, exactly, but the writer's intention:

The reason every one now tries to avoid it, to deny that it is important, to make it seem vain to try to do it, is because it is so difficult. Too many factors must combine to make it possible. . . . The kind of writing that can be done. How far prose can be carried if anyone is serious enough and has luck. There is a fourth and fifth dimension that can be gotten. [And if a writer can get this] . . . Then nothing else matters. It is more important than anything he can do. The chances are, of course, that he will fail. But there is a chance that he succeeds. . . . It is much more difficult than poetry. It is a prose that has never been written. But it can be written, without tricks and without cheating. With nothing that will go bad afterwards. . . . First, there must be talent, much talent. Talent such as Kipling had. Then there must be discipline. The discipline of Flaubert. Then there must be the conception of what it can be and an absolute conscience as unchanging as the standard meter in Paris, to prevent faking. Then the writer must be intelligent and disinterested and above all he must survive.

Such, or something such, is the conception of himself which

Hemingway would like to project into the public mind. It is an interesting conception.

A novelist, of admitted literary merit, who lacks all the equipment generally expected of a practitioner of his art except a certain artistic scrupulousness and poetic sense, is something of a phenomenon. And while one would hardly suppose Hemingway could be considered as, intrinsically, a very important writer, yet, it is obvious, his purely symptomatic significance is considerable. For what does Hemingway represent but that, in a special form, which might be termed the *proletarianization* of literature: the adaptation of the technical artistic conscience to the sub-average human consciousness? Sociologically considered, Hemingway seems to me to epitomize a phase of culture in which all the inward values which have sustained that culture in the past are vanishing, and nothing much is left but the empty shell of civilization – the shell of technique. The characters of Hemingway reflect accurately the consciousness of the depersonalized modern man of the totalitarian era, from whom all inward sources have been withdrawn, who has become alienated from his experience and objectivized into his environment.

*

C. S. Lewis, in his *Preface to Paradise Lost*, drawing a distinction between the Primary Epic of Homer and the Secondary Epic of Virgil and Milton, points out that the former kind is deprived of the great subject possessed by the latter because 'the mere endless up and down, the constant aimless alternations of glory and misery, which make up the terrible phenomenon called a Heroic Age', admit of no historical pattern or design, which can only be given 'when some event can be held to effect a profound and more or less permanent change in the history of the world, as the founding of Rome did, or still more, the fall of man'.

> No one event is really very much more important than another. No achievement can be permanent: today we kill and feast, tomorrow we are killed, and our women led away as slaves. Nothing 'stays put', nothing has a significance beyond the moment. Heroism and tragedy there are in plenty, therefore good stories in plenty; but no 'large design that brings the world out of the good to ill'. The total effect is not a pattern, but a kaleidoscope. . . .

Primary Epic is great, but not with the greatness of the later kind. In Homer, its greatness lies in the human and personal tragedy built up against this background of meaningless flux. It is all the more tragic because there hangs over the heroic world a certain futility. 'And here I sit in Troy,' says Achilles to Priam, 'afflicting you and your children.' Not 'protecting Greece', not even 'winning glory', not called by any vocation to afflict Priam, but just doing it because that is the way things come about. . . . Only the style – the unwearying, unmoved, angelic speech of Homer – makes it endurable. Without that the *Iliad* would be a poem beside which the grimmest modern realism is child's play.

It does not seem far-fetched to perceive some points of similarity between the Heroic Ages of the past and our own bloodstained epoch as it moves into an increasingly bleak future, and between the bards who recited the deeds of the ancient heroes and such a novelist as Hemingway – bearing in mind the retrogressive character of our own 'heroism', and, of course, putting the disparity between Homer and Hemingway into some proportion with that existing between, say, Hector or Agamemnon and Harry Morgan.

II

IN any serious considerations of the writings of Ernest Hemingway the fact must not be lost sight of that their author belongs to that generation of men whose formative adult years were spent on the battlefields of Europe during the first world war. It would scarcely be too much to say that Hemingway's special type of outlook is *a product of the battlefield*. Hemingway's comments upon war as a subject for the writer have already been noted. And it is a revealing fact that his two most coherent and most successful books, *A Farewell to Arms* (1929) and *For Whom the Bell Tolls* (1941), upon which his fame largely rests, are both 'novels of love and war'.

Each of these novels stands apart from the bulk of Hemingway's work by virtue of its embodiment of a sustained pathos; and this pathos, it is evident, is an aspect of its interior connection with Hemingway's own personal experience and vision of life. While much of Hemingway's writing is the product of a somewhat uneasy attitudinizing, *A Farewell to Arms* impresses one with its surprisingly genuine and unforced quality. It is naïve rather than cynical, bewildered rather than 'tough', and there is a minimum of deliberate sensational violence. Although published ten years after the end of the first world war, its clearly autobiographical character would seem to justify its being related to the early and comparatively unformed Hemingway, the Hemingway who was himself, in youthful immaturity, thrust by circumstances into the scarifying circumstances of war and left to digest his experience as best he could.

For a novelist with no coherent inner vision of human existence, the problem of form must present almost insuperable difficulties: difficulties which may be envisaged from a reading of Hemingway's two chaotic lesser novels, not considered here – *The Sun Also Rises* and *To Have and Have Not*. But in *A Farewell to Arms* this problem is solved by the exterior pattern of the events in which the curiously nameless hero is passively involved. The story is straightforward. An American enlisted in the medical section of the Italian Army, the hero meets, near the front, an English nurse called Catherine Barkley. They are indifferently attracted to one another, and there is a rather flat emotional encounter between them, very well described. (Catherine is mourning for her lover, killed in France, to whom she had put off her marriage.) Then the American is wounded and sent back to a hospital where he is nursed by Catherine, and they fall into an intimate sexual relationship. After his recovery, the American returns to the battle-front, but is involved in a disorderly retreat, is arrested and about to be shot by military police, but he frees himself, and 'through' with the war, makes his way to the town where Catherine is living and escapes with her down the lakes to neutral Switzerland. Here, away from the war and in outwardly idyllic circumstances, the whole accidental, haphazard series of events reaches its meaningless, accidental conclusion with Catherine's death at the maternity hospital in giving birth to a stillborn infant.

In this novel, the war, of which the central character is a more or less acquiescent and occasionally involved onlooker, is only the background and setting for the central story of the relationship between the soldier and the nurse. There is a real suggestion of pathos in the impersonal, unimpassioned account of their forlorn, uncomprehending, tacit endeavour to maintain

C

the illusion of the happiness and meaningfulness of their fortuitous relationship against their own deeper apprehension of
lovelessness, frustration and fatality, although the emphasis is
entirely on the objective occurrences, and the inward significance is never directly touched upon. The following passage
will provide an example of Hemingway's honest realism in
dealing with his 'love interest':

We walked down the corridor. The carpet was worn. There
were many doors. The manager stopped and unlocked a door and
opened it.

'Here you are. A lovely room.'

The small boy in buttons put the package on the table in the
centre of the room. The manager opened the curtains.

'It is foggy outside,' he said. The room was furnished in red
plush. There were many mirrors, two chairs and a large bed with
a satin coverlet. A door led to the bathroom.

'I will send up the menu,' the manager said. He bowed and
went out.

I went to the window and looked out, then pulled a cord that
shut the thick plush curtains. Catherine was sitting on the bed,
looking at the cut-glass chandelier. She had taken her hat off
and her hair shone under the light. She saw herself in one of the
mirrors and put her hands to her hair. She did not look happy.
She let her cape fall on the bed.

'What's the matter, darling?'

'I never felt like a whore before,' she said. I went over to the
window and pulled the curtain aside and looked out. I had not
thought it would be like this.

'You're not a whore.'

'I know it, darling. But it isn't nice to feel like one.' Her voice
was dry and flat.

'This was the best hotel we could get in,' I said. I looked out of
the window. Across the square were the lights of the station.
There were carriages going by on the street and I saw the trees in
the park. The lights from the hotel shone on the wet pavement.
Oh, hell, I thought, do we have to argue now?

'Come over here, please,' Catherine said. The flatness was all
gone out of her voice. 'Come over, please. I'm a good girl again.'
I looked over at the bed. She was smiling.

I went over and sat on the bed beside her and kissed her.

'You're my good girl.'

'I'm certainly yours,' she said.

There is, too, a queer, twisted pathetic quality in the lovers' final interview, when Catherine is on her deathbed.

'Do you want me to get a priest or anyone to come and see you?'

'Just you,' she said. Then a little later, 'I'm not afraid. I just hate it.'

'You must not talk so much,' the doctor said.

'All right,' Catherine said.

'Do you want me to do anything, Cat? Can I get you anything?'

Catherine smiled, 'No.' Then a little later, 'You won't do our things with another girl, or say the same things, will you?'

'Never.'

'I want you to have girls, though.'

'I don't want them.'

These short passages are enough perhaps, to make plain something of the novel's relatively sympathetic quality. There is an absence of deliberate harsh violence; what violence there is comes, unsought, from the external circumstances of war, and is received passively. This is in keeping with the character of the young man, who is not a proletarian tough, but an average young bourgeois American. He is – not a sufferer, for although he endures suffering he refuses to accept it – but a victim, who has not yet become hard and cynical and addicted to violence as an end in itself. If, at the beginning of the story, he has a philosophy, it is a simple one of self-centred enjoyment, although towards the end, and after Catherine's death, this gives place to a naïve 'tragic' outlook, which is expressed in such reflections as these:

Often a man wishes to be alone and a girl wishes to be alone too and if they love each other they are jealous of that in each other, but I can truly say we never felt that. We could feel alone when we were together, alone against the others. It has only happened to me like that once. I have been alone while I was with many girls and that is the way that you can be most lonely. But we were never lonely and never afraid when we were together. I know that the night is not the same as the day: that all things are different, that the things of the night cannot be explained in the day, because they do not then exist, and the night can be a dreadful time for lonely people once their loneliness has started. But with Catherine there was almost no difference in the night except that it was an even better time. If people bring so much courage to this world the world has to kill them to break them, so of course it kills them. The world breaks every one and afterward many are strong in the broken places. But these that will not break it kills. It kills the very good and the very gentle and the very brave impartially. If you are none of these you can be sure it will kill you too but there will be no special hurry.

The harsh note of suppressed grief on which this story closes expresses the fatalistic stoicism which arises in the young American out of his inherent inner passivity as it is affected by his sense of futility and of loss. At such an intensity of suffering there are usually only two courses open to the human heart, a receptive softening or a cynical hardening. But we already know that a desperate, bitter hardness is a characteristic of Hemingway's work as a whole.

A survey of the ground covered by the greater part of Hemingway's writings shows it to be that indicated in the first part of this essay – the delineation of an eviscerated, chaotic world of futility and boredom lit up with flashes of violent action, where life is brought into a sensational vividness only by contrast with the nullity of death. The bulk of Hemingway's writing expresses consciously an outlook on life which is negative to the point of nihilism. Yet, abruptly, at the conclusion of the Hemingway opus we find a work – *For Whom the Bell Tolls* – of an undeniably sustained and positive character, which has been widely received as revealing a profound and positive insight into the human condition and the life of our time. What sort of enigma have we here?

That there is a reversal of attitude of a decisive kind is quite clear. For in this latter book we have a pattern, not of aimlessness, but of positive direction and sense of purpose, and a depiction, not of nihilistic despair, but of lyrical acceptance, where futility is replaced by meaningfulness, and instead of merely factual externality there is a significant, organic pattern to sustain the interior structure of the narrative. The pathos with which the story is imbued is a pathos quite different in quality from that of the Italian novel – it is a pathos which derives, not from a negative sense of victimization at the hands of life, but from a kind of subdued, lyrical ecstasy of acceptance.

The story concerns a young American, Robert Jordan, who

espouses the cause of the Republicans in Spain during the Civil War, enlists with the Government forces as a dynamiter, and is entrusted with a mission, involving almost certain death, behind the enemy lines. Under the guidance of the old peasant, Anselmo, he reaches the hiding-place, a cave in the mountains, of the group of guerrillas who are to assist him in blowing the bridge on the specified day. There he encounters a mixed group of primitive people, including Pablo, the surly and untrustworthy leader of the group, Pilar, his powerful, earthily-sagacious wife, and a girl, Maria, whom they have rescued, after she has been raped, from the fascists, and with whom he quickly establishes an intimate relationship. The atmosphere among the little group is tense, partly because of the antagonism which arises between Jordan and Pablo, and partly owing to the necessary hazards of existence in enemy territory. But what contributes most to the psychical intensity which permeates the life of this little group and draws them together in bonds of intimacy is their nearness to the fatality felt to be involved in the accomplishment of the mission which has brought them into combination with the newcomer. After surviving some hazardous circumstances, Jordan, with the others, blows the bridge, but is wounded while escaping and left to face certain death from the approaching enemy, which he does with a gun in his hand and in his sustained mood of subdued ecstasy.

Nothing more clearly brings out the completeness of the alteration of attitude in the later novel than the juxtaposition of the following passages from each book, the Italian and the Spanish, concerning the heroes' attitudes towards the emotional aura that surrounds every cause for which men are prepared to kill and to die.

This is from the earlier book:

> I did not say anything. I was always embarrassed by the words sacred, glorious and sacrifice and the expression in vain. We had heard them, sometimes standing in the rain almost out of earshot, so that only the shouted words came through, and had read them, on proclamations that were slapped up by billposters over other proclamations, now for a long time, and I had seen nothing sacred, and the things that were glorious had no glory and the sacrifices were like the stock-yards at Chicago if nothing was done

with the meat except to bury it. There were many words that you could not stand to hear and finally only the names of places had dignity. Certain numbers were the same way and certain dates and these with the names of the places were all you could say and have them mean anything. Abstract words such as glory, honour, courage or hallow were obscene beside the concrete names of villages, the numbers of roads, the names of rivers, the numbers of regiments and the dates.

Nothing could be more opposed to this than such sentiments as these expressed in the later novel:

> At either of those places you felt that you were taking part in a crusade. That was the only word for it although it was a word that had been so worn and abused that it no longer gave its true meaning. You felt, in spite of all bureaucracy and inefficiency and party strife, something that was like the feeling you expected to have and did not have when you made your first communion. It was a feeling of consecration to a duty toward all of the oppressed of the world which would be as difficult and embarrassing to speak about as religious experience and yet it was authentic as the feeling you had when you heard Bach, or stood in Chartres Cathedral or the Cathedral at Leon and saw the light coming through the great windows; or when you saw Mantegna and Greco and Breughel in the Prado. It gave you a part in something that you could believe in wholly and completely and in which you felt an absolute brotherhood with the others who were engaged in it. It was something that you had never known before but that you had experienced now and you gave such importance to it and the reasons for it that your own death seemed of complete unimportance; only a thing to be avoided because it would interfere with the performance of your duty. . . .

That a very peculiar transposition of emotional attitudes has been effected somewhere between the two novels is obvious. But by what agency has this startling reversal been brought about?

The answer is not far to seek. The characters in this novel prove on examination to be characters no less elementary than those in Hemingway's previous books, but to their elementary, stripped humanity has been added a rudimentary political sense. *Politics* appears to be the pivot which has enabled Hemingway to swing from a completely negative emotional polarity towards life to a positive one.

If this is the case, then it would appear that the claim of the

Spanish novel to real and positive significance – a claim which has not been backward in coming from certain quarters – depends very largely upon the quality of the political consciousness displayed in it. Now, a political awareness of such a valid and enlightening character must, it is plain, be something very complex and organic to its possessor's personality, must at least affect, or be affected by, many other departments of its possessor's mind. Can this be said of Hemingway's political consciousness? It cannot.

I must pass over here the question of Hemingway's own political affiliations, of which I know little except that in 1936, with his compatriot, the socialist novelist, John Dos Passos, Hemingway visited Loyalist Spain* and came back a strong Communist sympathizer. In his writings, however, apart from a propagandist play entitled *The Fifth Column*, the first work of Hemingway's to show any social awareness is the novel *To Have and Have Not*, published in 1937, which is a crude chronicle of violent action (there are nine killings) upon which is superimposed, towards the end, a 'social' moral of the most elementary nature – a series of mechanical contrasts of the lives of certain members of the parasitical bourgeoisie with the underprivileged workers. The hero, an individualist adventurer named Harry Morgan, after a number of violent illegal escapades, dies, shot in the stomach, uttering the following profound observations:

'A man,' Harry Morgan said, looking at them both. 'One man alone ain't got. No man alone now.' He stopped. 'No matter how a man alone ain't got no bloody chance.'

He shut his eyes. It had taken him a long time to get it out and it had taken him all of his life to learn it.†

* . . . Where, according to an article in the then radically leftist *Partisan Review* (April 1938) ' . . . Dos Passos found bombs horrifying, bloodshed gruesome, anarchists hounded by a Stalinist camarilla, the People's Front conceding to Anglo-French imperialism and suppressing socialism; [and where] Hemingway found bombs intriguing, bloodshed exciting, anarchists treasonable, the People's Front noble, socialism nonsense . . .' etc. etc.

† It seems to have taken Hemingway quite a long time, too. In *Green Hills of Africa*, published only a year previously, he was writing in this vein: 'If you serve time for society, democracy, and the other things quite young, and declining any further enlistment make yourself responsible only to yourself, you exchange the pleasant, comforting stench of comrades for something you can never feel in any other way than by yourself' . . . etc.

In *For Whom the Bell Tolls*, the rudimentary quality of Robert Jordan's political consciousness is barely disguised, and we may safely take it that the quality of Jordan's insight accurately reflects Hemingway's own.

> You're not a real Marxist and you know it. You believe in Liberty, Equality and Fraternity. You believe in Life, Liberty and the pursuit of happiness. Don't ever kid yourself with too much dialectics. They are for some but not for you. You have put many things in abeyance to win a war. If this war is lost all of those things are lost. But afterward you can discard what you do not believe in. There is plenty you do not believe in and plenty that you do believe in.

So much, then, for the quality of Hemingway's political insight, which, from its appearance in his works, would seem to be very meagre indeed. It is enough, however, to justify a black-and-white taking of sides in an armed struggle. But politics is the pivotal point only for what is in effect a total transposition of emotional attitude. What the nature is of that reorientation which, it is plain to see, gives this novel its organic structure, and its sustained, epical positiveness, can now be made clear.

It is here that we touch upon the seeming paradox which makes it possible to speak of Hemingway's as a 'static' development. For what has occurred between the two novels is not a development, or unfoldment, at all, but a psychological shifting which has made possible a *retrogressive recapitulation* of an essentially identical theme. *For Whom the Bell Tolls* actually represents the same basic emotional situation as that stated in *A Farewell to Arms*, but turned, as it were, outside in. Whereas the accidental circumstances of war, sex and death, the poles of experience which provide the focal points for the emotional pattern, impose, in the earlier book, an external pattern on the narrative, reflecting the attitude of the central character as a passive victim, those identical circumstances are, in the later book, given an inward, positive significance and made intrinsic to the story, which attains thereby an interior coherence which is expressed stylistically in the rapt, exalted quality of the writing. It is exactly as though an emotional fixation, impressed on the mind by a certain original pattern of experience as the mind moved outward centrifugally to life, has determined, after a period of immobility, not a development, but an inward, centripetal, recapitulative movement, in which the accidentals become intrinsic; the negatives positive; the mechanical and outward the organic and inward. This whole process of reversal is aptly conveyed in the embarrassingly rhapsodic style of the Spanish novel, emotionally orientated as it is towards the central cult-acceptance of sexuality and death, which is in interesting contrast to the emotional and verbal asceticism of the Italian book.

Death provides the primary emotional focal point of the novel. From the moment he appears it is plain that Robert Jordan is going to his death. His own awareness of this fact serves not only to intensify his sense of the vivid immediacy of the little life which remains to him, but to throw depths of fortuitous significance into his physical union with the girl, Maria. Just as in the earlier novel, here too the emotional series is brought to an end by death. But for the death, accidental and as it were peripheral, of Catherine – death experienced as meaningless objective fact and deprivation – is here substituted a death which is deliberate and essential, embraced by the central character himself as the ultimate factor of subjective experience. And not only death is here embraced positively, and emotionally sanctioned, but also those other pivotal points of the Hemingway situation – sexuality (or 'love') and war.

The relationship of Catherine and the American 'Tenente' in the Italian novel is that of equals, and it retains some vestiges of human dignity which bring it within measurable distance of love, as distinct from animal sexuality. But that of Maria and Robert Jordan is one of uncontaminated animality, so uncontaminated indeed that Hemingway finds it possible to endow it with an absolute, 'mystical' significance. 'When I am with Maria,' ruminates Jordan, 'I love her so that I feel, literally, as though I would die, and I never believed in that nor thought that it could happen.' The emotional orgasm stimulated by his sense of proximity to death elevates every experience for Jordan into a realm of pseudo-mystical excitement. The mystico-sexual experiences of Robert Jordan reveal their nature, if that is in any doubt, by their existence in a psychic void, they

have no connection with and no effect upon his other activities –
although that perhaps is inaccurate, for there would appear to
be a direct connection with death and with killing. And here
the third significant transposition of attitude makes itself felt.
The hero of *A Farewell to Arms*, passively involved in war, as
passively accepts killing, and even himself dispassionately kills
when the necessity seems forced on him – which happens only
once in the book. And the context is not unfavourable to such
animadversions on war as the following:

'Tenente,' Passini said, 'we understand you let us talk. Listen.
There is nothing as bad as war. We in the auto-ambulance cannot
even realize at all how bad it is. When people realize how bad it
is they cannot do anything to stop it because they go crazy. There
are some people who never realize. There are people who are
afraid of their officers. It is with them that war is made.'
'I know it is bad, but we must finish it.'
'It doesn't finish. There is no finish to a war.'
'Yes, there is.'
Passini shook his head.
'War is not won by victory. What if we take San Gabriele?
What if we take the Carso and Monfalcone and Trieste? Where
are we then? Did you see all the far mountains today? Do you
think we could take all them too? Only if the Austrians stop
fighting. One side must stop fighting. Why don't we stop fighting?
If they come down into Italy they get tired and go away. They
have their own country. But no, instead there is a war.'
'You're an orator.'
'We think. We read. We are not peasants. We are mechanics.
But even the peasants know better than to believe in a war.
Everybody hates this war.'

In the later novel, however, war and killing are much more
enthusiastically undertaken.

'My rabbit,' Robert Jordan said and held her as close and as
gently as he could. But he was as full of hate as any man could be.
'Do not talk more about it. Do not tell me any more for I cannot
bear my hatred now.'
She was stiff and cold in his arms and she said, 'Nay, I will never
talk more of it. But they are bad people and I would like to kill
some of them with thee if I could. But I have told thee this only
for thy pride if I am to be thy wife. So thou wouldst understand.'

'I am glad you told me,' he said. 'For tomorrow, with luck, we will kill plenty.'

'But will we kill Falangists? It was they who did it.'

'They do not fight,' he said gloomily. 'They kill at the rear. It is not them we fight in battle.'

'But can we not kill them in some way? I would like to kill some very much.'

'I have killed them,' he said. 'And we will kill them again. At the train· we have killed them.'

But there is no need for the multiplication of instances. So much must suffice. If the earlier and typical Hemingway, the underlying factors of whose work I have done my best to bring to light in the first part of this essay, represents an aspect of the widespread sickness of our civilization, the Hemingway of *For Whom the Bell Tolls* reveals that sickness in an advanced stage, sickness masquerading as health, and, accepted as such, precluded from the possibility of being resisted. Of social, or 'political' insight, in this book, there is none. Hemingway's sole claim to such insight rests upon his perception, of dubious worth in the context, of the inadequacy of individualism – 'No matter how a man alone ain't got no bloody chance' – and the superiority of what he had previously been pleased to term, in revulsion, 'the pleasant, comforting stench of comrades'. Hemingway's ostensibly 'profound' realization of the fact of human solidarity – which is all of moral insight that can be said to emerge from the Spanish novel – permitting, as it does, under scanty 'political' justification, the division of men and women into two armed camps equipped and ready for mutual slaughter – hardly possesses any intimate relationship to the epigraph from John Donne from which the novel takes its title.

As for the consequences of Hemingway's peculiar retrogression – a certain loss of sincerity and asceticism of style, the proneness to a peculiar sentimentalism, and the readiness to entertain the cheap substitutes for thought manufactured by political factions – we can safely leave these to the enjoyment of that enormous public which Hemingway has now found, and which, one presumes, shares, to a measurable extent, his outlook and values.

E. M. FORSTER

IN view of the present popular eminence of E. M. Forster, it
is a striking reflection that the five novels upon which his
public reputation is based were, with one exception, composed within a period of six years during the first decade of
the present century. And even the exception, *A Passage to India*,
although not published until 1924, was drafted some twelve
years before that date.* E. M. Forster, it appears, is an Edwardian novelist, surviving into the contemporary world as a public
personality on the basis of a past creativity which has been
outlasted by its early products. In spite of this, Forster's is a
name which 'counts': his books are reprinted in popular cheap
editions, he lectures, broadcasts, contributes to symposia on
such subjects as 'What I Believe', sits on committees, and in
other ways represents 'culture' in the regions where it shades off
into the realms of practical life. It is clear from all this that in
some way Forster is a representative figure. When he makes
public pronouncements, he voices the mind of a group and a
class. As Rose Macaulay, a far from unsympathetic critic, has
said of his later political writings, ' . . . in all of them he
speaks with the voice of cultured, sensitive and democratic
liberalism rather than with his own peculiar note, or rather, he
is speaking with that part of his voice which sings in the choir
with cultured, sensitive and democratic liberalism'. An examination of his mind should, therefore, lead us beyond the
particular case to the general principles underlying it.

How Forster regards himself, or likes to be regarded by others,
may be discovered from a reading of an essay on his work by
Peter Burra which he has chosen to introduce the Everyman
edition of *A Passage to India*. In this essay, asking why did
Forster, who has 'felt so oppressively the attractions of abstract
presentation', ever adopt the novel at all, Burra replies:

It is that he has ideas which need a more distinct articulation

* *Vide The Writings of E. M. Forster*, by Rose Macaulay.

than music or abstraction can make. He is an artist on the fringe of social reform. He is interested in causes. He has never cut himself off, as most artists sooner or later do, from the political and economic questions of the outer world. While he has never deliberately written, like Dickens, a novel with a purpose – an irrelevancy to the dangers of which this art form is particularly exposed – the fact nevertheless remains that *A Passage to India* is 'a book which no student of the Indian question can disregard' . . . Probably the writing of novels has not been the most important element in his life. We are constantly given the impression that there are better things in the world to do.

And this appreciation (it is hardly criticism), winding its laudatory course, concludes:

It is the Anonymous Prophecy that will remain with us, the transcendent beauty of the Mosque and Temple, and the athletic body of Stephen. It would be perhaps merely stupid to ask, in conclusion, for more. It is possible that the mind which saw so visionarily the significance of Stephen, and which could tell the Wilcoxes that 'nothing has been done wrong', has achieved their own wisdom; that the organism, being perfectly adjusted, is silent.

It is an odd explanation of a novelist's prolonged uncreativeness, this attribution of it to some perfect inner adjustment which has rendered speech superfluous! In the present exegesis a directly contrary view will be maintained: namely, that Forster's creative sterility from 1910 to 1924, and subsequently, is the result, not of inner adjustment, but of an inner exhaustion.

Forster is a significant writer. But significant writers are of two kinds. There are those, and they are the greater ones, whose creative work proceeds from an achieved centre of being, and whose continual creativeness is the expression of the constant extension of their grasp upon and penetration into reality. And there are those others, necessarily more numerous, whose work takes its shape from the exteriorization of an inner conflict – which derives, that is to say, from a condition which is antecedent to an achieved inner integration. These latter writers work out, in the course of their art, a more or less significant personal logic, and with its conclusion, if they have not succeeded in achieving a valid inner integration which will remove them to the plane of the creators, they relapse into nonsignificance. Forster is a writer of the latter type, and it will be

my purpose here to reveal the significant pattern which underlies his work and his silence.

The interest of that pattern lies in the fact that it takes us to
the heart of the liberal dilemma, the liberal confusion, and it is
the interest of Forster's novels that they reveal very clearly to
the perceptive eye the inner motions which preclude an attachment to the liberal outlook.

What are the characteristics of the liberal approach to life?
First of all, the liberal mind is a *medium* mind, a mind which fears
extremes and which therefore is predisposed towards compromise. It inhabits a middle region of life, that of people, and therefore its characteristic expression is a social and political one;
but it is incapable of moving beyond people, as they appear on
the social level, to an understanding of the principles and forces
which govern their lives, and this incapacity applies both to
spiritual and economic realities. The compromising tendency
of liberalism causes it to give mental hostages both to the realm
of ideals and to the world of affairs, but it is rooted in the latter
and in a crisis it is the latter which proves the stronger. Liberalism is a half-hearted creed, born out of stable and comfortable
material circumstances, in which it puts its main trust, making
a gesture of greater or less sincerity towards spiritual values –
but nothing more than a gesture, however sincere. Those
spiritual values, however, tend to become something rather less
than the ultimate and therefore terrifying ones. The absolute is
carefully excluded from the liberal way of life. The gesture
towards the spirit is arrested, and modified into a gesture towards culture; that, in turn, resolves itself into a salute to
civilization, and in times of stress the process of deterioration
will not always stop there.

The 'cultured, sensitive and democratic liberalism' which is
explicitly voiced by Forster's later journalistic writings is so
muddled and bewildered an affair that to examine it seriously
is to risk making oneself ridiculous. In his pamphlet, *What I
Believe* (1939), we find Forster reiterating his belief in 'personal
relationships', although personality itself has for him no ultimate
significance, and on his own admission 'Psychology has split
and shattered the idea of a "Person"'. Tolerance, good temper,
sympathy – 'these', says Forster, 'are what matter really'. But

it transpires that these liberal demi-semi-values exist only on the sufferance of 'force', which really upholds society. As to the social question, Forster would prefer, we gather, to any social change, a perpetuation of the old order of 'democratic' capitalism. But he praises 'democracy' while showing no awareness of its capitalistic and therefore incipiently totalitarian substructure: 'democracy' is considered solely from a superficial political point of view, the façade (Parliament, the Press) is naïvely accepted at its face-value. One is reminded of his treatment of 'the Indian question' in his fifth and last novel, where the ugly realities underlying the presence of the British in India are not even glanced at, and the issues raised are handled as though they could be solved on the surface level of personal intercourse and individual behaviour.

But the liberal confusion has another and graver aspect, in which it appears not as a failure merely but as a betrayal. 'I hate the idea of causes,' wrote Forster in 1939, 'and if I had to choose between betraying my country and betraying my friend, I hope I should have the guts to betray my country. . . . Probably,' however, he adds, 'one will not be asked to make such an agonizing choice.' Evidently Forster was not asked, for after the outbreak of war appeared *Nordic Twilight* (1940), an indictment, not very difficult to make in the circumstances, of Nazi culture and an exhortation addressed primarily, one supposes, to writers and those professing a concern with cultural values, to line up and join in the general totalitarian holocaust of total war – for the sake of 'culture'.

That 'cultured, sensitive and democratic liberalism' is not so innocent, so admirable, and so pleasant as it would represent itself to be becomes apparent only upon a much closer examination than is usually accorded it. Such an examination will be implied in what follows. Liberalism rests upon a fundamental spiritual failure, a spiritual equivocation, a spiritual betrayal. It is the outcome of an absence of faith in the spiritual realities which lie at the back of the variable values to which it presents its dubious salutations. Forster, in *What I Believe*, cleverly attempts to discredit faith by attributing that quality to the blind collective hysteria of the dupes of totalitarianism, thereby making it responsible for the evil and violence in the modern world. This, an age of unfaith, and consequently of greedy materialism and the worship of brute force, is characterized by Forster as 'an age of faith'. 'A child of unbelief,' as he elsewhere names himself, he begins his liberal Credo with the sentence, 'I do not believe in Belief', and wittily informs us that: 'My motto is: "Lord, I disbelieve – help thou my unbelief." '

The point of departure for the liberal betrayal cannot be put more clearly than in these words.

I

E. M. FORSTER's first novel, *Where Angels Fear to Tread*, was published in 1905. In 1907 there appeared *The Longest Journey* and this was followed, in 1908, by *A Room With a View*. Each of these novels is concerned with the dual theme of personal salvation and the conflict of good and evil. Of the three it is *The Longest Journey* which is the most emotionally intense and personal, the others being more objectively conceived novels of social comedy, and here it may be convenient to consider the first and the third novels together – and perhaps this has even a chronological justification, for we are informed by Rose Macaulay that a draft of the first half of *A Room With a View* was made as early as 1903.

In each of these novels we have two opposed worlds or ways of life, and characters who oscillate between the two worlds. In *Where Angels Fear to Tread* the contrast and the conflict are between the world of 'Sawston', that is, of smug, respectable conventionality, and that of 'Italy', representing the free play of genuine natural feeling. Sawston is personified in Mrs. Herriton, insincere, calculating, cold, and moved by snobbery and her fear of public opinion; Italy by Gino, affectionate, impulsive and natural, a primitive whose very vulgarity has charm and warmth. In the drama that is played out between these opposites, it is Philip Herriton and Caroline Abbott who suffer the conflict between the two sets of values. Italy and the dramatic events which take place there have the effect of drawing out the nobility and passion of Miss Abbott's quiet nature, and it is through her that Philip, hitherto a man who has hovered distantly on the edge of existence, is drawn into life itself and given reality.

All through the day Miss Abbott had seemed to Philip like a
goddess, and more than ever did she seem so now. Many people
look younger and more intimate during great emotion. But some
there are who look older, and remote, and he could not think
that there was little difference in years, and none in composition,
between her and the man whose head was laid upon her breast.
Her eyes were open, full of infinite pity and full of majesty, as if
they discerned the boundaries of sorrow, and saw unimaginable
tracts beyond. Such eyes he had seen in great pictures but never
in a mortal. Her hands were folded round the sufferer, stroking
him lightly, for even a goddess can do no more than that. And it
seemed fitting, too, that she should bend her head and touch his
forehead with her lips.

Philip looked away, as he sometimes looked away from the
great pictures where visible forms suddenly became inadequate
for the things they have shown to us. He was happy; he was
assured that there was greatness in the world. There came to him
an earnest desire to be good through the example of this good
woman. He would try henceforth to be worthy of the things she
had revealed. Quietly, without hysterical prayers or banging of
drums, he underwent conversion. He was saved.

In *A Room With a View*, the antithesis is similar, but this time,
although the first part of the book is set against the background
of Italy, it is the radical Emersons, father and son, who represent life, truth, sincerity. The heroine, Lucy Honeychurch, is
torn between the values which they represent and those of the
pretentious, bookish Cecil Vyse and the insincere and intriguing
Charlotte Bartlett. Lucy has a moment of intense happiness in
Italy when she is kissed against a prospect of primroses by
George Emerson, but, a victim of the false proprieties as ex-
pounded and embodied by her cousin, Charlotte, she is impli-
cated in a system of falsehoods. Persuading herself that she has
been outrageously insulted by a 'cad', she denies her natural
feelings, and shortly after becomes engaged to Cecil Vyse. The
Emersons, by a coincidence, come to live near Lucy's family in
Sussex, and after a game of tennis, when an incident occurs to
remind both George and Lucy of the previous episode in Italy,
George kisses her again, and afterwards pleads for her love.
Lucy deliberately repulses George, denying and suppressing
again her genuine feelings, and that same evening breaks off

D

her engagement to Cecil, after which, lifeless and empty –

> . . . She gave up trying to understand herself, and joined the
> vast armies of the benighted, who follow neither the heart nor the
> brain, and march to their destiny by catch-words. The armies are
> full of pleasant and pious folk. But they have yielded to the only
> enemy that matters – the enemy within. They have sinned against
> passion and truth, and vain will be their strife after virtue. As the
> years pass, they are censured. Their pleasantry and their piety
> show cracks, their wit becomes cynicism, their unselfishness
> hypocrisy; they feel and produce discomfort wherever they go.
> They have sinned against Eros and against Pallas Athene, and
> not by any heavenly intervention, but by the ordinary course of
> nature, those allied deities will be avenged.
>
> Lucy entered this army when she pretended to George that
> she did not love him, and pretended to Cecil that she loved no
> one. The night received her, as it had received Miss Bartlett thirty
> years before.

In each of these novels, there is a spiritual conflict. In
Forster's words, describing Lucy's inner struggle,

> The contest lay not between love and duty. Perhaps there never
> is such a contest. It lay between the real and the pretended. . . .

The 'real', however, seems to be associated with the natural;
the 'pretended', with the falsities of convention which deny and
frustrate the natural impulses and passions.

Italy makes no appearance in *The Longest Journey* (according
to Rose Macaulay, ' . . . at once the most personal and the
most universal of the five novels; and obviously the most autobiographical . . .'), which is divided into three sections,
'Cambridge', 'Sawston', and 'Wiltshire'. Once again, these
localities have their counterparts in the personalities of certain
of the characters. Cambridge, which clearly represents the
author's naïve conception of the good life, has its counterpart
in the figure of Stewart Ansell; Sawston, again representing
insincere conventionality, pretentious 'culture' and the worship
of the false gods of prestige and success, has its human embodiment in the schoolmaster, Herbert Pembroke, and his sister,
Agnes; while Wiltshire, which stands for the basic touchstone
of nature, reality, the earth, is humanly projected into the
figure of Stephen Wonham, the healthy, unreflective pagan.

Rickie, the little lame hero of the book, is drawn in turn into the orbit of each of these worlds and undergoes an inward struggle which, although it is more desperate and emotionally intensified, is not unlike that of Lucy Honeychurch in *A Room With a View*.

In many respects the theme of *The Longest Journey* recapitulates that of *Where Angels Fear to Tread* and *A Room With a View*: but its development is more complex, and the spiritual drama more intense. It is, no doubt, this intensity which gives the book its overcharged emotional atmosphere and its consequent queer iridiscence as of something faintly morbid or perverse.

For the intensity does not seem justified by the terms of the drama. Which means that the drama itself is emotionally worked up to a point at which it becomes false to the terms of reference within which the mind of the novelist is operating.

Throughout all of Forster's writings there is to be seen an unfortunate tendency to lapse, at moments when the author feels the necessity to indicate something beyond the level of human relationships in their social setting (a level upon which alone he is perfectly at ease), into 'poetical' vagueness of the most embarrassing kind. An example of this is to be found early in *The Longest Journey*, when Rickie glimpses Agnes and her lover, Gerald Dawes, at a moment of erotic passion.

> Rickie limped away without the sandwiches, crimson and afraid. He thought, 'Do such things actually happen?' and he seemed to be looking down coloured valleys. Brighter they glowed, till gods of pure flame were born in them, and then he was looking at pinnacles of virgin snow. While Mr. Pembroke talked, the riot of fair images increased. They invaded his being and lit lamps at unsuspected shrines. Their orchestra commenced in that suburban house, where he had to stand aside for a maid to carry in the luncheon. Music flowed past him like a river. He stood at the springs of creation and heard the primeval monotony. Then an obscure instrument gave out a little phrase. The river continued unheeding. The phrase was repeated, and a listener might know it was a fragment of the Tune of Tunes. Nobler instruments accepted it, the clarionet protected, the brass encouraged, and it rose to the surface to the whisper of violins. In full unison was Love born, flame of the flame, flushing the dark river beneath him and the virgin snow above. His wings were

infinite, his youth eternal; the sun was a jewel on his finger as he passed it in benediction over the world. Creation, no longer monotonous, acclaimed him, in widening melody, in brighter radiances. Was Love a column of fire? Was he a torrent of song? Was he greater than either – the touch of a man on a woman?

Forster's books abound in passages of this sort, which, however, represent merely an intensification of his normal 'sensitive' and 'charming' style. The prevalence of this sort of false, over-ripe writing indicates some basic uncertainty in Forster's grasp of life, and to apprehend the roots of that uncertainty it is necessary to investigate the disparity between the religious drama which he unfolds and the ultimate principles to which it is referred.

What are the characteristics of this religious drama? First of all, it proffers the possibilities of salvation or of damnation, as we may see in the cases of Philip Herriton and Lucy Honey-church in the other novels. Philip, granted a vision of 'infinite pity and . . . majesty' (which, incidentally, had an erotic source), 'underwent conversion. He was saved.' Lucy, conse-quent upon a denial and a lie, joins 'the vast armies of the benighted' and 'the night received her'. In *The Longest Journey* there are indications that the issue of salvation depends upon the acceptance or rejection of a 'symbolic moment'.

> It seems to me [says Rickie] that here and there in life we meet with a person or incident that is symbolical. It's nothing in itself, yet for the moment it stands for some eternal principle. We accept it, at whatever cost, and we have accepted life. But if we are frightened and reject it, the moment, so to speak, passes; the symbol is never offered again.

The symbol, for Rickie, was his illegitimate half-brother, Stephen. When his kinship with Stephen is revealed to him (although he is then under the mistaken impression that Stephen was the child of his father, whom he hated) he is inexpressibly shocked and disgusted, but his better impulse is to acknowledge him honestly and to inform him of the relation-ship. The impulse is quashed by Agnes, and Rickie succumbs inwardly to the false life represented by Sawston. When a later opportunity presents itself of acknowledging Stephen, and he again fails at the crisis, we are told that 'he remained conscientious and decent, but the spiritual part of him proceeded towards ruin'.

His inner ruination continues, but is interrupted by Stephen's appearance at Sawston, coincident with that of Ansell; who – when Stephen is callously turned away by Agnes – publicly denounces the inhumanity and hypocrisy of Rickie; and there follows Rickie's abandonment of the Sawston life and his reconciliation with Stephen, in which we must presumably see his movement towards 'salvation'.

Stephen, then, in this novel, is the touchstone of reality. He is the 'elemental character' who 'sees straight through perplexities and complications, who is utterly percipient of the reality behind appearance, both in matters of general truth and of incidents in the story', to quote from Burra's essay: and as this essay has Forster's own approval it may be illuminating to consider what further is said in it about Stephen.

In the person of Stephen [writes Burra] physical strength is exalted into the most exciting beauty and the whole novel reminds one constantly of the work which Lawrence produced a few years later. When he makes his first appearance, a third of the way through the book, the writing is lifted up like music to herald his approach. He is the product of an intensely passionate imagination working upon closely recorded detail of behaviour and conduct. He is life, at the centre and at the circumference – he is the world's essential simplicity, transformed by the author's vision. His significance is clear to the reader at once; no other character – except Mrs. Failing when the mood is on her – perceives it, until Ansell, the articulate philosopher, sums him up.

And this is how Ansell sums him up – possibly it is an illustration of how the writing is 'lifted up like music' when he appears:

A silence, akin to poetry, invaded Ansell. Was it only a pose to like this man, or was he really wonderful? He was not romantic, for Romance is a figure with outstretched hands, yearning for the unattainable. Certain figures of the Greeks, to whom we continually return, suggested him a little. One expected nothing of him – no purity of phrase nor swift-edged thought. Yet the conviction grew that he had been back somewhere – back to some table of the gods, spread in a field where there is no noise, and that he belonged for ever to the guests with whom he had eaten.

This, then, is the touchstone of reality and of salvation which Forster proposes and it is not difficult to penetrate its glaring inadequacies: it in no way justifies the emotional intensity of the drama which is indicated as taking place in Rickie's soul. Between the poles of conventionality and naturalness there is room for drama of a sort, but not a drama insufflated with the highly-pitched emotional excitement of *The Longest Journey*, or even indeed that of the other two novels. This is not to say that the drama which is proposed is intrinsically unreal; only that it is made unreal by being set in such limited and lateral perspectives: the drama is too intense for the slight terms of reference. A spiritual conflict is imported into a naturalistic framework, and the effect is one, inevitably, of sentimentality and falsification.

This confusion of the spiritual and the natural runs throughout the earlier novels. As in D. H. Lawrence (who, however, avoided Forster's irrelevant sweetness and charm), spiritual attributes are conferred upon biological phenomena. Thus in *Where Angels Fear to Tread*, Philip's 'conversion' follows upon the erotic emotions stirred in Caroline Abbott by the frankly sensual Gino. Similarly, in *The Longest Journey*, not only is Rickie's personal drama initiated by his witnessing of the erotic passage between Agnes and Gerald Dawes, but the 'acceptance' upon which his salvation depends centres around the result of his dead mother's illicit intercourse with her farmer lover – a Lady Chatterly situation. The importance which Forster confers upon sexual passion is shown both by the excessive excitement with which he approaches it, and the way in which he connects it with violent death – the finality of death being utilized to confer something of its own ultimate, absolute character upon the emotion stirred by sex.

To endow conventionality with all the attributes of the powers of darkness is, of course, grossly to overstate the matter. The world represented by the word 'Sawston' has genuine undercurrents of evil which we are made to feel, but which are simply not explicable in the terms of Nature versus Convention which are proposed. When we encounter such a sentence as this –

> Then he [i.e. Rickie] . . . prayed passionately, for he knew that the conventions would claim him soon . . .

we at once feel the somewhat ridiculous inadequacy of the antithesis which provides the frame of reference for the novel.

Not only in *The Longest Journey* is the question of salvation (raised in the action of the narrative and brought to an arbitrary conclusion there) left with a good many loose ends flying: the same is true of the other novels. What is to happen to Philip Herriton, now that his eyes have been opened to the wonder and beauty of life? What will happen to Lucy and George Emerson now that their difficulties are over and they are happily married? It is hard to see any more finality in their 'saved' state than that implied in the insufficient and question-begging symbol, towards the end of *The Longest Journey*, of 'Wiltshire' – the life of pastoral satisfactions.

The incompleteness and indeed the reversibility of Forster's moral symbolism is shown in his 'realistic' confusion of the attributes of the 'good' and 'bad' types. Having said, as Burra says in the essay already referred to, that Forster introduces an 'elemental' character into each of his books, whose wisdom 'puts into ironic contrast the errors and illusions of the rest', and having pointed out that 'In the case of the men the stress is laid on the athletic, of the women on the intuitive', one can point to characters who possess the external evidences of these qualities, and who yet turn out to be on the wrong side of the moral fence. George Emerson, Gino and Stephen may be said to be athletic', and therefore on the side of the 'real'. But equally athletic, though by no means on the side of the real, are Gerald Dawes and Agnes, while Stewart Ansell, undoubtedly a touchstone of values, is not athletic at all. Similarly in the case of the 'intuitive' women. Of them Mrs. Moore and Mrs. Wilcox and perhaps Mrs. Honeychurch are recognizably 'good' characters, while Mrs. Failing, a woman of the same basic type, and who possesses the additional symbolical advantage of living in Wiltshire, is as recognizably 'bad'. One might compare also Cecil Vyse with Philip Herriton and Stewart Ansell. This confusion is true to life, no doubt, but it is not true to the symbolical pattern of the novels, and it is necessary to ask what are the reasons for this ambivalence.

The most plausible explanation of Forster's 'realistic' confusion of good and bad types (a confusion which, it must be repeated, is out of place in a symbolical setting) lies in the very plain fact that the middle-class existence which Forster portrays, the life of the irresponsible, moneyed, parasitical bourgeoisie, is false, because it is based upon social falsehood, and nothing can ever be made really right within it. Consequently, no stable system of moral symbolism can be erected upon it.

This is not to say that his characters are by that fact deprived of the possibility of spiritual struggle; only that such a struggle which takes place within a spiritual arena circumscribed by its reference to the framework of their false social order, and whose outcome does not result in an overthrowing or a repudiation of the limits set around their lives by their privileged social and economic position, is thereby rendered devoid of real and radical significance. The life of Forster's characters, as members of the English upper middle-classes, is based on falsehood because it is based on unearned income, derived from nameless and unmentioned sources, and all their independence, freedom, culture, 'personal relationships' are only made possible by this fact. Their lives are lived in a watertight system abstracted from the larger life of society as a whole. They are out of touch with humanity, carefully, though for the most part unconsciously, preserving themselves, by means of their mental circumscriptions and social codes, from all encroachment of the painful and upsetting actualities which make their privileged existence possible. Unlike the rich of other times, their privileges carry with them no burden of responsibility, and thus possess no concrete social sanction. The penalty they pay for their social advantages is a heavy one – a fundamental unreality which vitiates the personal dramas which take place in the closed social circuit to which they are condemned. For an inner spiritual change which affects one's attitude to one or two other selected persons only, and does not extend itself to include every other human being irrespective of social distinction, is invalidated from the start. But at the point at which some attempt to deal with this question would seem necessary, Forster brings his stories to a close.

It is not difficult to perceive the connection existing between the false social circumstances which set limits to reality for the sake of their own perpetuation, and the inhibiting factors which prevent Forster from reaching out to ultimates for the validation of his religious drama. The novelist, despite his perception of the reality of personal struggle towards salvation, is himself unable to transcend the pattern imposed on reality by the self-interest of the class to which he belongs, and instead, therefore, of permitting the drama with which he is concerned to break through the pattern and centre itself within the perspectives of reality, he curtails the perspectives themselves and attempts to persuade himself and his readers that the drama takes place between the poles of Nature and Convention, with Nature filling the place of God, or the Absolute.* The novelist's own awareness that this will not justify a real spiritual dynamism in his characters must eventually follow.

II

IT is possibly the realization of something of this which led Forster to abandon the narrow personal drama and to embrace the social issues which are clearly displayed in his fourth novel, *Howards End* (1910). There is no doubt whatever as to the social orientation of this novel and its characterization, nor as to its bearing upon the logic of Forster's development. From the point reached in *The Longest Journey* there were two possible paths for one in Forster's situation: either to affirm the reality of the spiritual, and thus to justify the drama of personal salvation, by placing the individual (and thus by inference his social circumstances) in the ultimate perspectives of existence; or to affirm the primary reality of the social and to reduce the spiritual to an epiphenomenon dependent upon the social pattern. The first alternative would have made possible a continuation and development of the personal drama; and thus, conceivably, the transformation of Forster into a genuine

---

* Of all the characters in the early novels who represent 'the real' as against 'the pretended', not one derives his sanction from any other than a natural principle. Stephen and Gino are a direct appeal to biological, not to say physiological, values. In the case of Stephen it is made clear that he is a crude atheist, while Ansell is evidently an ethical materialist. Old Mr. Emerson, a religious figure, is an old-fashioned agnostic radical. The clearest insight, however, into Forster's religiosity is to be derived from a study of his early short stories where Nature is deified as Pan and conventionalism is contrasted with the amoral universe of dryads, mermaids and satyrs.

creator: the second could only have necessitated a transition from the personal to the social level, a movement from the centre to the periphery; which was, in fact, the result.

Howards End must be interpreted from this point of view. Here is an evidently allegorical contrast between the inner world of personal existence, represented by the cultured sisters Helen and Margaret Schlegel, and the outer world of the practical organization of living represented by the business-like, British-to-the-backbone, empire-building Wilcoxes. But before we move on to a consideration of the relationship between the two families, the focal point of the novel must be considered.

That focal point is money. Hardly are the Schlegels introduced before the subject of their investments is touched upon. Money, indeed, is the *leit-motif* which accompanies the Schlegels throughout the book. And it is poverty, in the character of Leonard Bast, which underscores their wealth and culture. The significance of this bringing to the surface of what, in order to permit the strictly personal drama, had hitherto been kept in concealment, hardly needs to be emphasized. *Howards End* is in one of its aspects a justification of economic privilege; but the recognition of the individual's dependence upon social circumstances destroys the possibility of the drama of personal salvation, and substitutes the drama of social relationships.

Leonard rises, spectre-like and accusing, from the depths of the world outside the social hot-house of the economically and culturally privileged, to confront the Schlegels with the harsh realities of their situation. But how subjectively and with what a suspicious bias he is presented will appear from the manner in which he is pushed on to the scene by his author:

> The boy Leonard Bast, stood at the extreme verge of gentility. He was not in the abyss, but he could see it, and at times people whom he knew had dropped in, and counted no more. He knew that he was poor, and would admit it: he would have died sooner than confess any inferiority to the rich. This may be splendid of him. But he was inferior to most rich people, there is not the least doubt of it. He was not as courteous as the average rich man, nor as intelligent, nor as healthy, nor as lovable. His mind and his body had been alike underfed, because he was poor.

Because he does not enjoy the financial advantages of the

Schlegels, Leonard Bast's aspirations towards culture are made to appear pathetic in their hopelessness. But the character of Leonard Bast is not the result of authentic, disinterested observation of life; he is unconsciously falsified, in a manner which will be considered below, to fit within the preconceived interpretation of reality which underpins the structure of the novel.

The argument of *Howards End*, at all times implicit and at times declared, is that culture and the good life depend upon economic security, which in the capitalistic world of the time means privilege. 'To trust people is a luxury in which only the wealthy can indulge; the poor cannot afford it' – such statements as this are intermittent in the early parts of the book. In Chapter VII the following conversation takes place between Margaret Schlegel and her aunt, Mrs. Munt, a conversation which sets the course for Margaret's progression throughout the story:

'I hope to risk things all my life.'

'Oh, Margaret, most dangerous.'

'But after all,' she continued with a smile, 'there's never any great risk as long as you have money.'

'Oh, shame! What a shocking speech!'

'Money pads the edge of things,' said Miss Schlegel. 'God help those who have none.'

'But this is something quite new!' said Mrs. Munt, who collected new ideas as a squirrel collects nuts, and was especially attracted by those that are portable.

'New for me; sensible people have acknowledged it for years. You and I and the Wilcoxes stand upon money as upon islands. It is so firm beneath our feet that we forget its very existence. It's only when we see someone near us tottering that we realize all that an independent income means. Last night, when we were talking up here round the fire, I began to think that the very soul of the world is economic, and that the lowest abyss is not the absence of love, but the absence of coin.'

'I call that rather cynical.'

'So do I. But Helen and I, we ought to remember, when we are tempted to criticize others, that we are standing on these islands, and that most of the others are down below the surface of the sea. The poor cannot always reach those whom they want to love, and they can hardly ever escape from those whom they love no longer. We rich can. Imagine the tragedy last June if Helen and Paul

Wilcox had been poor people, and couldn't invoke railways and motor-cars to part them.'

'That's more like Socialism,' said Mrs. Munt suspiciously.

'Call it what you like. I call it going through life with one's hand spread open on the table. I'm tired of these rich people who pretend to be poor, and think it shows a nice mind to ignore the piles of money that keep their feet above the waves. I stand each year upon six hundred pounds, and Helen upon the same, and Tibby will stand upon eight, and as fast as our pounds crumble away into the sea they are renewed – from the sea, yes, from the sea. And all our thoughts are the thoughts of six-hundred-pounders, and all our speeches; and because we don't want to steal umbrellas ourselves, we forget that below the sea people do want to steal them and do steal them sometimes, and that what's a joke up here is down there reality——'

. . .'Do tell me this, at all events. Are you for the rich or for the poor?'

'Too difficult. Ask me another. Am I for poverty or for riches? For riches. Hurrah for riches!'

'For riches,' echoed Mrs. Munt, having, as it were, at last secured her nut.

'Yes. For riches. Money for ever!'

'So am I, and so, I am afraid, are most of my acquaintances at Swanage, but I am surprised that you agree with us.'

That conversation occurs after the Schlegels' first encounter with Leonard Bast. After a second encounter, at which they find out something of his private life, the Schlegels attend a debating society at which the question is discussed of how a philanthropic millionaire ought to dispose of his money. 'Mr. Bast' is taken as the hypothetical poor man whose condition is to be improved by the millionaire's bounty, and Margaret, after listening to various propositions, intervenes with the suggestion that he should be given the money itself.

'Money's educational. It's far more educational than the things it buys. . . . When your Socialism comes it may be different, and we may think in terms of commodities instead of cash. Till it comes give people cash, for it is the warp of civilization, whatever the woof may be. The imagination ought to play upon money and realize it vividly, for it's the – the second most important thing in the world. It is so slurred over and hushed up, there is so little clear thinking – oh, political economy, of course, but so few of us think clearly about our own private incomes, and admit that independent thoughts are in nine cases out of ten the result of independent means. Money: give Mr. Bast money, and don't bother about his ideals. He'll pick those up for himself.'

On the other side of the Schlegels to Leonard Bast, however, and representing the organized, coercive practical life which guarantees to them that private income which makes their cultured existence possible, stands Henry Wilcox, efficient, practical, masterful, but spiritually and emotionally uninte-grated. But the Wilcoxes' guarantees have a spiritual aspect – that of the 'outer life' which Forster takes as antithetical to the 'inner life' represented by the Schlegels. The Wilcoxes are introduced on this very note, which is struck almost immediately after Helen's return, at the beginning of the tale, from her visit to Howards End, Mrs. Wilcox's country house, where she has had a brief erotic passage with the Wilcoxes' youngest son, Paul.

'To think that because you and a young man meet for a moment, there must be all these telegrams and anger,' supplied Margaret. Helen nodded.

'I've often thought about it, Helen. It's one of the most interest-ing things in the world. The truth is that there is a great outer life that you and I have never touched – a life in which telegrams and anger count. Personal relations, that we think supreme, are not supreme there. There love means marriage settlements, death, death duties. So far I'm clear. But here's my difficulty. This outer life, though obviously horrid, often seems the real one – there's grit in it. It does breed character. Do personal relations lead to sloppiness in the end?'

'Oh, Meg, that's what I felt, only not so clearly, when the Wilcoxes were so competent, and seemed to have their hands on all the ropes.'

'Don't you feel it now?'

'I remember Paul at breakfast,' said Helen quietly. 'I shall never forget him. He had nothing to fall back upon. I know that personal relations are the real life, for ever and ever.'

'Amen!'

The respective positions of Leonard Bast and Henry Wilcox have an obvious symbolic importance, in that the leanings of the Schlegel sisters are divided between the two. The impulsive and idealistic Helen reacts vehemently against Mr. Wilcox, and her reaction drives her towards Leonard Bast, who has suffered as a result of the business-man's human irresponsibility (and whose character as a *victim* is further emphasized by the revelation that his bedraggled wife was once Mr. Wilcox's mistress). Margaret, on the other hand, wiser and more level-headed, so we are told, is drawn towards the Wilcox family and led to associate herself with the values they represent.

> 'If Wilcoxes hadn't worked and died in England for thousands of years, you and I couldn't sit here without having our throats cut. There would be no trains, no ships to carry us literary people about in, no fields even. Just savagery. No – perhaps not even that. Without their spirit life might never have moved out of protoplasm. More and more do I refuse to draw my income and sneer at those who guarantee it.'

The dramatic action of the book develops out of the schism which takes place between the Schlegel sisters as each moves further along her chosen path, Margaret towards the acceptance of the 'outer life', expressed in her engagement to the widowed Mr. Wilcox, and Helen towards her pursuit of a somewhat vaguely conceived 'ideal'. The scales are, however, heavily weighted against Helen, who is used as a mere foil to her sister's maturer wisdom. That Helen's antagonism to her sister's engagement to Mr. Wilcox is a modified one, and that inwardly she is reconciled to it and even approves of it, appears from a conversation between the sisters following an outburst of Helen's to Mr. Wilcox on the subject of his responsibility for the misfortunes of Leonard Bast.

> Margaret . . . gave her sister a thorough scolding. She censured her, not for disapproving of the engagement, but for throwing over her disapproval a veil of mystery. . . . Helen was silent for a minute, and then burst into a queer speech, which cleared the air. 'Go on and marry him. I think you're splendid; and if anyone can pull it off, you will.' Margaret denied that there was anything to 'pull off', but she continued: 'Yes, there is, and I wasn't up to it with Paul. I can only do what's easy. I can only entice and be enticed. I can't, and won't, attempt difficult relations. . . . But you, you're different. You're a heroine. . . . You mean to keep proportion, and that's heroic, it's Greek, and I don't see why it shouldn't succeed with you. Go on and fight with

him and help him. Don't ask *me* for help, or even for sympathy. Henceforward I'm going my own way. I mean to be thorough, because thoroughness is easy.'

The morality of the story and the conclusion we are supposed to draw from it are plain. 'Only connect . . .' exhorts the book's epigraph; and Margaret it is, we are asked to believe, who accomplishes the connection.

In this novel, however, once again Forster's work suffers artistically as the result of the confusion between the symbolical and the realistic treatment of his subject. A clearer and deeper mind, we can safely assume, taking the theme of the relationship of the inner life to the outer, would manipulate somewhat different symbols from 'Wilcoxes' and 'Schlegels' and would reach somewhat different conclusions from those of *Howards End*. For Forster has not in fact stated the real issue either helpfully or sincerely. What he has succeeded in doing, and in doing quite clearly enough, is to reveal, in the pre-determined and therefore falsified treatment of his subject, the central predicament and equivocation inherent in the compromising liberal mentality.

The crucial falsification is not that of the characters of the Wilcoxes, who are presented honestly and objectively enough, but of the Schlegels and Leonard Bast. And it is here, perhaps, that we touch upon the psychological compulsion which inclined Forster's mind towards his admixture of the symbolical and the realistic – namely, in its effect in securing the falsification of symbolical truth necessary for the adaptation of the realities represented by the words 'culture' and 'poverty' to the far from disinterested preconceptions of the bourgeois liberal point of view.

'It is private life that holds out the mirror to infinity; personal intercourse, and that alone, that ever hints at a personality beyond our daily vision.' Such, in characteristically Forsterian phraseology, is the Schlegel viewpoint. Suppose we grant, then, what is so almost squeamishly proffered – that, symbolically, the Schlegels represent the inner life of personality in contrast to the outer life of organization represented by the Wilcoxes. The question follows: Can there in fact ever be such a reconciliation between the two as is symbolized by Margaret's marriage to Mr. Wilcox? To speak more explicitly, can Culture only save itself from inward debility by an alliance with the State, can the life of the spirit maintain and strengthen itself only by a compromise with the Prince of this world?* Is such a reconciliation, or compromise, a spiritual achievement or a betrayal?

From the spiritual, personal and cultural point of view it is clearly a betrayal; it is the equivocal and deluded attempt to serve two masters which is spoken of in the New Testament. That Forster is uneasy about this is shown not only by his splitting of the Schlegel viewpoint into two, but also by his hesitant treatment of the relations between Margaret and Mr. Wilcox, for their relationship crashes on a critical issue, and is only saved, rather unconvincingly, by the entirely fortuitous circumstances which make Henry Wilcox, at the last moment, a 'broken man', and drive him humbly to his wife for protection.

What, indeed, is this 'connection', but the bridging of the two worlds which were, in the earlier novels, held apart as spiritual antitheses: the world of falsity and convention and the world of the genuine and natural: the 'pretended' and the 'real'? Twists of presentation aside, in what essential respect can the Wilcoxes be said to differ from the Pembrokes of *The Longest Journey*? Yet while, in the earlier novel, for the sake of the personal drama which is enacted between those antitheses, the Pembrokes are represented as something at all costs to be eschewed and shunned, in the later book, where the personal drama gives place to the social, the same type, with a few changes, is represented as admirable and to be courted.

What is the reason for this change of attitude and the decision to compromise? The answer, it is not difficult to perceive, lies in the weakness and invalidity of the inner life, of 'the real', as conceived by Forster, which, presented in naturalistic terms, has not sufficient inner vitality to maintain itself as a centre of spiritual energy in independence of the outer region of practical life. Forster's fundamental error consists of invoking the spiritual principle and then referring it for its ultimate sanction not to

* *Vide* Chapter XXVII: 'Talk as one would, *Mr. Wilcox was king of this world*, the superman, with his own morality, whose head remained in the clouds.' (My italics.)

God, to the supernatural – a resort which would have had the effect of thoroughly disequilibrizing Forster's mental pattern and bringing it to a new and revolutionary centrality – but to Nature. That Forster's ethical naturalism will not bear the spiritual burdens which are placed upon it we have already seen. This inability to support the personal values represented by the Schlegels by an appeal to any higher order of being than that embodied in the mundanely 'mysterious' figure of the first Mrs. Wilcox with her tiresome wisp of hay (with the dew still on it) deprives the antithesis between Schlegels and Wilcoxes of its absolute character and therefore of all real value as a statement of the relationship between the inner and outer realms of existence – or the realm of subjectivity and that of objectivization. For neither can the Schlegel sisters really be accepted as adequately symbolizing the life of the spirit, nor can Leonard Bast be regarded as a truthful representation of the urge towards culture unsupported by economic privilege. The Schlegels are simply what they are 'realistically' represented to be – two specimens of the leisured bourgeois parasite upon culture. And all that the book leaves us with is a statement of the real relations between 'cultured, sensitive and democratic' liberalism and the capitalistic structure of Edwardian society which permits and guarantees its harmless, ineffectual and even charming existence.

Here it is that Forster's confusion of symbolical and realistic treatment serves the purposes of so doctoring the issue that it conforms to the pre-requirements of an outlook obviously conditioned by its liberal bourgeois background. Forster's realistic presentation of the Schlegels enables him to get around the responsibility of declaring that his novel is an allegory of the inner life. Quite so. But if the Schlegels are only – the Schlegels, nothing more or less, then the book is deprived of inner significance. Forster's confused method enables him to retain the overtones of symbolical significance while presenting an apparently straightforward realistic narrative: it is no wonder that the book has been popular.

Perhaps we may exonerate Forster of the charge of sinister intent in deliberately falsifying his presentation of the Schlegels, at the price of denying them the symbolical significance which

E

they are presumed to possess. But it is much more difficult to avoid making the charge in the case of his presentation of Leonard Bast; and there is the further reflection to which this leads, namely, that Leonard is presented in such a way as to emphasize the Schlegels' claim to symbolical significance as the bearers of cultural values and the inner life. For the implication of Leonard's failure, owing to inferior social advantages, to attain the inner life, is that the inner life itself is made possible only by the possession of social advantages such as those the Schlegels enjoy, and from this it follows that, in the author's mind, the Schlegels do therefore possess symbolical significance.

Forster's evident determination that Leonard Bast should be made to fit the preconception that culture is secondary to economic security leads him to draw a portrait which is the least convincing fabrication in the book, and the one which most plainly calls into question the author's fundamental seriousness and responsibility as an artist. Now, it simply is not true that an inferior social position automatically deprives its victim of the possibility of attaining to the inner life, any more than it is true that the possession of social advantages guarantees spiritual development. It is not even true that the average rich man is, as Forster states, more courteous, intelligent and lovable than the average poor man.

The wretched Leonard is a lay figure, an effigy made to walk and talk in such a way as to bolster up the liberal philosophy which inspires the book. For culture is *not* dependent upon wealth; it is only to the parasites of the spirit that it appears as an object which can be externally appropriated. Nor can Forster's pressing of this point home find any response in the mind of the genuine champion of the dispossessed, for the depth of his concern with the sufferings of the underprivileged masses may be judged from the fact that it is Henry Wilcox with whom Margaret, 'keen to derive the modern capitalist from the warriors and hunters of the past', 'connects'.

Leonard is disposed of by death, and his elimination glossed over with an outburst of Forster's special lyricism:

. . . the time for telegrams and anger was over, and it seemed wisest that the hands of Leonard should be folded on his breast and be filled with flowers. Here was the father; leave it at that. Let Squalor be turned into Tragedy, whose eyes are the stars, and whose hands hold the sunset and the dawn.

III

THE foregoing delineation of the inner development of Forster's mind as revealed in his novels should have clarified the nature of the compromise or betrayal which lies at the root of 'cultured, sensitive and democratic liberalism', a compromise which cannot but vitiate its perpetrator's grasp of reality and deprive his mind of creative purpose. But if my interpretation of the interior dialectic of Forster's novels has any validity, then it follows that *A Passage to India* (1924) must have its relation to it. What, briefly, is that relationship?

With the resolution of the conflict between what is called, in *A Room With a View*, 'the real and the pretended', signified by the union of the Schlegels with the Wilcoxes, the novelist's own inner thought-conflict, expressing the inner conflict which lies at the bottom of all the novels, comes to an end, and there is no longer any imperative urge towards fictional creation. Forster has exhausted his theme, and the dramatic materials are lacking. More, his interest has moved outward, peripherally, from the personal drama to a concern with the generalized problems of society, and it is now possible to speak of him (*vide* Burra) as 'an artist on the fringe of social reform'. The only way in which the novelist can finally exploit his basic situation is by transporting his mechanical dramatic apparatus to some external situation which it happens approximately and fortuitously to fit. And so, in *A Passage to India*, we have the Anglo-Indian world of Turtons and Burtons on the one side and on the other that of Aziz and his compatriots, with Cyril Fielding, the liberal educationalist, in between, and Mrs. Moore, the counterpart of Mrs. Wilcox, anomalously bridging both worlds. But the apparatus hardly fits the drama, which, indeed, exiguous as it is, takes place, not in the battlefield of any individual soul, but on the plane of external action and political issues, where it is brought only to a precarious and inconclusive termination. The conflict is external to the author's mind.

A Passage to India is written at the extreme edge of Forster's creative impulse. It is hard to see how any but a mechanical and inwardly meaningless work of fiction could have succeeded it, and the fact that it has been followed by silence need cause us no great surprise. Certain features of the novel, however, have an interest in the light of the interpretation of Forster which I have proposed.

If the book can be said to have a hero, that hero must be Cyril Fielding, a character who evidently embodies his creator's own outlook upon life. In Fielding, we find a union of the qualities seen as separate in *Howards End*. Fielding is humane, cultured, enlightened, progressive, but he is also capable, reliable, and self-assured: he has a sense of the importance of 'personal relationships' but he also has 'grit' and his hands are definitely 'on the ropes'. Ideally, then, he should be an harmonious figure. Yet it seems that there is some dissatisfaction on his author's part with the finality of the values which he embodies.

> . . . he felt dubious and discontented suddenly, and wondered whether he was really and truly successful as a human being. After forty years' experience he had learnt to manage his life and make the best of it on advanced European lines, had developed his personality, explored his limitations, controlled his passions – and he had done it all without becoming either pedantic or worldly. A creditable achievement; but as the moment passed, he felt he ought to have been working at something else the whole time – he didn't know at what, never would know, never could know, and that was why he felt sad.

Those feelings of self-dissatisfaction are again touched on at the end of the book, where Fielding is speaking to Aziz of his marriage to Mrs. Moore's daughter, Stella, who, he feels, unlike himself, is 'after something' – the 'something', whatever it is which is included in this vague gesture, being that, evidently, which is outside the scope of his limited, rationalistic scheme of life.

But the most significant factor in the novel is the emotional background provided by the Marabar Caves, around which the action centres. It is the visit of Aziz, Mrs. Moore and Miss Quested to the caves which precipitates the drama, and throughout the novel the echoing *'Boum-boum'* of the caves supplies an insistent undercurrent to the moods and thoughts of the characters.

The caves' horrible echo, is, however, a more elaborate repetition of something which has evidently lurked always at the edge of Forster's mind, for it has found expression in previous writings. It is indicated by the description of the infernal region in which a character in an early story finds himself after death, through his smug, unheroic life; and it is indicated also in the metaphor of the goblins 'walking quietly over the universe' to describe the Beethoven Symphony in *Howards End*. ('Panic and emptiness', the message of the goblins, being the words which Helen has previously applied to the inner life of the Wilcoxes.) The caves reiterate the same message of meaninglessness and nullity, but more insistently and overpoweringly. The echo murmurs: 'Pathos, piety, courage – they exist, but are identical, and so is filth. Everything exists, nothing has value.' And the terror of the Marabar lay in the fact that it 'robbed infinity and eternity of their vastness, the only quality that accommodates them to mankind'. Not only does the echo of the caves prolong itself throughout the story to which it provides such a menacing undertone, but it has the effect of undermining and disintegrating Mrs. Moore's hold on life, and ultimately, of destroying her. When we recollect that Mrs. Moore is to *A Passage to India* what Mrs. Wilcox is to *Howards End* – that she is the 'elemental character' who represents what appears to be the highest value to which Forster can appeal to sanction his interpretation of life, the metaphorical implications of her disintegration and its occasion are ominous, to say the very least. Nor is there anything in Forster's occasional and miscellaneous writings of the past twenty years to dispel the misgivings to which a consideration of the sequence of his novels, ending on this ominous note, gives rise.

VIRGINIA WOOLF

I

AMONG the women writers of our time there is none whose *prestige* stands higher than that of Virginia Woolf. It is because I believe this prestige to be unfounded that I am here proposing a drastic revaluation of her work. The legend of Virginia Woolf as an 'artist' pure and simple, projecting, in an experiential vacuum, sensitive and delicate word-patterns devoid of all but the most essentially aesthetic content, is one which can have taken root only in a society in which there exists the most lamentable indifference both to life and art. The following passage from a review of a typically adulatory book about Virginia Woolf's novels is representative of the prevalent inert and thoughtless acceptance of this legend:

> Of Mrs. Woolf's style this book does not directly treat, yet . . . here, if anywhere, the style *is* the writer . . . her best work is a sequence of illuminating moments woven into a complete design; and for that design her imagination used its own language – an impressionistic, highly charged, emotive prose that differs at times little, if at all, from poetry; its texture shot with grace, sensitivity, and subtle awareness. Over a human landscape of deliberately limited dimensions her delicate rhythms drift and play like soft clouds through which gleams the dappled sunlight of her pity and her humour, her sympathy for the sorrows and frustrations of her fellow men and women, and her ironic smile at their weaknesses and foibles. . . .

To the question, 'Yes – but what are Virginia Woolf's novels *about*? What view of life do they reflect? What particular insights do they display?' one receives no satisfactory answer.

That Virginia Woolf's novels are tenuous, amorphous and vague, that her prose expresses a state of sensitized generality, is true. Nevertheless, this condition has definite psychic roots, and in itself raises the question of value. What I shall attempt to do in this essay, therefore, is simply to lay bare the interior psychological pattern which runs through the series of her novels. It will then appear that beneath the imprecisions, vaguenesses and generalities of the particular work there is an underlying, basic preoccupation which gives rise to those qualities: that the merely aesthetic approach to her work begs the question, and that beneath the aesthetic surface there runs a theme of a totally non-aesthetic character. In bringing this theme to light, in revealing the unconscious psychological process which determines the aesthetic form of the work, my aim is to explode the theory of aestheticism, and to show that no artistic work can exist in independence of its maker's human preoccupations and beliefs. All that is necessary to this end is to expose the interior logic of Virginia Woolf's development, which aestheticism is both unwilling and powerless to penetrate.

Virginia Woolf's work as a novelist falls roughly into three periods. There is the early period of conventional fictionalizing represented by her two first novels, *The Voyage Out* and *Night and Day*. There is the period of experiment marked by the discarding of those fictional properties which she was unable to utilize, and issuing in *Jacob's Room* – the first novel in what was to be recognized as her characteristic manner – and later, in an ascending scale, in *Mrs. Dalloway* and *To the Lighthouse*. And lastly, there is the descent into an increasingly despairing vacuousness and dissipation of perception through *The Waves*, *The Years*, and finally *Between the Acts*, marked by a disintegration of form expressing a surrender of all significance to the accidental process of time.

The Voyage Out (1915) and *Night and Day* (1919) are dull, third-rate novels in the conventional manner, interesting only because they reveal quite plainly the nature of the disabilities under which Virginia Woolf laboured. These two novels reveal that she lacked the first requirements of a good novelist: the ability to create living, credible characters whose life is projected into an interesting and significant narrative pattern. The structure of the first novel is incoherent. In substance, it is the story of Rachel Vinrace, an inexperienced girl of the professional classes, who is taken out to an island on the Amazon where there is a colony of holiday-making Europeans, and who makes a variety of haphazard human contacts, ponders on the meaning of life, is flustered by her discovery of sex, falls vaguely in love, goes on a picnic up the river, where she becomes ill and dies. The narrative is neither coherent nor sustained. Characters are introduced, become the focus of the action, and are then dropped. Indeed, it is not until she is nearly half-way through the book that the author makes up her mind that the story is to centre around Rachel, and not around one of the other half-dozen characters to whom, up to that point, no less attention has been paid.

Night and Day is a somewhat more orderly and externally competent piece of work. Here we have four chief characters, two young men and two young women, and the story is kept within the limits of their relationships, which are worked out to a conventional conclusion. It is, however, a story of no interest whatever, revealing no insight into the principles of human conduct – the dramatic movement is occasioned by the commonplace device of the 'love-interest' – and padded out (it is a work of five hundred pages) with irrelevant asides, descriptions and soliloquies. *Night and Day* might well qualify as the dullest novel in the English language. There can be few readers who have really traversed the book from beginning to end.

The uncertainty which characterizes Virginia Woolf's grasp of human character, experience, relationships, finds unintentionally ludicrous expression in her treatment of the relationship of her lovers, whom she presents as moved by the most comically unmotivated attractions and repulsions. The 'misty state of mind' in which Katharine Hilbery, the book's heroine, avers she had accepted William Rodney's offers of marriage, it is only too apparent is the common mental condition of Virginia Woolf's characters. Ralph Denham, the second male partner in this conventional foursome, for instance, explains to Katharine that –

> 'You can force me to talk as if this feeling for you were an hallucination, but all our feelings are that. The best of them are half illusions.'

This sense of vagueness and unreality is itself connected with an underlying sense of the planlessness of existence. A minor character, Evelyn Murgatroyd, in *The Voyage Out*, left alone after receiving a proposal of marriage, reflects, 'What did matter then? What was the meaning of it all?' and this question is never far from the lips of any character in these two novels.

Towards the close of *Night and Day*, impelled to snatch at a meaningful conclusion for her otherwise random narrative, the author secures it with the simple overt statement that the lovers, Ralph and Katharine, merely by coming together, had somehow achieved valid intimations of the elusive 'significance' of human life.

> She had turned before she answered him. She had no wish to see anyone tonight; it seemed to her that the immense riddle was answered; the problem had been solved; she held in her hands for one brief moment the globe which we spend our lives in trying to shape, round, whole and entire from the confusion of chaos.
>
> 'It's all so easy – it's all so simple,' Katharine quoted, remembering some words of Sally Seal's, and wishing Ralph to understand that she followed the track of his thought. She felt him trying to piece together in a laborious and elementary fashion fragments of belief, unsoldered and separate, lacking the unity of phrases, fashioned by the old believers. Together they groped in this difficult region, where the unfinished, the unfulfilled, the unwritten, the unreturned, came together in their ghostly way and wore the semblance of the complete and the satisfactory. The future emerged more splendid than ever from this construction of the present.

Beneath *The Voyage Out* and *Night and Day*, it is obvious, are preoccupations of a quite basic and elementary kind with the primary conditions of human existence. And the first condition for existence at all is that implied in what we mean by the word 'belief'.

There is, in David Daiches' little book on Virginia Woolf, a discerning passage on this question of a writer's belief and its relation to method and style.

> . . . Virginia Woolf, unlike Jane Austen [says Daiches] was writing in a world in which there was no consensus of opinion concerning what 'reality' was, and, unlike some of her contemporaries, she was very much aware of that lack of agreement. The second and third decades of the twentieth century, which saw Virginia Woolf's flowering as a novelist, saw also the final dissolution of that common background of belief and attitude that made it possible for a writer to talk of Smith and Liverpool while

assuming certain unarticulated preconceptions concerning the nature and value of human life which made communication on what Virginia Woolf called the 'materialist' level at the same time statements about reality. Virginia Woolf had, as it were, to start from scratch, to provide each character with a world view in the light of which it was to be interpreted. The events recorded in her novels were not acted out against a solid background of belief, a stable emotional and intellectual pattern; they had, on the contrary, to be invested with their own philosophic and emotional background. Virginia Woolf had come face to face with the problem that challenged so many of her contemporary artists, the problem of producing significant art in an individualistic and sceptical age.

Art without belief – without, that is, community belief – is not easy to create. For here the artist has to throw his own sensibility around each work in such a way as to provide the reader or beholder with a philosophic background sufficient to serve as a key to the patterning of that particular work. As that key is no longer provided by the civilization in which both writer and reader live, it is up to the writer to provide one himself. Virginia Woolf has, therefore, to find a method of writing which enables her to tell a story while at the same time indicating the particular view of 'reality' which gives that story significance. This is the explanation of her constant concern with 'reality'.

. . . In an essay entitled 'How it strikes a Contemporary' she discusses this very point, the relation of art to community belief. Referring to the 'sense of security' that emerges from the work of Wordsworth, Scott and Jane Austen, she asks, 'From what, then, arises that sense of security which gradually, delightfully, and completely overcomes us?' And her reply is worth noting: 'It is the power of their belief, their conviction, that imposes itself upon us. . . . They have their judgment of conduct. They know the relations of human beings towards each other and towards the universe. Neither of them (i.e., Jane Austen and Scott) probably has a word to say about the matter outright, but everything depends upon it. . . . To believe that your impressions hold good for others is to be released from the cramp and confinement of personality.'

And this is precisely the point. The moderns, as Virginia Woolf saw them, lived in an age without common belief, and therefore could not be free from the cramp and confinement of personality. 'Our contemporaries afflict us because they have ceased to believe,' she complains in the same essay. Yet there was a way out of the difficulty. It might be possible to make a virtue of necessity, to find a way of writing which would call for dependence on the writer's personality, a way of writing out of a personal sense of truth so as to convey that sense to the reader as he reads. That is the course that Virginia Woolf took.

These remarks have their relevance: but it seems necessary to question the far too easy way in which they accept a writer's inert dependence upon beliefs which he receives at second-hand from 'society'. For where does 'society' in turn get those beliefs? Granted that the society to which Virginia Woolf belonged was without common beliefs, to explain the inner nature of her work by this is precisely equivalent to saying that she had no creative originality, that she passively and vacuously reflected, in personal terms, the spiritual decadence of that society. Daiches, however, evidently does not suppose that the question of belief is, in itself, of real and determining significance. He attributes to it nothing much more than an aesthetic *function*. The explanation of Virginia Woolf's 'constant concern with "reality" ', however, is something much more pressing than the need for finding 'a method of writing which enables her to tell a story while at the same time indicating the particular view of "reality" which gives that story significance'.

The question of belief in its most obvious form is occasionally touched on in *The Voyage Out*.

'I always think religion's like collecting beetles,' she said, summing up the discussion as she went up the stairs with Helen. 'One person has a passion for black beetles; another hasn't; it's no good arguing about it. What's *your* black beetle now?'

And again:

'They believe in God,' said Rachel as they regained each other. She meant that the people in the crowd believed in Him; for she remembered the crosses with bleeding plaster figures that stood where foot-paths joined, and the inexplicable mystery of a service in a Roman Catholic church. 'We shall never understand!' she sighed.

The Voyage Out was written, it is not hard to see, by someone with no particular beliefs about existence. The state of flux to which a general absence of belief necessarily leads is indicated in the following significant passage:

> Rachel felt much as Terence had felt that Evelyn was too close to her, and that there was something exciting in this closeness, although it was also disagreeable. She was spared the need of finding an answer to the question, for Evelyn proceeded, 'Do you *believe* in anything?'
>
> In order to put an end to the scrutiny of those bright blue eyes, and to relieve her own physical restlessness, Rachel pushed back her chair and exclaimed, 'In everything!' and began to finger different objects, the books on the table, the photographs, the fleshly leaved plant with the stiff bristles, which stood in a large earthenware pot in the window.
>
> 'I believe in the bed, in the photographs, in the pot, in the balcony, in the sun, in Mrs. Flushing,' she remarked, still speaking recklessly, with something at the back of her mind forcing her to say the things that one usually does not say. 'But I don't believe in God, I don't believe in Mr. Bax, I don't believe in the hospital nurse. I don't believe——' She took up a photograph and, looking at it, did not finish her sentence.

In *Night and Day* the problem of belief becomes somewhat more urgent. Of Mary Datchet in that novel her author writes –

> Having no religious belief, she was the more conscientious about her life. . . .

But, it later transpires –

> She could not see the world divided into separate compartments of good people and bad people, any more than she could believe so implicitly in the rightness of her own thought as to wish to bring the population of the British Isles into agreement with it. She looked at the lemon-coloured leaflet and thought almost enviously of the faith which could find comfort in the issue of such documents . . . feeling that faith, faith in an illusion, perhaps, but at any rate, faith in something, was of all gifts the most to be envied.

And we have seen that the lovers, towards the end of the same story, given an apparent, elusive intimation of life's 'significance', try to 'piece together . . . fragments of *belief*'.

Belief is inseparable from *meaning* and *reality*. And it is meaning and reality (or rather, her sense of life's meaninglessness and unreality) which trouble Virginia Woolf in her first two novels. As a novelist, Virginia Woolf began, not with any clear and steady vision of a pattern in human life, but with apparently no more compelling impulse than a mere desire to write, and a trust that the process of writing would assist towards the discovery of some inherent pattern in the random sequence of experience. The disorder and incoherence which, in her first novel, resulted from this aimless procedure, she endeavoured to overcome, in her second, by the imposition of a conventional pattern of character-relationships and, at the last, a hasty and unconvincing iteration of 'significance'.

II

THAT this solution failed to satisfy her appears from the immediately following period in her career, which is one of transition, marked by theorising and experiment directed towards the finding of a method of composition adapted to the limitations of her severely restricted perception of life. To this period belong the short tales and sketches which were collected in the little volume *Monday or Tuesday* (1921), and the well-known essay on 'Modern Fiction', in which she expressed her dissatisfaction with conventional writing and tentatively defined an attitude and a programme for the future of the novel.

This essay begins with a perfunctory reference to the classic English novelists and passes on at once to Wells, Bennett and Galsworthy, for whom she had conceived a marked distaste, representing as they did for her the most eminent and successful practitioners of the 'conventional' novel which had proved its inadequacy to the view of life that she increasingly considered it her task as a novelist to convey.

. . . Admitting the vagueness which afflicts all criticism of novels [she writes in this essay], let us hazard the opinion that for us at this moment the form of fiction most in vogue more often misses than secures the thing we seek. Whether we call it life or spirit, truth or reality, this, the essential thing, has moved off or on, and refuses to be contained any longer in such ill-fitting vestments as we provide. Nevertheless, we go on perseveringly, conscientiously, constructing our two and thirty chapters after a design which more and more ceases to resemble the vision in our minds. So much of the enormous labour of proving the solidity, the likeness to life, of the story is not merely labour thrown away but labour misplaced to the extent of obscuring and blotting out the light of the conception.

And then comes the well-known and portentous passage which points forward to her own later method of composition:

> Look within and life, it seems, is very far from being 'like this'. Examine for a moment an ordinary mind on an ordinary day. The mind receives a myriad impressions – trivial, fantastic, evanescent, or engraved with the sharpness of steel. From all sides they come, an incessant shower of innumerable atoms; and as they fall, as they shape themselves into the life of Monday or Tuesday, the accent falls, differently from of old; the moment of importance came not here but there; so that, if a writer were a free man and not a slave, if he could write what he chose, not what he must, if he could base his work upon his own feeling, and not upon convention, there would be no plot, no comedy, no tragedy, no love interest or catastrophe in the accepted style, and perhaps not a single button sewn on as the Bond Street tailors would have it. Life is not a series of gig lamps symmetrically arranged; life is a luminous halo, a semi-transparent envelope surrounding us from the beginning of consciousness to the end. Is it not the task of the novelist to convey this varying, this unknown and uncircumscribed spirit, whatever aberration or complexity it may display, with as little mixture of the alien and external as possible? We are not pleading merely for courage and sincerity; we are suggesting that the proper stuff of fiction is a little other than custom would have us believe it.
>
> . . . Let us record the atoms as they fall upon the mind in the order in which they fall, let us trace the pattern, however disconnected and incoherent in appearance, which each sight or incident scores upon the consciousness. Let us not take it for granted that life exists more fully in what is commonly thought big than in what is commonly thought small.

These paragraphs will repay the closest attention, for they mark the point of departure for the whole of their author's subsequent course as a novelist. Their personal application, as with all of Virginia Woolf's criticism ostensibly dealing with contemporaries, is evident. The description of the writer constrained 'not by his own free will but by some powerful and unscrupulous tyrant who has him in thrall' to write in such and such a way, is an apt one, not at all of Wells, Bennett or Galsworthy, but of Virginia Woolf herself, struggling with the composition of *Night and Day*, which she had just completed.

Virginia Woolf has been hailed as a prospector into new territory in the novel. In view of the claims made for her by admirers, it is interesting to recollect that she herself accepted the basic assumptions of the realistic writers of her period and departed from their methods only because forced to do so by her inability to extend her powers to their breadth of scope. Her method was one of retraction rather than extension – a narrowing of focus to take in only that which readily lent itself to appropriation by her extraordinarily limited vision. In a pamphlet, *Mr. Bennett and Mrs. Brown*, for example, written as late as 1924, we find her point of departure to be an unqualified agreement with a statement of Arnold Bennett's concerning the fundamental importance of the creation of 'character' to the novel; her reply to Bennett's criticism of the 'younger novelists', on the ground that they were incapable of the creation of character, taking the curious line that 'on or about December 1910', that is, at about the time these younger novelists (Virginia Woolf herself among them) began writing, 'human character changed', and consequently they were faced with entirely new problems of presentment, which their elders, Bennett, Galsworthy and Wells, owing to their overwhelming preoccupation with the material environment and political question were unable to help them to solve. For this reason, she concludes, doubtless with her own predicament still determining her words, 'we must reconcile ourselves to a season of failures and fragments'.

Jacob's Room (1922) is the first novel in which Virginia Woolf endeavours to put something of her new way of seeing and method of composition into practice. To 'record the atoms as they fall upon the mind in the order in which they fall' is not really a workable theory. And her actual method was a compromise between the practice of the conventional novelist and adherence to her own tentative formula. In *Jacob's Room* one notices less any innovation of a positive order than the simple and drastic employment of omission. There is no plot – the reader simply follows Jacob through this and that planless permutation in his history from childhood to his death in the war. The design of the novel follows from the mere juxtaposition of one passage of intrinsically trivial particularities with another, separated by a jump in time. While this simple omission is preferable to the accumulation of meaningless detail which had padded out the previous novel, there is no added intensity of vision, no motivating passion which might give the book an organic centre and thus create for the novel a significant form. The narrative comes to a blank space, Jacob's death (off-stage) and then abruptly stops. The novelist never comes to close quarters with her chief character, but portrays him in a wooden, detached, external manner which takes note of his way of sitting down, of reading a book, of lighting a pipe, and so forth, but which is powerless to evoke his inner life. Jacob is as void of content as any 'tough' character of Ernest Hemingway's, but instead of being precipitated into a region of violent external agitation, he moves with puppet-like impassivity through scenes of domesticated calm. It is a novel in two dimensions, and the general effect is of a silent shadow-play.

III

IT is not until *Mrs. Dalloway* (1923) that we reach a work in which it is possible to trace the drawing together in Virginia Woolf's mind of the impulsion towards belief on the one hand and on the other the inability to make any decisive movement of belief and thus to discriminate which led to the narrowing of vision to the elementary conditions of momentary experience. *Mrs. Dalloway* is curiously compounded of this dual movement of belief and unbelief.

In the early essay on 'Modern Fiction', Virginia Woolf charges the 'conventional' novelists whose manner she had attempted to follow, with writing of unimportant things, with spending their skill and industry on 'making the trivial and the transitory appear the true and the enduring'. 'For us at this moment,' she wrote, 'the form of fiction most in vogue more often misses than secures the thing we seek. Whether we call it life or spirit, truth or reality, this, the essential thing, has moved off.' What, then, is the enduring, the true, which it is the

novelist's task to capture? She does not know; but she ventures
to suppose that it may be found by a form of passive receptive-
ness to experience. 'Let us not take it for granted,' she wrote in
that early essay, 'that life exists more fully in what is commonly
thought big than in what is commonly thought small.' Unable
to distinguish between this value and that she takes the barest
unit of disparate experience and concentrates upon it, in the
supposition or the hope that within that, if anywhere, must lie
the secret of life's *indigenous* significance.

The inability to discriminate between levels of life, to make
choices between 'good' and 'bad', 'right' and 'wrong', or
'desirable' and 'undesirable', besides thrusting the individual so
affected back upon the naked and isolated moment of perception, places him furthermore in a position where, if any kind
of positive 'significance' is to be attempted (and life can be
endowed with significance only by an interior act of affirmation
– of *belief*), then, inevitably, undifferentiated, elementary life
has to be accepted unreservedly and in its totality. In *Mrs.
Dalloway* we see not only the results of the period of experimental, impressionistic, *momentary* writing applied to the novel;
we also see the attainment of a sustained, though of course
ultimately spurious, 'significance' through the continuous act
of complete and undiscriminating acceptance of every moment
of undifferentiated existence, each separate atom of which is
presumed to contain an equal fragment of *indigenous* meaning.

In *Mrs. Dalloway*, in fact, the specific absence of belief which
is shown in the earlier novels is revealed in its reverse aspect.
It takes on the appearance of belief – a positive acceptance and
affirmation, not of any particular level of reality, but of *everything*, without discrimination: except, significantly enough, of
that which would imply the possibility, or the need, of discrimination. 'One can only hope that they will have the same vision
and the same power to believe, without which life would be so
meaningless,' writes old Mrs. Hilbery, of Katharine and her
fiancé in *Night and Day*: to believe, that is, not in any specific
reality or value, but simply to believe, in everything, perhaps;
in 'life'. And one can only take Clarissa Dalloway as exemplify-
ing this 'belief' – a belief so total that it engulfs the whole of
experience, and which on examination turns out to be a positive

F

inversion of unbelief. Besides representing the combination of *happiness* and *belief*, Clarissa Dalloway is an incarnation of life itself, the stream and efflorescence of natural, material, feminine existence. A sentimental, worldly sort of average sensual woman, she is presented lyrically and quite uncritically through a rose-tinted haze, the trivialities of her pointless, sensational life inflated to universal proportions.

> But to go deeper, beneath what people said (and these judg-ments, how superficial, how fragmentary they are!) in her own mind now, what did it mean to her, this thing she called life? Oh, it was very queer. Here was So-and-so in South Kensington; some one up in Bayswater; and somebody else, say, in Mayfair. And she felt quite continuously a sense of their existence; and she felt what a waste; and she felt what a pity; and she felt if only they could be brought together: so she did it. And it was an offering; to combine, to create; but to whom?
>
> An offering for the sake of offering, perhaps. Anyhow, it was her gift. Nothing else had she of the slightest importance; could not think, write, even play the piano. She muddled Armenians with Turks; loved success; hated discomfort; must be liked; talked oceans of nonsense; and to this day, ask her what the Equator was, and she did not know.
>
> All the same, that one day should follow another; Wednesday, Thursday, Friday, Saturday; that one should wake up in the morning; see the sky; walk in the park; meet Hugh Whitbread; then suddenly in came Peter; then these roses; it was enough. After that, how unbelievable death was! – that it must end; and no one in the whole world would know how she had loved it all; how every instant . . .

The loquacious, breathlessly chattering style is a perfect medium for the expression of the reflections of this empty-headed, middle-aged bourgeoise matron, so ostentatiously and rhapsodically thrilled by the mere continuous fact of existence (though it is a leisured, idle, comfortable enough existence to be sure). What is so curious about it is its quite genuine spontane-ity, the essence from it of any hint of irony, of detachment, which might reveal some disparity between the life-outlook embodied in the character, and that of her creator. Here is belief, then, on its most primitive level: a belief in 'life' – in

the successive moments of unco-ordinated sensational experience – as a 'good' in itself. Mrs. Dalloway is a child in her
unreflective responsiveness to each moment of experience, but
a child grown middle-aged, in whose deliberate retrogression to
innocence there is a subdued strain of hysteria.

How far from the primal innocence of childhood Clarissa
Dalloway has travelled is shown in such passages as the following, where the theology of middle-aged innocence is appropriately sketched in:

> Oddly enough, she was one of the most thorough-going
> sceptics he had ever met, and possibly (this was a theory he used to
> make up to account for her, so transparent in some ways, so
> inscrutable in others), possibly she said to herself, As we are a
> doomed race, chained to a sinking ship (her favourite reading as a
> girl was Huxley and Tyndall, and they were fond of these nautical
> metaphors), as the whole thing is a bad joke, let us, at any rate,
> do our part; mitigate the sufferings of our fellow-prisoners (Huxley
> again); decorate the dungeon with flowers and air-cushions; be
> as decent as we possibly can. Those ruffians, the Gods, shan't have
> it all their own way – her notion being that the Gods, who never
> lost a chance of hurting, thwarting and spoiling human lives, were
> seriously put out if, all the same, you behaved like a lady. That
> phase came directly after Sylvia's death – that horrible affair.
> To see your own sister killed by a falling tree (all Justin Parry's
> fault – all his carelessness) before your very eyes, a girl too on the
> verge of life, the most gifted of them Clarissa always said, was
> enough to turn one bitter. Later she wasn't so positive, perhaps;
> she thought there were no Gods; no one was to blame; and so she
> evolved this atheist's religion of doing good for the sake of good-
> ness. . . .

Such, then, is the centre, if centre it can be called, around
which Clarissa Dalloway's manner of responding to life coheres,
or fails to cohere. And it has something in common with the
aimless openness to life of the deranged consciousness of her
alter ego, Septimus Warren Smith, the neurasthenic war-victim
who darkly underscores her buoyancy with his submergence
and her total acceptance of life with his total rejection – for he
is to kill himself by jumping from a top-storey window on to
the area railings.

The vague, fluid characters in this book – Clarissa herself, her whimsical, Puckish lover, Peter Walsh, and Septimus Warren Smith – are bathed in the tender warmth of their author's undiscriminating sympathy. It is interesting, that being so, to find that there are also portrayed two characters who are given at least potential definition by the decisiveness of their attitude to life, in which they stand in polar opposition to the indecisive fluidity of the other chief characters. And it is intriguing to watch the manner in which these two characters are pursued by their creator with a gratuitous vindictiveness which seems at first sight unaccountable.

To Clarissa Dalloway is opposed the maliciously-drawn minor figure of Miss Kilman, her daughter's teacher, who, she fears, is alienating the girl's affection from her. Between Mrs. Dalloway and Miss Kilman there is an unspoken but vibrant antagonism, which flashes out as Miss Kilman, leaving Mrs. Dalloway's house with the girl, encounters her employer on the landing.

> . . . Love and religion! thought Clarissa, going back into the drawing-room, tingling all over. How detestable, how detestable they are! For now that the body of Miss Kilman was not before her, it overwhelmed her – the idea. The cruellest things in the world, she thought, seeing them clumsy, hot, domineering, hypo-critical eavesdropping, jealous, infinitely cruel and unscrupulous dressed in a mackintosh coat, on the landing; love and religion. Had she ever tried to convert anyone herself? Did she not wish everybody merely to be themselves? And she watched out of the window the old lady opposite climbing upstairs. Let her climb upstairs if she wanted to; let her stop; then let her, as Clarissa had often seen her, gain her bedroom, part her curtains, and disappear again into the background. Somehow one respected that – that old woman looking out of the window, quite unconscious that she was being watched. There was something solemn in it – but love and religion would destroy that, whatever it was, the privacy of the soul. The odious Kilman would destroy it. Yet it was a sight that made her want to cry.

Subsequently Miss Kilman is made to disgrace herself before Mrs. Dalloway's daughter, and is left, a pathetic figure, covered with humiliation.

Humiliation is the portion also of the other character who is so unsympathetic as to possess a definite, formulated attitude to life. Sir William Bradshaw, the nerve specialist who is called in to deal with the neurasthenic Septimus, is presented as a thick-skinned, domineering egotist, who applies to human beings a sovereign test of normality and sense of proportion.

> Proportion, divine proportion, Sir William's goddess, was acquired by Sir William walking hospitals, catching salmon, begetting one son in Harley Street by Lady Bradshaw, who caught salmon herself and took photographs scarcely to be distinguished from the work of professionals. Worshipping proportion, Sir William not only prospered himself but made England prosper. . . .
> But Proportion has a sister, less smiling, more formidable, a Goddess even now engaged – in the heat and sands of India, the mud and swamp of Africa, the purlieus of London, wherever in short the climate or the devil tempts men to fall from the true belief which is her own – is even now engaged in dashing down shrines, smashing idols, and setting up in their place her own stern countenance. Conversation is her name and she feasts on the wills of the weakly, loving to impress, to impose, adoring her own features stamped on the face of the populace. At Hyde Park Corner on a tub she stands preaching; shrouds herself in white and walks penitentially disguised as brotherly love through factories and parliaments; offers help, but desires power; smites out of her way roughly the dissentient, or dissatisfied; bestows her blessing on those who, looking upward, catch submissively from her eyes the light of their own.

In so mild a writer the vehement bitterness of this is surprising. It would seem that just as Clarissa Dalloway and Septimus Warren Smith are linked in an unconscious psychic sympathy, representing as they do the human mind's state of fluid and unprincipled openness to the undifferentiated phenomena of elementary existence, so the decisive attitudes of Miss Kilman and Sir William Bradshaw converge – and converge upon that threatening imperative towards *conversion*, the imposition of a definite view of life upon the fluid, the indefinite, which is felt as inexpressibly menacing to everything that Clarissa Dalloway herself values and represents. Pondering on Miss Kilman, and the challenge she is seen to present to her own undiscriminating acceptance, Mrs. Dalloway asks herself:

Why creeds and prayers and mackintoshes? when . . . that's the miracle, that's the mystery: that old lady, she meant, whom she could see going from chest of drawers to dressing-table. She could still see her. And the supreme mystery which Kilman might say she had solved, or Peter might say he had solved, but Clarissa didn't believe either of them had the ghost of an idea of solving, was simply this: here was one room; there another. Did religion solve that, or love?

Sir William Bradshaw, like Miss Kilman, is disgraced. When Septimus Warren Smith is in a condition of intense neurotic excitement, he insists upon entering his room, with the result that Septimus flings himself out of the window and is killed. Towards the end of the story, at Mrs. Dalloway's party, the climax of her day, she learns from Sir William Bradshaw, who is one of the guests, of the young man's death.

What business had the Bradshaws to talk of death at her party? A young man had killed himself and they talked of it at her party – the Bradshaws talked of death. He had killed himself – but how? Always her body went through it first, when she was told, suddenly, of an accident; her dress flamed, her body burnt. He had thrown himself from a window. Up had flashed the ground; through him, blundering, bruising, went the rusty spikes. There he lay with a thud, thud, thud in his brain, and then a suffocation of blackness. So she saw it. But why had he done it? And the Bradshaws talked of it at her party!

. . . But this young man who had killed himself – had he plunged his treasure? 'If it were now to die, 'twere now to be most happy,' she had said to herself once, coming down, in white. Or there were the poets and thinkers. Suppose he had had that passion, and had gone to Sir William Bradshaw, a great doctor, yet to her obscurely evil, without sex or lust, extremely polite to women, but capable of some indescribable outrage – forcing your soul, that was it – if this young man had gone to him, and Sir William had impressed him, like that, with his power, might he not then have said (indeed she felt it now), Life is made intolerable; they make life intolerable, men like that?

Then (she had felt it only this morning) there was the terror; the overwhelming incapacity, one's parents giving it into one's hands, this life, to be lived to the end, to be walked with serenely; there was in the depths of her heart an awful fear. Even now, quite often if Richard had not been there reading the *Times*, so that she could crouch like a bird and gradually revive, send roaring up that immeasurable delight, rubbing stick to stick, one thing with another, she must have perished. She had escaped. But that young man had killed himself.

Such then is the psychological structure of *Mrs. Dalloway*. Although, as a novel, it represents the peak of Virginia Woolf's achievement, just as it marks the highest, most buoyant point on the graph of her emotional progression, it shows no authentic advance over her earlier works: no movement of the mind, that is, into new territory. Apparently, affirmative in mood, its innocency is in fact, retrogressive and corrupt. And its apparent affirmation of life is merely the reverse aspect of its rejection of that which alone could give life meaning and value: i.e., a positive, spiritual affirmation which, facilitating the introduction of a principle of choice, of discrimination, would make life subject to differentiation and thus to the realization of meaning.

IV

AND yet, despite its at times cloying sentimentality, *Mrs. Dalloway* is perhaps Virginia Woolf's most satisfactory novel, for it has an organic structure which derives from the successful dramatic presentation of a view of life. It is in fact the only novel of Virginia Woolf's in which tension is achieved through the opposition of characters embodying contrary principles of conduct. The lack of such tension in the rest of her work results from the monistic conception of existence which sets all characters alike within the same undifferentiated flow of life, and makes inward and outward conflict alike inconceivable.

In the next novel, *To the Lighthouse* (1927), there are already signs of disintegration of form, concurrent with a loosening grasp upon experience which finds expression in a depletion of emotion. A buoyant, dashing surrender to the flux of life has given place to an anxious, anguished questioning of the flux. If *Mrs. Dalloway* is indicative of a state, however illusory, of achieved *being*, *To the Lighthouse* reveals an alienation from that being expressed as a concern for *meaning*.

The sentimentality of *Mrs. Dalloway* was communicated through the author's uncritical identification of her own viewpoint with that of her central character. But it is clear that such an identification could be effected only by a suppression of those mental qualities which in point of fact must have distinguished the 'intellectual' Virginia Woolf from such a feather-pated creature as Clarissa Dalloway is shown to be. *To the Lighthouse* is so much more subdued in tone than *Mrs. Dalloway*, and so lacking in the former novel's cloying and breathless sentimentality, precisely because there is no such simple identification of the writer with her central character. A significant alienation of identity appears in the presentation of Mrs. Ramsay, a modified and graver equivalent of Mrs. Dalloway, at one remove. Instead of being presented from *within*, she is approached externally, through the hazy and tremulous thoughts and emotions of her worshipper, Lily Briscoe.

Those critics, are, I think, mistaken who have supposed that the theme of this novel is contained in the story of the trip to the lighthouse. While that story indubitably provides a framework of incident for the support of the novel's content to which, however, it is not organically connected the substance of the book is contained in the verbal hoverings and quiverings around the relationship between Lily Briscoe and Mrs. Ramsay. Thus, the first part is devoted to Lily Briscoe's immediate thoughts and feelings about the living woman, who represents for her some mysteriously satisfying relationship with life that she herself, hovering on the edge of things, can hardly hope to achieve – for Mrs. Ramsay, *being* itself; for Lily Briscoe, *perception* of being: significance. The second part, 'Time Passes', records parenthetically the death of Mrs. Ramsay. And the final section of the novel concerns Lily's attempt to achieve a synthetic vision of existence, in which her memories of Mrs. Ramsay, and the wholeness, the integration of which she is emblematic, play a preponderating part. Finally, the climax of the book comes at the moment when it seems to her that Mrs. Ramsay actually returns to the house – she has a vision of her sitting placidly in her chair, knitting.

It is, assuredly, with Lily Briscoe's, if with anyone's, that the author identifies her point of view. To this detached, ineffectual spinster, with her 'artist's eye' – to her, the substantial, homely Mrs. Ramsay, with her house, her husband, and her eight children, represents a solid, tangible, satisfying rootedness in

life which is so foreign to her experience as to be positively
endued with mystery; and it is, consequently, with an aura of
mysteriousness, of wonder, that she surrounds her in her reflections. Mrs. Ramsay is the exact counterpart of those matronly
female characters who, in E. M. Forster's novels, represent
those same 'mysterious' values of natural continuity, of unquestioning rootedness in the tangible, immemorial natural
order.

In the first part of the book, near to the living woman, yet
quite unable to penetrate into her character, Lily reflects upon
her in such terms as these:

> Was it wisdom? Was it knowledge? Was it, once more, the
> deceptiveness of beauty, so that all one's perceptions, half-way to
> truth, were tangled in a golden mesh? Or did she lock up within
> her some secret which certainly Lily Briscoe believed people must
> have for the world to go on at all? Every one could not be as helter
> skelter, hand to mouth as she was. But if they knew, could they
> tell one what they knew? Sitting on the floor with her arms round
> Mrs. Ramsay's knees, close as she could get, smiling to think that
> Mrs. Ramsay would never know the reason of that pressure, she
> imagined how in the chambers of the mind and heart of the woman
> who was, physically, touching her, were stood, like the treasures
> in the tombs of kings, tablets bearing sacred inscriptions, which if
> one could spell them out would teach one everything, but they
> would never be offered openly, never made public. What art was
> there, known to love or cunning, by which one pressed through
> into those secret chambers? What device for becoming, like waters
> poured into one jar, inextricably the same, one with the object
> one adored? Could the body achieve it, or the mind, subtly
> mingling in the intricate passages of the brain? Or the heart?
> Could loving, as people called it, make her and Mrs. Ramsay one?
> For it was not knowledge but unity that she desired, not inscrip-
> tions on tablets, nothing that could be written in any language
> known to men, but intimacy itself, which is knowledge, she had
> thought, leaning her head on Mrs. Ramsay's knee.
>
> Nothing happened. Nothing! Nothing! as she leant her head
> against Mrs. Ramsay's knee. And yet, she knew knowledge and
> wisdom were stored in Mrs. Ramsay's heart. How then, she had
> asked herself, did one know one thing or another thing about
> people, sealed as they were? Only like a bee, drawn by some
> sweetness or sharpness in the air intangible to touch or taste, one

haunted the dome-shaped hive, ranged the wastes of the air over the countries of the world alone, and haunted the hives with their murmurs and their stirrings; the hives which were people. Mrs. Ramsay rose. Lily rose. Mrs. Ramsay went. For days there hung about her, as after a dream some subtle change is felt in the person one has dreamt of, more vividly than anything she said, the sound of murmuring and, as she sat in the wicker arm-chair in the drawing-room window she wore, to Lily's eyes, an august shape; the shape of a dome.

'It was not knowledge but unity that she desired.' But nowhere, in this first section of the book, does Lily succeed in 'pressing through into those secret chambers', in 'becoming . . . one with the object she adored'. The pattern is of frustration – a frustration reflected in the narrative in the postponement of the expedition to the lighthouse. In the ensuing vacant lapse of ten years, Mrs. Ramsay's death supervenes. And in the final section the novelist is faced with the formidable task of bringing the whole novel to a meaningful conclusion.

Deprived of the sense of secure certainty provided by the adored figure of Mrs. Ramsay, Lily Briscoe, on her return to the house with Mr. Ramsay, two of the children, and old Mr. Carmichael, the poet, is impelled to establish some kind of relationship with her – or, more accurately, with that which she represents – in spite of her death. For with Mrs. Ramsay and her unquestioning rootedness in the natural order has come to be associated the whole significance of life, so that with her obliteration from the scene, that significance has disappeared. So it is that this section of the book is devoted principally to Lily's bewildered and even passionate questionings for life's 'significance'. And the achievement of 'significance' is equivalent, it appears, to an actual *return* of Mrs. Ramsay.

Mrs. Ramsay, she thought, stepping back and screwing up her eyes . . . Mrs. Ramsay. When she thought of herself and Charles throwing ducks and drakes and of the whole scene on the beach, it seemed to depend somehow upon Mrs. Ramsay sitting under the rock, with a pad on her knees, writing letters. (She wrote innumerable letters, and sometimes the wind took them and she and Charles just saved a page from the sea.) But what a power was in the human soul! she thought. That woman sitting there, writing under the rock resolved everything into simplicity; made

these angers, irritations fall off like old rags; she brought together
this and that and then this, and so made out of that miserable
silliness and spite (she and Charles squabbling, sparring, had been
silly and spiteful) something – this scene on the beach for example,
this moment of friendship and liking – which survived, after all
these years, complete, so that she dipped into it to re-fashion her
memory of him, and it stayed in the mind almost like a work of
art.

'Like a work of art,' she repeated, looking from her canvas to
the drawing-room steps and back again. She must rest for a
moment. And, resting, looking from one to the other vaguely, the
old question which traversed the sky of the soul perpetually, the
vast and general question which was apt to particularize itself at
such moments as these, when she released faculties that had been
on the strain, stood over her, paused over her, darkened over her.
What is the meaning of life? That was all – a simple question; one
that tended to close in on one with years. The great revelation had
never come. Instead there were little daily miracles, illuminations,
matches struck unexpectedly in the dark; here was one. This, that,
and the other; herself and Charles Tansley and the breaking wave;
Mrs. Ramsay bringing them together; Mrs. Ramsay saying 'Life
stands still here'; Mrs. Ramsay making of the moment something
permanent (as in another sphere Lily herself tried to make of the
moment something permanent) – this was of the nature of a
revelation. In the midst of chaos there was shape; this eternal
passing and flowing (she looked at the clouds going and the leaves
shaking) was struck into stability. Life stands still here, Mrs.
Ramsay said. 'Mrs. Ramsay! Mrs. Ramsay!' she repeated. She
owed this revelation to her.

What is the meaning of life? The emphasis here is very different from that in *Mrs. Dalloway*. Life, no longer a 'lark' and a
'plunge', as in the opening sentence of that novel, but a dark
enigma, hides its purpose from its puzzled and groping creatures.
But 'the great revelation had never come . . . perhaps never
did come'. There were only little fragments, little flashes, of
'significance', united by the presence of Mrs. Ramsay, typifying
the inscrutable natural order. But perhaps, after all, this *was*
a revelation. Perhaps, that is to say, there was no larger meaning, but only a succession of little elusive fragments of 'significance', and one must make the most of these. Thus, it appears,
we are back at the state of affairs which preceded the fervent

and enthusiastic acceptance of momentary sensation which gave *Mrs. Dalloway* its special character.

It is hardly surprising that this meagre 'revelation' should be felt by Lily Briscoe to be still unsatisfactory. It contents her for a very short while. And then, a little further on, this exasperated clutching at life's elusive 'significance' is taken up afresh in her impassioned inward questioning of Mr. Carmichael.

Against her will she had come to the surface, and found herself half out of the picture, looking, a little dazedly, as if at unreal things, at Mr. Carmichael. He lay on his chair with his hands clasped above his paunch not reading, or sleeping, but basking like a creature gorged with existence. His book had fallen on to the grass.

She wanted to go straight up to him and say, 'Mr. Carmichael!' Then he would look up benevolently as always, from his smoky vague green eyes. But one only woke people if one knew what one wanted to say to them. And she wanted to say not one thing but everything. Little words that broke up the thought and dis-membered it said nothing. 'About life, about death; about Mrs. Ramsay' – no, she thought, one could say nothing to nobody. The urgency of the moment always missed its mark. Words fluttered sideways and struck the object inches too low. . . .

'What does it mean? How do you explain it all?' she wanted to say, turning to Mr. Carmichael again. For the whole world seemed to have dissolved in this early morning hour into a pool of thought, a deep basin of reality, and one could almost fancy that had Mr. Carmichael spoken, a little tear would have rent the surface of the pool. And then? Something would emerge. A hand would be shoved up, a blade would be flashed. It was nonsense of course. . . .

. . . She addressed old Mr. Carmichael again. What was it then? What did it mean? Could things thrust their hands up and grip one; could the blade cut, the fist grasp? Was there no safety? No learning by heart of the ways of the world? No guide, no shelter, but all was miracle, and leaping from the pinnacle of a tower into the air? Could it be, even for elderly people, that this was life? – startling, unexpected, unknown? For one moment she felt that if they both got up, here, now on the lawn, and demanded an explanation, why was it so short, why was it so inexplicable, said it with violence, as two fully equipped beings from whom nothing should be hid might speak, then, beauty would roll itself up; the space would fill; those empty flourishes would form into shape; if they shouted loud enough Mrs. Ramsay would return. 'Mrs. Ramsay!' she said aloud, 'Mrs. Ramsay!' The tears ran down her face.

The conclusion, the moment of vision, to which these questionings lead, is, although it provides the climax of the novel, strangely indeterminate and unconvincing.

Suddenly the window at which she was looking was whitened by some light stuff behind it. At last then somebody had come into the drawing-room; somebody was sitting in the chair. For Heaven's sake, she prayed, let them sit still there and not come floundering out to talk to her. Mercifully, whoever it was stayed still inside; had settled by some stroke of luck so as to throw an odd-shaped triangular shadow over the step. It altered the composition of the picture a little. It was interesting. It might be useful. Her mood was coming back to her. One must keep on looking without for a second relaxing the intensity of emotion, the determination not to be put off, not to be bamboozled. One must hold the scene – so – in a vice and let nothing come in and spoil it. One wanted, she thought, sipping her brush deliberately, to be on a level with ordinary experience, to feel simply that's a chair, that's a table, and yet at the same time, It's a miracle, it's an ecstasy. The problem might be solved after all. Ah, but what had happened? Some wave of white went over the window pane. The air must have stirred some flounce in the room. Her heart leapt at her and seized and tortured her.

'Mrs. Ramsay! Mrs. Ramsay!' she cried, feeling the old horror come back – to want and want and not to have. Could she inflict that still? And then, quietly, as if she refrained, that too became part of ordinary experience, was on a level with the chair, with the table. Mrs. Ramsay – it was part of her perfect goodness – sat there quite simply, in the chair, flicked her needles to and fro, knitted her reddish-brown stocking, cast her shadow on the step. There she sat.

Lucy, the artist, is able to finish her picture. And, in conclusion:

Yes, she thought, laying down her brush in extreme fatigue, I have had my vision.

'Symbolically,' writes Mr. Daiches in his estimation of it, 'the past returns and shapes the present. Mrs. Ramsay comes back into Lily Briscoe's picture, as she had been part of the original design ten years before, and out of this meeting of two very different personalities across the years the final insight results. Across the water at the same moment Mr. Ramsay, by his praise of James's handling of the boat, is exorcising the ghost of James's early resentment, also ten years old, and all the threads of the story are finally coming together. It is a masterly piece of construction.' But, really, does this fleeting appearance of a phantom Mrs. Ramsay do anything of the kind? And what, after all, does it imply – in what way does it answer Lily Briscoe's protracted questioning of 'the meaning of life'? What, finally, is the reader really meant to make of this whimsical apparition itself? These questions are simply not answered – are not, in fact, even asked by Lily Briscoe.

Had this 'vision', which is the climax of the book, any validity, it would mean that Virginia Woolf herself had at last achieved a creative inner integration, that her protracted quest for the meaning of experience had resulted in the attainment of a balanced and potent view of life which would provide a germinal point of departure for further and positive creation. The fact that it was in reality but a calculated, mechanical device for introducing a point into an otherwise pointless novel, is borne out not only by its own unsatisfactory effect but by its failure to provide a starting-point for a wider and more vital extension of meaning into Virginia Woolf's vision of existence.

v

THE principle which, in the foregoing pages, I have been trying to establish, is that at the centre of this novelist's work there lies, not some abstract 'aesthetic' principle, but a plain and simple preoccupation with the most primary and central necessity of human life – the necessity of belief.

To accept life, to respond to experience, without any prior belief in the primacy of this or that order of reality is to become the victim of utter inward disorder. And this is accentuated when the state of society is such as to provide no readily acceptable conventions of the good and the bad, the desirable and the undesirable. In such a case, only an original act of faith, a decisive and positively dynamic spiritual affirmation can provide a focal centre for the introduction of meaning into experience, which in turn will introduce a principle of order into life. Such an order presumes discrimination: an acceptance of *this* presumes a corresponding rejection of *that*: and thus there is erected a scale of values upon which may be built a more or less orderly and significant experiential pattern.

The discovery of meaning and the introduction of order depend upon an initial act, and upon subsequent, continual interior activity. They are introduced by the dynamism of the subject. Now the distinguishing feature of Virginia Woolf's apprehension of life lies precisely in its passivity; and furthermore, she subscribed unwittingly, as we have seen, to a view of life which placed a primary emphasis upon the object. One recalls the passive function ascribed to the mind ('The mind *receives* a myriad impressions') and the atomistic conception of experience ('From all sides they come, an incessant *shower of atoms*') revealed in the essay 'Modern Fiction'. This sort of initial inward inertia at once obviates the very possibility of meaning, which cannot conceivably subsist inherently in the world of objects. Virginia Woolf's search for 'significance' on the primitive level of primary sensational perceptions, therefore, was chimerical from the beginning. And indeed, it is a typical feature of the characters in her novels to be altogether lacking in the capacity for discriminating within experience. They are passively caught up in the stream of events, of 'life', of their own random perceptions. The furthest Virginia Woolf could move in the direction of a positive act of belief was towards the undiscriminating and finally pointless embracing of everything, which is featured in *Mrs. Dalloway* – a comprehensive gesture which itself obviated the very possibility of order achieved through discrimination, since it was precisely discrimination which was repudiated. This very gesture, when its perpetuation became impossible – and only two years after the affirmations of *Mrs. Dalloway* there came the questionings of *To the Lighthouse* – resulted in an inevitable surrender to eventual explicit meaninglessness.

A simple *monism*, let us call it, was fundamental to Virginia Woolf's outlook upon life. From this derives her incapacity to portray character. For the omission of a principle of differentiation in human life – a principle which is obviously dualistic in that its operation results in a continual extension of an *either/or* choice – makes quite impossible the definition of character, which is itself built up upon the tension of choice between this and that value, this and that course of conduct, and grows through inward affirmations, struggles, and decisions. This lax and vitiating monism is expressed in the absence from her characters of any interior struggle or development. At best they grope for an elusive 'significance' within the texture of atomized, elementary perception; at worst are helplessly caught away in the disintegral temporal stream. Being so void of interior definition, and having no points of opposition, such characters could hardly be expected to maintain dramatic relationships with each other. And this elementary monism, which renders it impossible to make distinctions of values, to introduce discriminations within the total process of life, to grasp the nature of personality, must have the effect, eventually, of merging everything in one vast, undifferentiated flux. It is exactly this which is to be seen in the last three novels, *The Waves*, *The Years*, and *Between the Acts*.

Experience in *The Waves* (1930) is generalized by being located in a void, out of which the six characters, or voices, take turns in delivering isolated, introspective monologues in a stylized diction, bearing upon their common lives. The narrative, thus taken up by each in turn, proceeds from their childhood through the several stages of their lives to beyond middle age, when the novel terminates with a melancholy, inconclusive summing-up. Each section of the novel is preceded by a piece of poetical prose expressing, in terms of the progress of the day from morning to night, the process of human life from childhood to age. Over the earlier parts of the book there preside the beams of a rising sun, while over the latter part fall the shadows of a world in which the sun is declining, while throughout there sounds the menacing beat of the Waves, signifying the primal flux out of which life emerges and into which it must dissolve.

So generalized and so shadowy is the novel that not much can profitably be said about it. It is a medley of impressionistic scenes, a complex of sometimes sensitive but unrelated observations, strung together only by a sense of the transience of life. The sense of realness, of tangible, common-sense, yet somehow mysterious and worshipful rootedness in life which had previously been projected into the figures of Mrs. Dalloway and Mrs. Ramsay, here surrounds the remoter, more abstract figure of Percival, who, himself silent, is presented only through the comments of the speaking characters.

Percival's death in India at the age of twenty-six (taking place, like Mrs. Ramsay's, off-stage) provides a climactic point in the book, and the deprivation in the lives of the six characters which his death brings is combined with the symbolism of the rising and declining day. With his death, the others are slowly permeated by the vaguely-suggested sense of the treacherousness of life, and towards the end the virtual surrender to meaninglessness is expressed by Bernard in his summing-up.

The Years (1937) is a more tedious, protracted and commonplace repetition of *The Waves*. In structure it shows a relapse to the conventional which is curious – it is *Night and Day* without the plot-structure, stretched out and dissolved in the featureless, disintegrating stream of sixty years. A diffuse group of characters, even shadowier in outline than those in any of the previous novels, are seen at various intervals in their passage through life, drifting emptily down the stream of time. But in spite of this surrender, there is no passionate concern with the nature and meaning of time. Nor is there even any nostalgic endeavour to capture and convey the subtler vibrations of 'period' atmosphere; and the selection of incidents seems quite desultory. The predominant mood is of a vacant lassitude. Formlessness reaches its apogee.

She had always wanted to know about Christiantity – how it began; what it meant, originally. God is love, The kingdom of Heaven is within us, sayings like that she thought, turning over the pages, what did they mean? The actual words were very beautiful. But who said them – when? Then the spout of the tea-kettle puffed steam at her and she moved it away. The wind was rattling the windows in the back room; it was bending the little bushes; they still had no leaves on them. It was what a man said under a fig tree, on a hill, she thought. And then another man wrote it down. But suppose that what that man says is just as false as what this man – she touched the press cuttings with her spoon – says about Digby? And here am I, she thought, looking at the china in the Dutch cabinet, in this drawing-room, getting a

G

little spark from what someone said all those years ago – here it comes (the china was changing from blue to livid) skipping over all those mountains, all those seas. She found her place and began to read.

But a sound in the hall interrupted her. Was someone coming in? She listened. No, it was the wind. The wind was terrific. It pressed on the house; gripped it tight, then let it fall apart. Upstairs a door slammed; a window must be open in the bedroom above. A blind was tapping. It was difficult to fix her mind on Renan. She liked it, though. French she could easily read of course; and Italian; and a little German. But what vast gaps there were, what blank spaces, she thought leaning back in her chair, in her knowledge! How little she knew about anything. Take this cup for instance; she held it out in front of her. What was it made of? Atoms? And what were atoms, and how did they stick together? The smooth hard surface of the china with its red flowers seemed to her for a second a marvellous mystery. But there was another sound in the hall. It was the wind, but it was also a voice, talking. It must be Martin. But who could he be talking to, she wondered? She listened, but she could not hear what he was saying because of the wind. And why, she asked herself, did he say we can't tell a lie to save our souls? He was thinking about himself; one always knew when people were thinking about themselves by their tone of voice. Perhaps he was justifying himself for having left the Army. That had been courageous, she thought; but isn't it odd, she mused, listening to the voices, that he should be such a dandy, too? He was wearing a new blue suit with white stripes on it. And he had shaved off his moustache. He ought never to have been a soldier, she thought; he was much too pugnacious. . . . They were still talking. She could not hear what he was saying, but from the sound of his voice it came over her that he must have a great many love affairs. Yes – it became perfectly obvious to her, listening to his voice through the door, that he had a great many love affairs. But who with? and why do men think love affairs so important? she asked as the door opened.

And so the vague thoughts drop from Christianity to teacups, from teacups to love-affairs, in a process of mental dissipation. Only towards the end (as in *The Waves*) does the imminence of her conclusion persuade the novelist to cast about for a few grains of 'significance'. And so, in the concluding section, those characters who are still surviving are suddenly endowed with a proclivity to ponder about Life. Eleanor Pargiter, to whose reflections we have just listened, first introduced in 1880 as a young girl, now an old woman, is made to reflect as follows:

My life, she said to herself. That was odd, it was the second time that evening that somebody had talked about her life. And I haven't got one, she thought. Oughtn't a life to be something you could handle and produce? – a life of seventy-odd years. But I've only the present moment, she thought. Here she was alive, now, listening to the fox-trot. Then she looked round. There was Morris; Rose; Edward with his head thrown back talking to a man she did not know. I'm the only person here, she thought, who remembers how he sat on the edge of my bed that night, crying – the night Kitty's engagement was announced. Yes, things came back to her. A long strip of life lay behind her. Edward crying, Mrs. Levy talking; snow falling; a sunflower with a crack in it; the yellow omnibus trotting along the Bayswater Road. And I thought to myself, I'm the youngest person in this omnibus; now I'm the oldest. . . . Millions of things came back to her. Atoms danced apart and massed themselves. But how did they compose what people called a life? She clenched her hands and felt the hard little coins she was holding. Perhaps there's 'I' at the middle of it, she thought; a knot; a centre; and again she saw herself sitting at her table drawing on the blotting-paper, digging little holes from which spokes radiated. Out and out they went; thing followed thing, scene obliterated scene. And then they say, she thought, 'We've been talking about you!'
     . . . Does everything then come over again a little differently? she thought. If so, is there a pattern; a theme, recurring like music; half remembered, half foreseen? . . . a gigantic pattern, momentarily perceptible? The thought gave her extreme pleasure: that there was a pattern. But who makes it? Her mind slipped. She could not finish her thought.
     . . . It's useless, she thought, opening her hands. It must drop. It must fall. And then? she thought. For her too there would be the endless night; the endless dark. She looked ahead of her as though she saw opening in front of her a very long dark tunnel.

Depressing as all this is, it remains vague and undefined. The nearest approach to a definite attitude within this pervasive general temper in which all the characters are monistically submerged is provided by a younger woman at the same party:

Peggy, marooned when the dance started, over by the bookcase, stood as close to it as she could. In order to cover her loneliness she took down a book. It was bound in green leather; and had, she noted as she turned it in her hands, little gilt stars tooled upon it. Which is all to the good, she thought, turning it over, because then it'll seem as if I were admiring the binding, . . . But I can't stand here admiring the binding, she thought. She opened it. He'll say what I'm thinking, she thought as she did so. Books opened at random always did

'*La médiocrité de l'univers m'étonne et me révolte*,' she read. That was it. Precisely. She read on . . . '*la petitesse de toutes choses m'emplit de dégoût.* . . .' She lifted her eyes. They were treading on her toes. ' . . . *la pauvreté des êtres humains m'anéantit.*' She shut the book and put it back on the shelf. 'Precisely,' she said.

After the aimless vacancy of the substance of the tale and such concluding reflections as these, the book's final sentence comes with a glib indication of a superimposed 'significance' almost shocking in its irrelevance.

Then she turned round into the room. 'And now?' she said, looking at Morris, who was drinking the last drops of a glass of wine. 'And now?' she asked, holding out her hands to him.

The sun had risen, and the sky above the houses wore an air of extraordinary beauty, simplicity and peace.

VI

THE annihilation of personality in the stream of non-personal being which is the logical consequence of Virginia Woolf's basic monism is expressed several times in *Night and Day*:

The great torrent of vans and carts was sweeping down Kingsway; pedestrians were streaming in two currents along the pavements. She stood fascinated at the corner. The deep roar filled her ears; the changing tumult had the inexpressible fascination of varied life pouring ceaselessly with a purpose which, as she looked, seemed to her, somehow, the normal purpose for which life was framed; its complete indifference to the individuals, whom it swallowed up and rolled onwards, filled her with at least a temporary exaltation.

This undisguised, but intermittent, note of individual personal immolation is kept at bay through *Jacob's Room*, *Mrs. Dalloway*, and *To the Lighthouse*, only to emerge once more on the downward emotional curve of *The Waves*.

'But listen,' said Louis, 'to the world moving through abysses of infinite space. It roars; the lighted strip of history is past and our Kings and Queens; we are gone; our civilization; the Nile; and all life. Our separate drops are dissolved; we are extinct, lost in the abysses of time, in the darkness.

In *The Years*, the process of time is confessed as sovereign. Human beings are simply and unresistingly swept away in the irreversible flux. It is the negation of spirit, the acceptance of dissolution, and it is perfectly in keeping with the incredible fragmentariness and incoherence of that novel.

The surrender to the process of time which had taken possession of Virginia Woolf's work from *To the Lighthouse* onwards, which is itself symptomatic of the relinquishment of meaning in personal life, is, in *Between the Acts* (1941) made absolute: but this enthroning of meaninglessness is effected in what is evidently a last desperate gesture towards the delineation of meaning. The book's 'extraordinary vacancy and pointlessness, the apparent absence of concern for any appearance of grasp or point', as F. R. Leavis describes it, is in fact the outcome of a pathetic gesture towards a final, desperate sort of significance. Here the time-pattern is extended to embrace, not one or two individual life-times, but the whole collective period of the human story. A naïve, self-cancelling 'significance' is indicated by a simple placing of the trivial moments of the inherently pointless characters in this tale against the immensities of racial history. The entire work is merely an elaboration of this intrinsically futile gesture, of which its inner story, that of the village pageant-play, is the type.

On the book's opening page, we have this immediate reference back to history:

Her family, she told the old man in the arm-chair, had lived near Liskeard for many centuries. There were the graves in the churchyard to prove it.

And on the second page:

From an aeroplane, he said, you could still see, plainly marked, the scars made by the Britons; by the Romans; by the Elizabethan manor house; and by the plough, when they ploughed the hill to grow wheat in the Napoleonic wars.

This historical and prehistorical background is reiterated at every opportunity:

> Only something over a hundred and twenty years the Olivers had been there. Still, on going up the principal staircase . . . there was a portrait. A length of yellow brocade was visible halfway up; and, as one reached the top, a small powdered face, a great head-dress slung with pearls, came into view; an ancestress of sorts. Six or seven bedrooms opened out of the corridor. The butler had been a soldier; had married a lady's maid; and, under a glass case, there was a watch that had stopped a bullet on the field of Waterloo.

The very boy who delivers fish has to be presented with a backward glance at his ancestry:

> Mitchell's boy – had to deliver right over the hill at Bickley; also round by Waythorn, Roddam, and Pyeminster, whose names, like his own, were in Domesday Book.

When someone knocks over a coffee-cup, the individual who catches it turns it over and sees, from the markings, that it was made at Nottingham at about 1760. Even the stones in the ground point a moral:

> This dry summer the path was strewn with stones, He kicked – a flinty yellow stone, a sharp stone, edged as if cut by a savage for an arrow. A barbaric stone; a prehistoric.

Old Mrs. Swithin, who on the day of the pageant is living in the village with her brother, Mr. Oliver, and his daughter, Mrs. Giles Oliver (Isa), at his country house, is awakened in the morning by the song of birds, and –

> . . . Forced to listen, she had stretched for her favourite ready – an Outline of History – and had spent the hours between three and five thinking of rhododendron forests in Piccadilly; when the entire continent, not then, she understood, divided by a channel, was all one; populated, she understood, by elephant-bodied, seal-knecked, heaving, surging, slowly writhing and, she supposed, barking monsters; the iguanodon, the mammoth, and the mastodon; from whom presumably, she thought, jerking the windows open, we descend.

The Pageant, a description of which forms the greater part of this peculiar novel, is designed by the producer, Miss La

Trobe, to show the villagers their organic continuity with history – their absorption, as it were, in the unbroken stream of time. That is the theory, which the novelist emphasizes as a fact at every opportunity.

> The audience was assembling. . . . Among them were the representatives of our most respected families – the Dyces of Denton; the Wickhams of Owlswick; and so on. Some had been there for centuries, never selling an acre. . . . Roughly speaking, had Figgis been there in person and called a roll call, half the ladies and gentlemen present would have said: '*Adsum*; I'm here, in place of my grandfather or greatgrandfather,' as the case might be.

The titled woman who patronizes the pageant is described as 'the old lady, the indigenous, the prehistoric':

> Then the great lady in the bath chair, the lady whose marriage with the local peer had obliterated in his trashy title a name that had been a name when there were brambles and briars where the Church now stood – so indigenous was she that even her body, crippled by arthritis, resembled an uncouth, nocturnal animal, now nearly extinct – clapped and laughed aloud – the sudden laughter of a startled jay.

It is all like that. The barn, in which refreshments are served during the interval, is 'the Barn, the Noble Barn, the barn that had been built over seven hundred years ago and reminded some people of a Greek temple, others of the middle ages, most people of an age before their own, scarcely anybody of the present moment'. And the climax of the moronic pageant is the section called 'Ourselves', when Miss La Trobe arranges for a host of actors with mirrors to flash them in the faces of the assembled audience.

The novel has one or two curious implications. To ascribe some peculiar sort of indwelling 'significance', not to the individual life, but to the collective history of mankind, the life of the race, is by emphasizing more continuity, to place human values at once within primarily biological categories. So it is that, oddly enough for this supposedly delicate and refined woman novelist, the biological pseudo-values of race, nature and sex are emphasized continually throughout her tale. During an intermission in the pageant, when Miss La Trobe is

anxiously waiting for something to fill the hiatus in the per-
formance, the emotional continuity is appropriately provided
by the mindless bellowing of a herd of cows:

> Then suddenly, as the illusion petered out, the cows took up the
> burden. One had lost her calf. In the very nick of time she lifted
> her great moon-eyed head and bellowed. All the great moon-eyed
> heads laid themselves back. From cow after cow came the same
> yearning bellow. The whole world was filled with dumb yearning.
> It was the primeval voice sounding loud in the ear of the present
> moment. Then the whole herd caught the infection. Lashing their
> tails, blobbed like pokers, they tossed their heads high, plunged
> and bellowed, as if Eros had planted his dart in their flanks and
> goaded them to fury. The cows annihilated the gap; bridged the
> distance; filled the emptiness and continued the emotion.

These 'values' are applied to the human characters.

Mrs. Giles Oliver (Isa), for example, is introduced with a
reference to her sexual yearnings for a certain gentleman farmer
she has met; a little later she reads in the current *Times* about
the brutal rape of a girl by some troopers, and this incident
recurs to her mind at intervals throughout the day. When her
husband, Giles Oliver, from whom she is estranged, comes to
the house from his work at London:

> 'He is my husband,' Isabella thought, as they nodded across the
> bunch of many coloured flowers. 'The father of my children.'
> It worked, that old cliché; she felt pride; and affection; then pride
> again in herself, whom he had chosen. It was a shock to find, after
> the morning's look in the glass, and the arrow of desire shot
> through her by the gentleman farmer, how much she felt when
> he came in, not a dapper city gent, but a cricketer, of love; and
> of hate.

This phrase is repeated at intervals up to the end of the book –

> . . . 'the father of my children,' she muttered. The flesh poured
> over her, the hot nerve wired, now lit up, now dark as the grave
> physical body.
> . . . Yet he was extraordinarily handsome. 'The father of my
> children, whom I love and hate.' Love and hate – how they tore
> her asunder! . . .

when, after the lengthy description of the pageant which is to fill the onlookers with a sense of their racial-historical continuity, Giles and Isa at last come together and,

> Left alone together for the first time that day, they were silent. Alone, enmity was bared; also love. Before they slept, they must fight, after they had fought, they would embrace. From that embrace another life might be born. But first they must fight, as the dog fights the vixen, in the heart of darkness, in the fields of night. . . .

Thus impersonality is transformed into animality. Meanwhile, old Mrs. Swithin has returned to her meditations.

> It was time to read now, her Outline of History. But she had lost her place. She turned the pages looking at pictures – mammoths, mastodons, prehistoric birds. . . . 'England,' she was reading, 'was then a swamp. Thick forests covered the land. On top of their matted branches birds sang.' . . . 'Prehistoric man,' she read, 'Half-human, half-ape, roused himself from his semi-crouching position and raised great stones.'

Finally, night descends.

> The house had lost its shelter. It was night before roads were made, or houses. It was the night that dwellers in caves had watched from some high place among rocks. . . .

So ends the last book of this 'pure artist'.

MARGIAD EVANS

A STUDY of the cultural products of the last hundred years reveals an amazing heterogeneity of modes of human life and thought. This is to be expected in a period during which, following widespread apostasy from Christianity, no common faith has existed to sustain and unify cultural endeavour, nor is this heterogeneity the result of a creative flowering, but of a process of dissolution. Human life is disintegrating into fragments, and the individual, instead of achieving, or at least pursuing, wholeness, tends to adopt a fragmentary view of life, which results in a distortion of personality and its submission to lower elements.

A remarkable and little apprehended stream of this kind, running through the culture of the present day, issues from a peculiar and distinctive cult of nature, a reversion to a pre-Christian immersion of the soul in the natural universe. John Cowper Powys and his brother Llewelyn are eminent contemporary representatives of this cult in the world of letters. Brief passages from a recent book of the former indicate some of the basic features of the cult. This writer, not without philosophical pretensions as the author of *In Defence of Sensuality* and *A Philosophy of Solitude*, advocates 'a philosophy of life which regards the whole purpose of this Dimension of the Multiverse as the fullest possible enjoyment of life in general by each individual in particular'. Of this 'fullest enjoyment' Powys says:

> The most intense as well as the most lasting enjoyment possible to man is not to be attained through love or lust or power or possession or action, but through a very special sort of sensation, the sensation of embracing the whole Inanimate Mystery of which our present Dimension is composed.

Rhapsodizing over the irresponsibility of old age, which, he claims, sets men and women free to devote themselves to this 'fullest enjoyment of living', he exclaims:

> But oh! the escape from the appalling debt we owe to our fellow-men that is offered by the inanimate or sub-animate!

The more we learn to eat it, drink it, ravish it, be ravished by it, fuse with it, merge with it, sink into it, lose ourselves in it, the more fully we shall possess our souls in peace, the better will our solitude be protected and our subtlest egoism fulfilled.

In these passages we have, allowing for idiosyncrasies of expression, a fairly typical presentation of some of the chief features of the cult of nature. A cult of solitude, of sensuality, of enjoyment, of biological vitality, and of merging, it is antipersonal and anti-social, anticultural and materialistic. It is sufficient here merely to indicate these matters and to comment on the didactic presentation of the principles of the cult in J. C. Powys' work. This presentation, presupposing a settled basis of formulated experience, distinguishes him from those who are themselves spiritually involved in a process of turning towards nature as a release from the burdens and strains of the distinctively human life which is frustrated by the conditions of the modern world.

Such a turning towards and dissolution of personality in the fluid universe of nature is to be seen in progress in the writings of D. H. Lawrence. Yet, because Lawrence was a complicated person, the progression in Lawrence's case was intricate. A much simpler, but no less revealing, example of the process of the repudiation of personal life and spiritual values for the sake of immersion in the life of nature is to be found in the work of a distinguished contemporary, Margiad Evans.

A writer of considerable force and honesty, her earlier books, *Country Dance*, *The Wooden Doctor*, *Turf or Stone*, and *Creed* – all novels of more than common merit – are bitter, passionate cries of protest against the frustrations of personal life. The mood of her work is curiously reminiscent of that of *Wuthering Heights*. These novels followed close upon one another, having been published within a period of five years. There was then a significant seven years' silence between the publication of her fourth novel, *Creed* (1936), and her last book, *Autobiography* (1943), which clearly bears the markings of an individual version of the cult of nature.

Not an autobiography in the usual sense of the word, this book is a series of nature articles and notes written under such headings as 'A Little Journal of Being Alone', 'The Winter Journal', 'The Autobiography of an Afternoon', containing nothing about the author except as she exists in relationship with nature. It is clear that this is not intended to be an appetizer for the special public that seems to delight in little volumes about the English countryside; the title 'Autobiography' has for the author a quite definite significance, implying nothing less than that life in relationship with nature is the true, the essential life. 'This autobiography,' she writes, 'is the record of my gravest (that is happiest) inner existence. . . .' She says early in the book:

> Oh, how long it is since I have looked at the greatness of Nature miserably, through my own dreariness! *Now* it is my great refuge, my independent godliness which I worship without self-pity. It's a beautiful change from the tortured symbolism in which creation is molten and twisted into the form of *self*, to the simple and ever open sight of love! The fields are my grass life, the sun, the wind, the weather. If this power over my solitary hours persist, I am blessed.

Such is the spirit of her book. In keeping with this, elsewhere in it she confesses, 'Life to me is solitude'; and again, 'Don't talk to me of morals. To draw a moral is to draw a bolt.'

> Writing saddens me. Vision is turned into effort. Only in the *inner physical* eye is the radiance reflected. Life to me is solitude. My senses are all solitary. Through solitude I breathe. Memory is solitude and seeing. My senses are all solitary. They desert me when I am not alone, or rather leave me paralysed at the point of desertion. I thought this as I turned into the wind. Leaning on a gate I looked up at the sky in joy of my loneliness. The earth was reared up against the tossing clouds. And as I achieved the stripped summit of the hill and my eye swept the vigorous lines, the spaced and wintry trees that made the identity of the place, I put from me the intermediate self and spoke to the spirit, I, asking it, to what is it apt? The answer came by sight and feeling – to the earth itself and not to the people of it. My passionate and only belief is in another order of being from my own: my joy is in the hills and the different notes of the wind, and the (to me) unbaptized stars.

II

THE novels of Margiad Evans glow with a dark, sombre, passionate light. This is in evidence in her first and shortest work, *Country Dance* (1932), a tale, purporting to be founded

upon an old manuscript diary kept by the central character of
the story, of a bitter rivalry between two jealous, surly men of
the Welsh Border over a girl, half Welsh, half English, as
sullenly passionate as they. Unlit by any gleam of love, it ends,
inevitably, in the murder of the girl by the rejected lover.
Beneath the tale itself runs an emotional awareness of the dark
grief of existence; the book's motto reads:

> . . . Place thy hand, unless thou believest me,
> Under my breast and beware of hurting me;
> Thou shalt hear if thou listen
> The sound of the little heart breaking.

Although written with a terse, incisive power, *Country Dance*
did not achieve any great degree of success with the reading
public.

The Wooden Doctor (1933), the second novel, won immediate
recognition for the author's talent as a writer and straightway
went into several impressions. This clearly personal novel is the
history, told in the first person, of the childhood, adolescence,
and youth of Arabella Warden, given a sporadic emotional
continuity by the description of her unrequited passion for a
middle-aged Irish doctor who is the one person in her desolate
childhood to show her human tenderness.

The note of desolation is sounded in the opening pages, and
the tale proceeds with a bitter, restless feverish ardour.

> In our home there was no peace. My father did more than
> drink occasionally; he was an habitual drunkard. No word was
> ever more accurately or deservedly applied; no family was ever
> rendered more miserable by its justice.
> . . . We grew up accepting him at first with terror and disgust,
> finally with bitter resignation. We have heard our mother called
> by names that would have shamed a harlot, not below the breath,
> but as one might sing praises. We have stood shivering behind
> bolted doors with our hands over our ears that we might not hear
> him scream of the horrors that he saw, and shut our eyes to those
> that were no delirious fancy.
> . . . Sometimes for our own sake, and his own, we have wished
> him dead, drowned, buried, or for ourselves that freedom. . . .
> . . . One and all, year in, year out, we nursed the prospect of
> escape. We quarrelled among ourselves, fretted, isolated by our

eccentricities, we sharpened our claws in one another's flesh. Our home among the quiet fields became a cage of savagery.

That note is sustained throughout the novel. Brought up in such surroundings, Arabella is morose, wild, and rebellious. In her teens she goes as a pupil-teacher to a school in France, but she is no happier there than at home.

> For years afterwards I hated the French. If I had been happy at the Cours Saint-Louis it might have dispelled my impression that the world was a grievous place.

Returning to England, she is attacked by a mysterious and painful malady:

> In the night the pain came back. It was like a fox in a bag scratching and rending to get out. My spirits trailed in the dust. The claws penetrated my sleep, dragged me awake and I sat up in my bed. I knew that I was ill. . . .
> One night we went to the cinema. . . . We were laughing. Suddenly out of the darkness the fox sprang with flaming feet and famished jaws, rending, biting, tearing. I wished that I could faint and be delivered from this agony, but my strength increased with the torture. A man in front of me had rather long hair. I wanted to seize it in both hands and pull his head backward: I felt I could have pulled it off.

Meanwhile she has drawn no nearer towards the doctor:

> One day after the doctor had gone my mother observed: 'He is beginning to look old.'
> Sadness filled me at these words. To me he was unchanged, but she was right, and I felt that living and loving were slipping by. . . .

There follows an incisive description of the experience of illness and the life of hospitals, written with savage stoicism. Then:

> One night I looked from my window. What a stormy sky I saw, and the moon shining livid behind black clouds; the hills rose up to them and mingled indistinguishably.
> There could be no comfort in humans. And my mind could find no god. I seized a pencil and wrote angrily.
> 'There's no doctor.'
> 'There's only me.'

'Am I to spend the rest of my life in the vapours? The gods forbid.'

In the morning I looked at what I had written with wonder. It was sunny.

All woes grow dim in the sun.

The Wooden Doctor learns of Arabella's passion for him and gently rejects her.

> . . . the cut was dealt to me that divided my life into two parts. The period I approach was one of intense misery to me: I cannot write about it now without trembling; yet I am urged to do it. . . .

She goes to stay with a married cousin.

> My cousin had a beautiful face. Those delicate features, those laughing, shining eyes, that cunning mouth, all that fascination so frequently before me, so contentedly blooming beside the husband she adored, tortured me. Savagely I envied her, not for what she had, but for what she might have had. To myself I cried: 'J'ai perdu, perdu, perdu; elle auriait gagnée!'
>
> Full bitterness was mine, but my habit of deception hid it all. Outwardly I led a commonplace and happy existence: inwardly I seethed with jealousy and shame, and an aching loss.
>
> I could not attract the man I loved: henceforth I should walk in utter humiliation. Twenty lovers would not atone for it. I look at those words now that I have written them down, admitting their truth. Arabella, from the heights of folly and the depths of despair I trounce you, denounce you, curse you, flout you for a fool.
>
> I wish I could inspire one half the devotion I have given!

Her inner state is one of isolation:

> I began to feel now more than ever before that confession was foolish and to be found out contemptible. That belief cut me off from all but superficial contact with other people.
>
> Heavily, heavily the days trundled by. I was glad when the hours passed quickly and the evenings came. I strained my eyes ahead, tugged at the leash . . . for what?
>
> I did not want to die – there were many things that interested me – but I did wish that I had never been born.

So the tale runs on. The portrait of Arabella is not a pretty one: tortured, rebellious, and proud, she is filled with 'fierce resentment' of the happiness of others. She begins to write a book, and to finish it goes to a farmhouse in Wales, where she meets a young man called Oliver, who makes love to her and begs her marry him. She promises to do so, but on returning home finds that her devotion to the doctor makes marriage impossible.

Abruptly the story closes:

> All this took place some time ago.
> My book was published.
> Oliver sends me red tulips on my birthday.
> And the Irishman married a young girl a few months after my return.
> And that's the end.

Clearly, this is a very simple novel, covering a restricted area of sensibility. Its merit is its passionate intensity and the savage honesty which presents a firmly limned outline of felt experience. Its limitations are as apparent as its virtues: what would seem to be lacking in the attitude to life which it reveals is any potentiality of development. The author's patent identification of herself with her heroine, who lives solely in her egoistic passional life, and who, utterly without humility and the capacity for self-forgetfulness, is unable in any way to transcend her particular circumstances, suggests an inadequate equipment for continuous fictional creation. The story in *The Wooden Doctor* is, in fact, slight, secondary entirely to the implicit attitude which it reveals toward experience. The nature of that attitude is sufficiently indicated by the extracts given above. The 'humiliation' of which it is a record is a measure of Arabella's pride which remains unaffected to the end. It even has a demoniac quality. The interest of the book centres entirely upon the presentation of events and scenes which group themselves around the inner passionate protest of Arabella. The protest is against existence itself, for not shaping itself to her egoistic desires. The result is a stark simplicity which, however, seems to hold within it no potential unfoldment, inasmuch as the book possesses no positive philosophical, moral, religious, or social content. There is no novelist's interest in human beings for their own sake: everything centres around the morose

Arabella and her exclusive preoccupation with her own sorrows.

Turf or Stone (1934) is a less successful work, although it has considerable emotional interest. The hero of the book, Easter Probert, a half-gipsy groom and outcast from society, although outwardly a wild, sullen, malicious creature, is really – though unconsciously – searching for a woman's tenderness and love. The story opens with a description of Easter's marriage to a rather superior, genteel girl whom he has seduced, Mary Bicknor, a companion-servant to a wealthy old lady. He treats her brutally from the time of the wedding, quarrelling with her outside the very church and leaving her to walk home while he jumps into a passing bus. Easter is groom for Matt Kilminster, an idle, bored, dissolute 'gentleman', married to a frivolous, luxury-loving, self-pitying wife with three children. Having conceived an attachment for Easter's wife, Matt arranges for the groom to be away from the house for three days in the week in order to indulge his passion for Mary. Denied the tenderness for which he is always hungering, Easter sinks further into a bitter, violent nihilism until at last Mary, incensed at his treatment of her, lays information of his cruelty with the police and applies for a separation. Matt's young daughter, Phoebe, goes to Easter's squalid lodging to plead with him to keep her father's name out of the matter to avoid disgrace: although he does not agree to do so, he keeps his mouth shut at the court hearing and makes no defence against Mary's charges. Shortly afterwards he is killed in a brawl.

Turf or Stone is again a novel of passion rather than of character. The characters move in a heavy, oppressive atmosphere of empty meaninglessness, lifted only by occasional outbursts of debauchery or rage. Their world is utterly without light or love. Existence drags painfully. Unable to look for grace from above, they are at the mercy of the dark forces which rise from the lowest depths of their natures. 'Morose', 'dreary', 'baleful', 'sullen', 'gloomy', 'threatening', 'brooding', 'sombre', and 'bitter' are adjectives which litter each page. Matt Kilminster typifies this picture of existence: he –

led an increasingly blank existence. He was sometimes tortured by the vacancy of everything. Lately he had taken to drinking. . . .

H

[He was driven] deeper, deeper, into a vague mental state where nothing held any significance.

'My blind island,' he called it to himself. . . .

He fell into a sombre calm, and his thoughts were all sad:

'How is it people are happy in this world, or even at their ease?'

By contrast with Matt and the others, it becomes clear as the tale proceeds that Easter in some way represents for the author the assertion of a value. As a hero, Easter recalls certain of the characters of D. H. Lawrence. Though presented in all his native viciousness and squalor, the only hint of idealization occurring in the retrospective glance at his childhood, it is nevertheless implied that circumstances have made him what he is and that in contrast to the other characters he has virtue. Besides being insolent, violent, and malicious, he has courage, animal gracefulness, and vitality.

If the story is told from the viewpoint of any one of the characters, it is that of Matt's eldest daughter, Phoebe. As the tale unwinds, there are subtle hints of the emotional significance which the groom holds for the growing girl. An example is the description of Phoebe's interview with Easter:

He put one foot on the bench, laid his elbow on his knee, and cupped his chin, while he stared at her eyes which she could not meet without a spasm of shame and something besides, something sharp and acute which stirred her so deeply that she began to shake. He desired Phoebe ardently, had done so for a long time, almost unaware; even as he sneered at the purity of her face it fascinated him. He experienced once more the voluptuous and painful craving for unsought caresses. The furious rancour which he had fostered for the last two years was beginning to give way before a sense of isolation which at times sapped his manhood and caused wild outbreaks of unconscious weeping at night. He was discovering that no creature of seven skins can be an outcast without suffering at least intermittent grief and yearning.

Phoebe was silent.

'There's no sense in your staying,' he resumed obstinately, 'why, God blast it all, you innocent toy, you don't know what you're asking of a man! It's my nature to be revengeful; you're asking me to change my nature . . . you might as well say "hop out of your skin, Easter, you'd be handsomer in a new one".'

'I do believe you have a cleaner skin underneath.' For the first time he was moved a little beyond his predatory senses. She heard him sigh.

'Perhaps,' he went on, 'But you wouldn't touch it! You don't even offer me anything. You'd make a new man if you could, but you won't take the new man near you and keep him against harm. You're Miss Kilminster and I'm a groom, and that's enough.'

He broke off, watching her. Her heart was beating so hard that he could see the throbs shaking her breast. Had he been aware to what extent she was fighting her own rising instincts he might have gone forward and taken his revenge on Matt without leaving the shed.

When Phoebe hears of his death, the story ends with the words: 'she began to cry dreadfully and heavily, in a deathly senseless manner, as if every sob would kill her'.

Turf or Stone, in so far as it is not written as direct auto-biography centring around the narrator, but as a drama concerning a group of characters, told in the third person, reveals in the author an increase in that objectivity necessary for novelistic creation, which makes possible the dramatic explication of a morality, the projection of a pattern of thought. Although the novel lacks structure, the character of Easter reveals a movement towards the dramatic presentation of an inner attitude, which alone gives significance to a novelist's work.

That inner attitude is seen clearly in the writer's subsequent novel, *Creed* (1936).

III

THIS bold title discloses that the novel, like all significant modern literature, is scriptural in character. Despite its lack of an overt morality, so is *The Wooden Doctor*, which discloses, although not in philosophical terms, a definite attitude toward experi-ence. In *Turf or Stone*, the attitude implicit in the earlier book is made more explicit; in *Creed* it is given full and definite expression. This is without doubt the best of Margiad Evans's novels. Considered aesthetically, it is one of the very few signi-ficant modern works of fiction. As the title implies, an attempt is made to formulate and express a religious attitude to life.

The chief character is Francis Dollbright, ironmonger's

clerk, a religious bigot, stern and upright, worshipper of a harsh, tyrannical Ancient of Days, the eternal Judge and condemner of human sin. The story opens with an account of a sermon preached by an old Welsh parson, Ifor Morriss, who is overcome by sincerity in his pulpit and preaches his own private gospel of the irrelevance of sin and the impossibility of damnation.

> 'Ah, I tell you man cannot perish! I know it, for God loves him; not as a saint but as a blackened sinner he is loved. . . .
>
> My friends, although we should be murderers and blasphemers, although we are eaten through with meanness, cowardice, deceit, cruelty and the unnamed sins of our lusts, we should never be afraid to lift our foreheads to His face: although we are conscious of a determined will to continue in our vile courses, let us worship and say:
>
> ' "Lord, I know you are in me, and I thank You for Your presence. In the midst of our wickedness and our resolution to continue, let us kneel and avow: I know that You have not abandoned me." '

Shocked by this blasphemy, Dollbright interviews and anathematizes the parson after his sermon. Morriss laughs at Dollbright, who returns home in a state of inner turmoil, which moves him to assert his moral values by severing connections with his employer, John Bridges, an ill-living, passionate, unbelieving man who lives with a woman to whom he is not married. Dollbright announces this decision to his wife, who bitterly resents the placing of the demands of his conscience before her well-being, despite which he notifies his employer of his intention to quit. Meanwhile his wife discovers that she is ill with cancer and must undergo an operation, while Dollbright finds that his action earns him the contempt rather than the respect of other people. Eventually he wavers, and the discovery of his wife's illness forces him to go hat in hand to Bridges to beg for the return of his job.

Interwoven with the story of Dollbright is that of the stricken, beseeching passion of the young Bellamy Williams for haunted, compassionate Menna Trouncer. They feel 'fated' to love each other, but Menna tries to run from her fate and to deny Bellamy.

'Oh, Menna, Menna, Menna, I'd scarcely be in such despair if I saw you dead or loving another man! Dead you'd be out of chance, and loving would give you substance and a heart which I'd twist towards me. But I can't strain at nothing, and nothing is all I've got to beg you by. What do you hold to? What can't you spare when you've spared everything? What's your most inner and last hope? I'll pray and implore you by that to take me and love me . . . love me. I want the looks that you hide from me, the time that you spoil, all the joys that you kill and keep back. I want my sleep from you, my life, my rest. I'm deserted and sleepless without you. I want your hands on my head – it's all pain and longing! Take me, Menna darling, dear love——!' Tightly as he held her, forcing her face close to his own with his hard right hand over her ear and his gasps crossing her lips, she scarcely felt the pressure on her living body. But each word melted her. She looked at him, lifted her hand and put it against his neck; then her eyes yielded and his own name seemed uttered in them rather than in sound. Neither would move; they were walled up in passion, in a rigid pause, a stricken knowledge of what was inevitable between them. All softness and elasticity departed, even the tremulousness of breathing. Their eyes were like callouses. At last he spoke, but with indescribable difficulty, as though something bolted and barred within him were making noises behind a door.

'Now . . . is it . . . love?'

She could not answer, could do nothing but gaze while her hand began to stir on his neck and she learned the line of his lips forever.

'If we two part,' he toiled on in the same weak, yet urgent tone, 'we shall always hanker after each other. You'll never forget me; I have burned into you.'

'Yes——'

In a desperate spasm they simultaneously clutched each other and stood blind and reeling with their faces stricken together. Then the strength ran out of them. Bellamy fell against the wall, covering his eyes, and Menna sank down on the floor at his knees.

In his bewilderment and inner struggle, Dollbright encounters Menna's hideous mother. This woman, powerfully drawn by the author, provides a spiritual centre for the book. Under the surface of their lives, all these characters, Dollbright, Ifor Morriss, Menna Trouncer, and Bellamy Williams, meet and are psychically united; their basic stuff is the same and finds its crude expression in the figure of Mrs. Trouncer.

Once more [Dollbright] noticed her short dirty neck disappear-
ing in the wrinkles of a silk handkerchief. Suddenly he felt an
abominable seduction dwelling in her swarthy flesh. She shook
. . . He looked at her with grim disgust.

'It isn't church and chapel and gory black hats that makes life,'
she said.

'Nor whiskey and the gutter,' he retorted.

'Talking of the gutter you name yourself. Sodding church-
warden!' she screamed, glaring and advancing as he shut the
inner door that Florence might not hear. When he turned round
he found her face almost touching his ear; the large pores stood
out like a rash, the nose was nearly black. Without the slightest
warning but the audible clash of her teeth, she shot her fist out
and struck him on the right arm above the elbow with her left.

He saw the blow whirling in the air like a chipped stone falling.
She did not repeat it, she was too breathless.

'You . . .!' he shouted, 'touch me again and I'll call a con-
stable.'

'If I'd the strength, I'd tear up the stones in the street to heave
at you. I'd squash your bloody nob in the Mill, myself the wheel,
and bless every fall of bad that comes your way . . . I'd stamp
you down in Hell, where I've been and seen not one devil but
ten thousand holding up their arms at the whole —— lot of us and
sending up rockets that burst your eyes. Blast you to ruins! My
tongue's gone down me gullet——'

Standing in the doorway she glared at him as if she would nail
him to the wall.

'Church bug – climb up the cross!'

The underlying psychic unity of these passion-driven characters expresses itself in Dollbright's fascinated recognition of that
which he has in common, despite appearances, with the terrifying, bestial drunkard, Mrs. Trouncer.

He could not find words to form his thoughts, nor images to
hold them. They were too vague, immense, and inevitable. He
had a sense of elemental diablerie quite apart from any human
will. Men and things were part of it, as agents but no more. It was
a dark illumination of the intellect, a search, a quest into the
wizard powers. It was a faith prouder than any, savagely intoler-
ant of happiness and goodness. It made Ifor Morriss smug,
Bridges empty as the skull he preached.

It made Mrs. Trouncer great.

Instincts go deeper than reasons, sin than sanctity. Dollbright was, he bitterly and fearfully acknowledged, a swaddled ignoramus before this woman's violent force. She made him ashamed of his religion, weary of it and distrustful; she interfused God and temptation. She was scored and branded. He hated her still, but he could think of her without the limitation of disgust. He ceased to curse himself for the abominable perversion of his desire. Self-blame was lost in an almost supernatural fear. He felt she was a giant figure in his destiny . . . she fated him.

What was she, less obviously than a blasphemous hag? She swilled spirits until her face was swinish and gloating, but what inexplicable look of initiation was that in her eye? Of what soul was her face the defiant scar? What end had she visioned and dared?

He knew that whatever these things were, they lay not in her, but beyond her; and that they had travelled to him through her.

. . . He was changed in the dark. All the time he was conscious of a new omnipotent idea of evil as a profound unearthly cause, a demonic over-soul, charged with life, and tangible only as breath.

As if to underline this discovery, to put beyond doubt her plain meaning, Margiad Evans makes a personal interpolation to the reader. 'I own that I am here. . . .'

I have never read any books on theology; but I have heard what I thought was God's voice in strange mouths. I have heard his name sound wonderful and holy in a furious row outside the pub, and I have heard sanctified congregations worshipping literature.

As for God – imaginations have bestowed the power and the glory upon him, but in fact he has only his name. He is like a madman, whose property very truly is his, only he is not allowed to make use of it. And like a madman is God in that to manifest his strength he has to break through the restraining bonds of those very ones who declare his calamitous insight, and fear his fires.

No. It requires not Christ to symbolize the poverty of God. It is so evident! With half the world pouring divinity on his altars, with all the building and decking of his houses, the painting of his revelations, he is still only a word among worse words.

His kingdom on earth is in oaths and men's deaths and despairs. He is in every man's mouth, though he die with each one. Where-ever there's shame and cruelty and wickedness, tongues drag him in as the one thing that can stand up to them – he is preached in all the sins and proclaimed in curses.

Dollbright fights in agony of mind against his conversion to this new and terrible 'faith'. In the throes of his struggle he is driven to the edge of suicide, further tormented by the importunings of his elderly lodger, Benjamin Wandby, who has chosen to make Dollbright judge over his inflamed conscience: he cannot forget that he was imprisoned years ago for attempted murder. Meanwhile Bellamy and Menna at last come together: Menna has turned on her mother, the obstacle to their union, now deliberately hastening her inevitable death through drinking. When for the first time Menna spends the night with Bellamy she returns home in the early morning to find Dollbright and Benjamin Wandby in the house and her mother dead, having fallen in a drunken stupor through an open trap door into the cellar. Wandby is astounded that Dollbright, the condemner of others' sin, has no word of reproach for Menna. Dollbright has come to the end of his struggle. The book concludes with this tremendous finale:

> He saw himself stooping over the monstrous figure lolling brokenly on the black mouldy steps, its garment slowly, slowly tearing from the nail. He smelled the horrible odour of drink and dirt and decay mixed with slimy wood and the rawness of stored potatoes. The hideous incident paused in his mind's eye, invoking horror, sickness . . . and deep unaccustomed pity. What staggering enforced journey had plunged her into that dark earthly hole with the fallen lantern shining on the brink? What whole abandonment by every human soul had she discovered in the night? She spoke of love?
>
> Unlike Benjamin, he was less affected by the tragedy of Menna's development than by her mother's ghastly end. She had crashed across his unchosen track like a lightning-stricken tree whose shadow was consumed by fire and death. This was her act in his destiny. This was the power over him which he had felt with a supernatural shrinking from the inevitable demonism of her eye, the demoniacal authority of her wild, half hinted speech, which was subterraneously linked to the breaking forth of his own fierce ungoverned spirit.
>
> That spirit had moved him all his life. Pounded down, subdued and overloaded, leashed and lashed by his inexorable unnatural

faith, he had struggled to make of that restless genitor a sacrifice to eternity. And it had burst upwards under his feet. And he had quoted it before he knew that he had heard its gagged voice speak. . . . For a long time he had not thought at all. Every day he had come and gone to his work, he had sat with his wife, he had suffered the terrible nothing in his breast and his brain. Last night, with blood on his hand and holding the matted head upon his arm, he had felt a great opening in his mind as though air were rushing into a vacuum. He could not think then: he was almost strangled, speechless in thought and undelivered.

Now words were working in him, excitement seized him. He felt his existence enclosed in a tremendous destiny. The knots in his breast relaxed in a rushing thaw. He shouted wildly, he walked about the empty shop like a man clean mad, possessed by freedom.

'I can lament or defy. And I'm defiant. From your millions you have lost me, and all your aeons will never bring me back. Order could not compel me; pain shall not subdue me, and tears are not repentance. The more powerful you, the weaker I; but the more you gather the less you never lose! Oh, God, I have taken separate existence from you, and you cannot pour my one soul back into your self!'

It grew dusky with a white, blind twilight, like the film of cataract. Benjamin Wandby came and knocked at the window. Dishevelled, passionate, Dollbright stood in the door.

'I thought I'd find you here,' said the other; 'I've come to tell you she's dead.'

'Dead, dead?' he echoed like a foreign word. He was free of death.

IV

THE meaning of *Creed* – that is, the significance of the inner orientation reached by Dollbright – is plain. But this meaning is by no means clearly apparent to the casual reader with no very clearly defined spiritual standards by which to measure the terms of the doctrine offered in this book.

It is easy for such a reader to run through the book and to read into it the conversion of Dollbright from proud religious bigotry to a humbler and more Christlike acceptance of suffering and sinful humanity. Yet the quotations given above should be sufficient to dispel this impression and to make clear he nature of Margiad Evans's creed. There is little point in maintaining a polite assumption that this novel has no necessary relation to its author's personal attitude. To repeat, between all the characters there is a profound psychic connection: Menna's and Bellamy's erotic passion, Dollbright's religious fervour, Ifor Morriss's creed, and Mrs. Trouncer's demoniac instinctive vitality – all these are aspects of one fundamental attitude, summed up in the author's declared acknowledgment of a deity who is 'preached in all the sins and proclaimed in curses'.

The religious argument of the book is that God is really to be identified with the telluric passionate depths of existence. That which Dollbright eventually comes to accept is a notion of the deity in which no separation is made between the divine and demoniac, holy and unholy. He finds himself no longer able to condemn, not because he has conquered intolerance with understanding and love, but because he has now no standpoint from which to make distinctions, between sin and sanctity, good and evil, salvation and perdition. All are fused in one passionate and insatiable act of undiscriminating acceptance, in which rings, however, a strange note of rebellion. This desperate creed is based upon and necessitates an exaltation of passion. But such an exaltation is inseparable from a fearful underlying boredom and vacuity. In this connection, the relationship between the feverish violence which distinguishes the characters in *Creed* and the dreary futility which is the pervasive emotional atmosphere of the preceding novel, *Turf or Stone*, should be considered. This exaltation of passion has nothing whatever to do with love: there is no question of love between Menna and Bellamy. It is a dark passion, in essence destructive and murderous – witness Bellamy's thoughts at the boxing match he attends, Menna having refused his solicitations:

> These weren't men. They were 'sports' who didn't know what it was to feel savage rage in your limbs and strangulation in your heart. Bellamy felt himself go rolling over and over, clenching that wet streaky body, hugging the breath out of it, cracking its ribs against the reef of his own bones. To break a man against yourself – that must be joy, to fly, to fell a tree, to beat a woman whom you passionately desired, to go to war . . . perhaps to go to war . . . that was a future. . . .

This exaltation of passion is connected with a lofty and intractable pride.

It is a characteristic of passion to be both destructive and self-consuming. It incinerates the energy on which it feeds. It leads not to renewal of passion, but to exhaustion, vacancy. It is bred in vacancy, flourishes in it, and burns out to leave the vacancy more achingly unbearable than before. Exalted into a 'faith', it is a creed of desperation. Personality and the personal values cannot flourish in its sultry atmosphere. It cannot lead to creativeness. Its direction is not lifeward but towards death and perdition. Margiad Evans's prolonged silence of seven years following the publication of *Creed* was thus not without significance. The creed of passion, bad in itself, is doubly bad for the novelist, if only for the obvious reason that it does not permit of the differentiation of character, its tendency being to merge individual personalities into a common emotional stream. *Creed* itself shows no subtle awareness of personality: each character is but a powerful projection of a certain aspect of the author's egoistic life-attitude. This raw stuff of passionate existence is monotonously the same wherever it is found. On these premises Margiad Evans would seem, as a novelist, to have little scope or variation, none for development, without a rupture in continuity. That her book is archetypal may be glimpsed from her treatment of Bellamy and Menna. They are powerless in the grip of their passion; the passion as a quality in itself rather than they as individual beings is the theme of her narrative. But passion as such has a monotonous uniformity. As a sincere and non-professionalized novelist, Margiad Evans would find little satisfaction, one presumes, in mere repetition. In this sense *Creed* represents the conclusion of an inner process, not a beginning; it contains no creative potentialities.

The conclusion to Margiad Evans's development, however, is to be found in her last book, not a novel, but an autobiography; not even an autobiography, but a sheaf of nature-notes. In fact, her *Autobiography* (1943) marks a final repudiation of personal values and calmly despairing desire for the merging of the soul into the life of the natural universe. Passion had faded out, leaving only the desire for rest, peace, and self-obliteration, which the author finds in an identification of herself with the phenomena of nature. The opening passages of the first section, 'A Little Journal of Being Alone', indicate the tone of the book.

> Midwinter and all dulled but the wind and the stars. The dead of the dark winter; stretching behind me the dim patch of silent days alone. The wind is a tooth in the breast . . . the dark suns give no light.
>
> There was no sky – only the breathy air and a heaviness behind the trees like the dull butt of an iron bar. I watch the moribund chickens standing about on one leg with their claws crimped like a bunch of twigs. A draught that seemed to splinter the bones, ran an icy tune along the hedge and leapt with the wind, dragging after it the straws combed by the brambles out of this morning's load. In, in, shut everything in. Oh, the happiness of being alone – it's like having only one door to yourself and that bolted and firm walls around. The taste of it is in my food, the sound of my foot-steps. I enjoy it even when terrified of my own alarming presence in the welcoming void.
>
> Down in the orchard getting wood, I said, 'That's the smoke of my fire.' In a moment I shall light my last candle and go to bed. I'm going to sleep on my elbow and my shadow lurches over the page. There's a noise far away in the dark which seems to know where I am. Why do all such things recall Death?

It needs no particularly sensitive ear to capture the melancholy undercurrent of this writing. To merge with nature is to merge with that which is transient, perishable; indeed this book smells of mortality.

> . . . One is in everything. One lives through the universe and beyond. Though I think what I see I don't see with my eyes alone. Never shall I see Nature passing without falling in with its order, myself mixing and coming to consciousness in all life.
>
> All existences merge, even physically. Things more than resemble one another, they are more than kin, they are one manifestation. Likenesses are symbols. How should we not grow like one another when the same element brims up in us all, when we ourselves are conscious sometimes that our separate existence is an intermittent form assumed, we cannot tell why?
>
> The life which is opposite to me, be what it is when I reach out to it, responds to me. There is no picture, no form of life, and in no form but as an unseen element, it floods the earth and sky. As nothing individual it returns. As nothing individual I go out.

Lapsing and losing myself I seem to breathe through distant trees; to look around the world from stones in the fields, and down on it from the budding mountain. It has seemed to me that ever since I was a child creation desired me as I desired creation. All of us sought one another.

The sympathy I longed for was not human sympathy, nor any human idea of it. It wasn't tenderness I wanted, nor mutual recognition, mutual pleasure; it was nothing I could describe in human language. I call it reciprocity, but that is apt to be too much. The further I can get from being a human being, the clearer can I feel in me the idea of an elemental conception. I need to feel it and have always needed it. I need and desire an extension, a plurality of being. . . . I don't wrap myself in solitude, I go naked in it. I discard my particularity, I discard myself. I don't want other humans to be solitary with me because their humanity on top of mine is too much for impersonality to discard. . . .

To make a full examination of this particular modern cult would require a volume; a brief comment is all that can be managed here. A life lived only in a relationship to nature, and not also in relationship to nature's complement, history, to say nothing of personal relationships, is less than half an existence. Devotees of the cult have, in the first place, little sense of personality and, in the second, little sense of history, of society; or, if they have a sense of these realities, it is negative and reactionary. An odd inner vacuity runs through most of the literary works of the cult, which at the same time evinces an absence of development. One who limits himself to that which he is in relationship with nature constricts his humanity; he becomes less than, not more than, human. Margiad Evans speaks of 'love', but the test of love is not a relationship with the inanimate, but with another person; for her, however, 'Life . . . is solitude'. The praise of solitude is found, too, in Richard Jefferies, whose *Story of My Heart* is a classic work of the nature cult, and in J. C. Powys. Books written from such an aspect can have no development, no form, because no beginning and no end; the writer inhabits a world in which time has been absorbed, or evicted, by space. *Autobiography*, despite the brilliant incisiveness of some of its descriptions, is finally tedious, because it is both repetitive and shapeless.

What is the value of simple descriptive jottings about the

trees and the weather, however incisively performed? What is the point of nature-writing?

> If you want to write with absolute truth and with the ease of a natural function, write from your eyes and ears, and your touch, in the very now where you find yourself alive wherever it may be. Carry your paper and book with you and conceal yourself in the fields. Watch and be in what you see or in what you feel in your brain. . . .

But to what end? If the essential meaning and value of life is to be found in this immediate communion with the natural universe, why reproduce one's observations, sensations, impressions, in the abstract mental medium of language? This is an inescapable problem for every despiser of society, of humanity, of culture, of the spirit. Margiad Evans continues her reflections:

> Even so there is a fading, a merging, a loss of something which no pondering and no effort can bring back. We are bound to return sometime and to begin 'copying out'. Once that starts . . . well to be within walls, even close under an open window where you can see rooks flying and calling under the clouds, is to be in comparative darkness. However light the room in which you work, it has few living shadows and little space compared to the field in which you saw so clearly. You may picture it with all the vividness in your power, but where is the grass you actually saw, the real grass with separate blades, with moss in it and roots and the light roughing it? It is not in you. Recollect the trees as you may, something is gone out of the vision. You cannot call up the colour of the bark, the seaminess, the firm flakes. A joy which rested on the ground and filled the sky, is not to be described. The brain wearies toiling with language, and the captive sight follows the bird's flight over the elm tops with a deep unconscious longing to return to the 'now' which seemed so unbreakable when you rested in the field only a short while ago.

Quite so. And silence would seem to be the inevitable conclusion of the inner dialectic to which the author has submitted herself. There is a point at which too emphatic a 'love of life', physically speaking, meets and merges with a longing for death. There is in the cult of nature an underlying dreariness, however it be disguised with a mask of 'joyousness' and 'optimism'. Margiad Evans reiterates her happiness, but the effect of her writing is of a deep hollow sadness. The transient sensual happiness on which some of the more superficial, dogmatic, and loquacious devotees of the cult place emphasis has a ghoulish character; it is a happiness snatched from the grave: nor can they altogether conceal from themselves their awareness of this fact. There is in nature not only a life-giving and a generative, but also a death-dealing principle, and an acceptance of nature as God implies the acceptance of both its aspects. In *The Story of My Heart* Jefferies's paeans to nature modulate insensibly into strains such as these:

> Could I have my own way after death I would be burned on a pyre of pine-wood, open to the air, and placed on the summit of the hills. Then let my ashes be scattered abroad – not collected in an urn – freely sown wide and broadcast. That is the natural interment of man – of man whose Thought at least has been among the immortals; interment in the elements. Burial is not enough, it does not give sufficient solution into the elements speedily; a furnace is confined. The high open air of the topmost hill, there let the tawny flame lick up the fragment called the body; there cast the ashes into the space it longed for while living.

The deathward trend of *Autobiography* is equally explicit. 'I used to feel,' writes Margiad Evans, 'that in some profound way my body was becoming my soul.' From that, the acquiescence, so foreign to the Christian consciousness, in annihilation, is not far distant: and so we find such paragraphs as this:

> It was pure delight to lie there with my dear home winds coming over the tops of the elms and my own country lapping around its incomparable hills . . . to lie and rest and wonder whether real death can be so perfect.

And this:

> Walking between the oak trees and the stile, I thought of death, as I do every day and every hour. Not death with its kneeling and services, and decay; but of short corruption to cleanness, and the white bone in its starry beauty on the turf. . . . I am not lonely. I should only be lonely if I happened alone, if I existed alone, if I had to make myself breathe. If I had created myself and must decide for myself when to die, then I should be lonely, and should

not ask myself why I didn't envy the strolling people their laughter, the children out of school their childhood. I don't envy them because on earth I find myself in everything, because in view of death we are all the same age.

Upon that note the Autobiography closes.

ALDOUS HUXLEY

THE reputation of Aldous Huxley – that initial reputation, through which his claim upon popular esteem still persists, was made, it should be recollected, in the era of post-Great War 'disillusionment', whose predominant mood was faithfully reflected in the bright and bitter humour, the sardonic portrayal of human futility, which marked the early novels and tales. In his earlier days Huxley was read with enthusiasm by many of his contemporaries, not only in England, who felt that, in his sophisticated hedonism, his freedom from outworn loyalties, even his licence, he spoke for a generation. He was detached, ironical, and he knew how to be amusing with that wryness which revealed an awareness of the corruption at the bottom of the glass of pleasure.

Huxley's work as a whole has taken the form of a thinly disguised autobiographical sequence; its shape has been determined by its author's changing attitude to life, which has always found its corresponding intellectual expression (reviewers were wont, as a matter of course, to prostrate themselves before his overwhelming 'intellect'); and the problem for the critic lies in the difficulty of keeping a just balance between the attitude to life underlying and conditioning the specific artistic productions; these productions (the novels) themselves; and the resultant ideas which the novelist has abstracted, as it were, from the creative process, and which he now arrays formidably and somewhat menacingly before his public.

For, as it happens, that early entertainer ('that different person', Huxley writes in a recent new preface to one of his old novels, 'who was oneself in youth . . .') is a figure from whom the later and at first glance strangely altered Huxley would wish rather pointedly to dissociate himself. Today there confronts us, not the sardonic portraitist of futility, but the prophet and the philosopher of Enlightenment, of Liberation, through

I   129

a species of contemplative mysticism, or mystical contemplation. And this prophet, or teacher, quite overshadows, if he has not finally liquidated, the artist.

What, in fact, is the nature of the teaching which emerges? It is rather a simple doctrine. Man's final end, according to Huxley's most recent work, a compendium entitled *The Perennial Philosophy* (1946), is nothing less than 'unitive love-knowledge of the Divine Ground', a knowledge which one must attain by 'making oneself loving, pure in heart and poor in spirit', through a 'discipline more arduous and unremitting than any imposed by ecclesiastical authority' – a discipline which involves, indeed, a total dying to self.

Salvation, deliverance, enlightenment are apostrophized; but always the emphasis, in this version of mysticism, is upon self-obliteration; and self-obliteration, it appears, in an impassive, non-personal, not-God (as with strange candour the 'Divine Ground' is here described). Time and all its works, being evil, must be annihilated: the goal is *Nirvana*, complete cessation of the pain which comes through individuation, separation from the abysmal One.

> Man must live in time in order to be able to advance into eternity, no longer on the animal, but on the spiritual level; he must be conscious of himself as a separate ego in order to be able consciously to transcend separate selfhood; he must do battle with the lower self in order that he may become identified with that higher Self within him, which is akin to the divine Not-Self; and finally he must make use of his cleverness in order to pass beyond cleverness to the intellectual vision of Truth, the immediate, unitive knowledge of the divine Ground.

The mystics – Catholics, Quaker, Hindu, Buddhist, Taoist, Sufi, and the rest – have pointed out the way; Huxley annotates it: we refuse it at our peril.

Whether in fact the new doctrine can be so completely dissociated from its literary antecedents is something which we owe it to truth and to ourselves to investigate rather than to take on trust. A hundred years ago Søren Kierkegaard in a masterly essay categorically described the fundamental disorientation which afflicts all human existence not lived under the rubric, Faith, as the 'sickness unto death'; the sickness unto death being – despair. To designate Aldous Huxley as the novelist of despair – if despair is the emotional potentiation of futility, the central theme of his work – will seem unquestionably fitting to the earlier 'Pyrrhonic aesthete', and if it should arouse some surprise, here and there, when applied with even greater emphasis to the later Huxley, in his 'Perennial' avatar, that surprise will, I trust, be modified in the light of what is said below.

That there is, in reality, more than a marked affinity between Huxley's earlier and his later work and ideas we shall discover if, disregarding whatever overt attitudes the abstract theorist would have us accept, we scrutinize the underlying structure of the novelist's and the thinker's world. The fictional universe which he creates and populates possesses certain well-defined features which might all be said to be explicable in the light of a fundamental *discontinuity*. If we say of Huxley's characters that they are static and isolated, that a certain impersonal detachment shows itself in their creator's attitude towards them, and that at the same time their existence presumes a context of pointlessness, we shall have sketched a readily recognizable picture of Huxley's constant frame of reference. For, by a curious irony, while Huxley himself would claim a radical discontinuity between the divergent attitudes to life – 'Pyrrhonic hedonism' and contemplative mysticism – which in turn grow out of and condition his earlier and his later work, in fact the two originate in a common dislocation of being: the one exaggeration of attitude finds its balancing counterpart in the other; and the irony is pointed in the fact that discontinuity itself can even be said to be the only continuous factor in decisive operation throughout Huxley's artistic career. Huxley's development follows not a spiral but an hour-glass pattern. The psychological structure underlying *Crome Yellow*, *Antic Hay*, and *Those Barren Leaves* becomes modified as the novelist's dissatisfaction with his non-committal relationship to life draws him towards a closer engagement, only to reassert itself with finality as he crosses over into a yet further detachment which is the obverse of the earlier attitude, and which reinforces its pronounced bias towards the impersonal, the non-human.

I

THE mental structure upon which Huxley was to raise his successive fictional edifices is discoverable with little difficulty in his first novel, *Crome Yellow* (1921). A dualism of mind and matter, of spirit and body, of the ideal and the actual is fundamental to it, and is the source at once of Huxley's pessimism, of the purely static and episodic quality of his work, and of his humour. Futility and frustration, humorously presented, the disparity between intention and accomplishment, are the themes of this slight, episodic narrative which tells of a short holiday spent by a young poet, Denis, at the country house of Crome, during the course of which he encounters a succession of interestingly odd characters, is pursued by a young female while himself unsuccessfully pursuing another, and eventually allows himself to be bundled off for home just as he seems to be within reach of amorous success. The appropriate note is struck in the opening paragraph:

> Oh, this journey! It was two hours cut clean out of his life; two hours in which he might have done so much, so much – written the perfect poem, for example, or read the one illuminating book. Instead of which – his gorge rose at the smell of the dusty cushions against which he was leaning. . . .

And it is maintained with fair consistency throughout.

The character of Denis is indeterminate. He is young and very uncertain of his own feelings and beliefs, and is moreover somewhat isolated from human contacts. Denis's response to living is involuntarily moralistic; theoretically he is a hedonist:

> 'I've always taken things as they come,' said Anne. 'It seems so obvious. One enjoys the pleasant things, avoids the nasty ones. There's nothing more to be said.'
> 'Nothing – for you. But, then, you were born a pagan; I am trying laboriously to make myself one. I can take nothing for granted, I can enjoy nothing as it comes along. Beauty, pleasure, art, women – I have to invent an excuse, a justification for everything that's delightful. Otherwise I can't enjoy it with an easy conscience.
> '. . . Pleasure is one of the mystical roads to union with the infinite – the ecstasies of drinking, dancing, love-making. As for women, I am perpetually assuring myself that they're the broad

highway to divinity. And to think that I'm only just beginning to see through the silliness of the whole thing!'

Of Huxley's two themes, the first, the disparity of the ideal and the actual, is expressed characteristically in the account from Mr. Wimbush's History of Crome, of the Elizabethan baronet's sanitary arrangements; 'the necessities of nature are so base and brutish that in obeying them we are apt to forget that we are the noblest creatures of the universe', so that accordingly the privy must be a book-lined room at the top of the house, commanding 'an extensive and noble prospect'. It finds expression also in the interpolated anecdote of the three lovely sisters who in public maintained a pretence of wan, etherial spirituality, while surreptitiously gorging themselves at elaborate private repasts in their chamber; while of the second, a deliberate hedonism coupled with an underlying sense of personal futility, Mr. Scogan in this novel is the mouth-piece:

'Worried about the cosmos, eh?' Mr. Scogan patted him on the arm. 'I know the feeling,' he said, 'It's a most distressing symptom. What's the good of continuing to function if one's doomed to be snuffed out at last along with everything else? Yes, yes. I know exactly how you feel. It's most distressing if one allows oneself to be distressed. But then why allow oneself to be distressed? After all, we all know that there's no ultimate point. But what difference does that make?'

We shall see that throughout his successive works Huxley has never departed from these foundations.

Antic Hay (1923) is at once more serious and more farcical, a mordant blaze of characters and incidents against a starker background of futility. Yet there is a pronounced thread of morality running through the tale's desperate gaiety. When we are introduced first to Theodore Gumbril we find him 'speculating, in his rapid and rambling way, about the existence and the nature of God', and then, a little later, disturbed by a pricking conscience over his 'first serious and deliberate lie' – in childhood.

The element of broad farce enters with Gumbril's invention and marketing of trousers with pneumatic seats. On the strength of his hopes from this venture he leaves his job as schoolmaster and embarks upon a random course of dissipation during which he encounters such exponents of depravity as Myra Viveash, whose voice 'seemed always on the point of expiring, as though each word were the last, uttered faintly and breakingly from a death-bed . . .'; Coleman, whose career of debauchery is carried out on principle and is accompanied by blasphemy; and Mr. Mercaptan, whose speciality is seduction according to the precepts of Crebillon *fils*, upon a white satin sofa in his tastefully decorated apartment. The thread of quasi-moral narrative – that which concerns Gumbril's relations of simple, genuine affection with the girl Emily, whom he is led to abandon at a whim of Mrs. Viveash's – is slight in proportion to the whole novel, which concerns the erratic futilities of Gumbril and the others as they are whirled around in the dry wind of boredom, vanity and despair.

Beneath the amusing surface there is a clear enunciation of the theme of futility:

> 'It's appalling, it's horrible,' said Gumbril at last, after a long, long silence, during which he had, indeed, been relishing to the full the horror of it all. Life, don't you know. . . .

And when, after his betrayal of Emily, he goes, with Mrs. Viveash, the dreary, anguished, pleasure-hunting round of night-clubs in an episode which palely reflects the Walpurgis-nacht scenes of *Ulysses*, the night perpetuates itself with yet further revelations of human depravity and the farcical point-lessness of things, until finally:

> 'Tomorrow,' said Gumbril at last, meditatively.
> 'Tomorrow,' Mrs. Viveash interrupted him, 'will be as awful as today.' She breathed it like a truth from beyond the grave prematurely revealed, expiringly from her death-bed within.

Those Barren Leaves (1925), the novel following, is the first to be written from a serious questioning of life. Each of the major characters who are gathered at the wealthy Mrs. Aldwinkle's Italian villa – Calamy the disenchanted man of the world, whose temper provides a point of location for the mood of the book, Cardan, and Chelifer – shares with the other two a common disillusionment with the human state. But whereas Cardan has pursued to the end a course of genial parasitical pleasure-seeking, Chelifer is a self-torturing romantic who takes a perverse delight in seeking out and identifying himself with life's most dingy aspects, while Calamy himself has simply wearied of the amorous round of the idle, affluent set, and is on the verge of a vaguely-envisioned quest for the 'way'.

' . . . It seems to me,' says Calamy, when Mr. Cardan, true to character, is praising 'love' as the most enjoyable of indoor sports, ' . . . that I'm beginning to have had enough of sports, whether indoor or out-of-door. I'd like to find some more serious occupation.' And he continues, in response to Mr. Cardan's profession of amorality, in this vein:

'You're fortunate. . . . It's not all of us whose personalities have such a natural odour of sanctity that they can disinfect our septic actions and render them morally harmless. When I do something stupid or dirty I can't help feeling that it is stupid or dirty. My soul lacks virtues to make it wise or clean.

'And I can't dissociate myself from what I do. I wish I could. One does such a devilish number of stupid things. Things one doesn't want to do. If only one could be a hedonist and only do what was pleasant! But to be a hedonist one must be wholly rational; there's no such thing as a genuine hedonist, there never has been. Instead of doing what one wants to do or what would give one pleasure, one drifts through existence doing exactly the opposite, most of the time – doing what one has no desire to do, following insane promptings that lead one, fully conscious, into every sort of discomfort, misery, boredom and remorse.

' . . . I don't like running after women, I don't like wasting my time in futile social intercourse, or in the pursuit of what is technically known as pleasure. And yet for some reason and quite against my will I find myself passing the greater part of my time immersed in precisely these occupations. It's an obscure kind of insanity.

' . . . And what's the most depressing of all . . . is the feeling that one will go on like this for ever, in the teeth of every effort to stop. I sometimes wish I weren't externally free. For then at any rate I should have something to curse at, for getting in my way, other than my own self. Yes, positively, I sometimes wish I were a navvy.'

While Mr. Cardan, for his part, in spite of his espousal of the theory and practice of hedonism, is forced continually to realize that he is in a blind alley, finding, towards the end of his career of pleasure, only bodily decrepitude and death. Alone, his reflections tend to take on a morbid tinge:

> It would be tiresome to end one's days with recurrent fever and an enlarged spleen. It would be tiresome for that matter, to end one's days anyhow, in one's bed or out, naturally or unnaturally, by the act of God or of the King's enemies. Mr. Cardan's thoughts took on, all at once, a dismal complexion. Old age, sickness, decrepitude; the bath-chair, the doctor, the bright efficient nurse; and the long agony, the struggle for breath, the thickening darkness, the end, and then – how did that merry little song go?

> > More work for the undertaker,
> > 'Nother little job for the coffin-maker.
> > At the local cemetery they are
> > Very busy with a brand new grave.
> > He'll keep warm next winter.

> Mr. Cardan hummed the tune to himself cheerfully enough. But his tough, knobbly face became so hard, so strangely still, an expression of such bitterness, such a profound melancholy, appeared in his winking and his supercilious eye, that it would have frightened a man to look at him.

The tone then is markedly more serious. And for the first time we find the disparity fundamental to Huxley's outlook emphasized as a cleavage between 'the flesh' and 'the spirit'. Thus, while Chelifer derives a mordant satisfaction from the ironic contrast which he delights to point between man's aspirations and the brute facts of his animal existence, the elderly Mr. Cardan's ruminations take a melancholy turn, and the disparity is seen like this:

> Only the tragedy of the spirit can liberate and uplift. But the greatest tragedy of the spirit is that sooner or later it succumbs to the flesh. Sooner or later every soul is stifled by the sick body; sooner or later there are no more thoughts, but only pain and vomitings and stupor. The tragedies of the spirit are mere struttings and posturings on the margin of life, and the spirit itself is only an accidental exuberance, the products of spare vital energy, like the feathers on the head of a hoopoo or the innumerable populations of useless and foredoomed spermatozoa. The spirit has no significance; there is only the body. When it is young, the

body is beautiful and strong. It grows old, its joints creak, it becomes dry and smelly; it breaks down, the life goes out of it and it rots away. However lovely the feathers on a bird's head, they perish with it; and the spirit, which is a lovelier ornament than any, perishes too. The farce is hideous, thought Mr. Cardan, and in the worst of bad taste.

But at this point we must pause to collect the threads which have so far been taken up, in order to trace them to their common centre in that basic disjunction of personality which is the psychological source of all the disjunctions in the Huxley world-picture. Let us begin with the two principal obsessions which have so clearly emerged this far – 'hedonism' and 'futility'.

Huxley's central character, whichever of his books we take up, is distinguished primarily by the fact that he places so little value upon his existence as a man that he is implicitly prepared to forgo his claim upon personal destiny and meaning, albeit with an uneasy conscience, for the immediate gain of a random succession of disrelated sensations. Inwardly inert, led this way and that by mere appetite, he becomes immersed consequently in a world which is deprived of value. Unaware that meaning and purpose do not reside as objective facts in the world of things but are interior realities which await for their realization upon interior dynamic movement, oblivious to the truth that personality is not a substance with which we are endowed by nature, but an inward integration which may be achieved only by the decisive choice of oneself, he arbitrarily attributes his own purposelessness to the universe as a whole. 'Hedonism' and 'futility' thus complement each other.

In *Crome Yellow* the chief character, Denis, is young, his hedonism an aspect of the common bewilderment of youth. Gumbril, in the second novel, is an older man, and hedonism gathers a cynical tinge, while futility is emphasized. Calamy, in the present novel, represents a further stage still – he is the disillusioned hedonist; and now the disparity of the Huxley world is presented from a new aspect. As a disillusioned hedonist Calamy has wearied of a life without *meaning*, he is beginning to look for another path, and hence the concept 'spirit' for the first time makes its appearance; but 'spirit' itself, superimposed upon the existing psychological pattern, takes the impress of the fundamental duality of mind, and appears as directly anti-thetical to 'matter', or 'the flesh', as something in some way beyond the limits of the sensual plane upon which human life is actually lived. Thus we find that Calamy unquestioningly assumes that the 'way' of which he is in quest must lie some-where beyond the region of ordinary human experience, and that it is to be found in opposition to the path of sensual indulgence from which that experience is inseparable.

He speaks in this manner to Chelifer and Mr. Cardan just prior to his departure for the mountain retreat:

' . . . there is a whole universe within me, unknown and wait-ing to be explored; a whole universe that can only be approached by way of introspection and patient uninterrupted thought. Merely to satisfy curiosity it would surely be worth exploring. But there are motives more impelling than curiosity to persuade me. What one may find there is so important that it's almost a matter of life and death to undertake the search.'

'H'm,' said Mr. Cardan. 'And what will happen at the end of three months' chaste meditation when some lovely young tempta-tion comes toddling down this road, "balancing her haunches", as Zola would say, and rolling the large black eye? What will happen to your explorations of the inward universe then, may I ask?'

'Well,' said Calamy, 'I hope they'll proceed uninterrupted.'

'You hope? Piously?'

'And I shall certainly do my best to see that they do,' Calamy added.

'It won't be easy,' Mr. Cardan assured him.

'I know.'

'Perhaps you'll find that you can explore simultaneously both the temptation and the interior universe.'

Calamy shook his head. 'Alas, I'm afraid that's not practi-cable. It would be delightful if it were. But for some reason it isn't. Even in moderation it won't do. I know that, more or less, by experience. And the authorities are all agreed about it.'

This brings us at last to the structure of Huxley's novels, all of which – it is one of their principal defects – are remarkable for their lack of total dramatic movement and impetus. And this is precisely explicable as a consequence of the absence of dynamic movement in the mind of the novelist himself, a defect which is naturally communicated to his creatures, whose intercourse with each other, prepared and sustained by the accidents of social life, is virtually confined, as we have often heard it remarked, to sexuality and cerebration. No character in the course of this novel undergoes in the course of it any modifications of outlook or temperament, each remains immobile within the limits marked out for it from the first. Of Calamy, we know nothing of the particular events and motives which move him towards the tentative renunciation which begins to take effect at the novel's close. Mr. Cardan is a lay figure as rigid as any in a morality play, and Chelifer is a study only in deliberate self-stultification. And such figures as the doctrinaire socialist, Mr. Falx, and the preposterous Mrs. Aldwinkle herself, are merely caricatures sardonically sketched by the satirist of social types. Only with the immature – in this case with Irene and the young Lord Hovingden, in their naïvely innocent courtship, does the novelist show any movement of human sympathy. Between such inwardly static characters, it is clear, there can be no dramatic interplay and thus no movement of the novel as an entity. So that instead of the movement of life we are presented with episodes, blocks of incident and conversation broken up peremptorily by external change.

But this is something which deserves further exploration, for it is evidently bound up with the whole question of movement and purpose. Movement in a work of fiction is required, of course, to be significant – to bear some purposeful relation to an end. In that vivid portrayal of purposeless activity, *Antic Hay*, the dance of futility is necessarily non-dramatic and presupposes the stasis of character – which in turn is static just because, according to the context, the possibility of purposeful movement is non-existent; life itself is purposeless. In the succeeding novel there is some endeavour to move beyond this static condition dictated by life's total futility. Yet all that the novel succeeds in doing in this respect is to lay bare at great length the absolute cleavage between 'matter' and 'spirit' which underlies the idea of pointlessness. Nowhere in it is there any questioning of the reality and the appropriateness of this dualism.

The novel ends inconclusively. Calamy retires to his mountain retreat, but it is uncertain whither his lonely quest will lead him; whether, indeed, it will lead anywhere. All we are told is that, looking at the distant skyline, he feels 'somehow reassured'.

II

THAT there is a progression of a sort within the first three novels is clear. And while *Point Counter Point* (1928) seems to show a divergence from what was later to appear as Huxley's main line of development, it nevertheless derives from the same basic pattern – though the emphasis is changed – while it continues the movement towards human responsibility already hinted at in the portrait of Calamy.

That *Point Counter Point* represents a movement away from the detached manipulation of puppet-characters towards a sympathetic approach to human life is a fact not entirely contradicted by the novel's ill-success in this aim, which is most signally exhibited by the emergence in its pages, for the first time, of a patently deliberate autobiographical character, the novelist Philip Quarles, whose personal views and problems, identical with Huxley's own, are placed directly before us.

The central problem in Philip Quarles's life is his personal isolation; 'All his life long he had walked in a solitude, in a private void, into which nobody, not his mother, not his friends, not his lovers had ever been permitted to enter.' Although, we are given to understand, he is a man of exceptional intellectual endowments, his convictions are fluid, his response to life indeterminate:

> If there was any single way of life he could lastingly believe in, it was that mixture of pyrrhonism and stoicism, which had struck him, an enquiring schoolboy among the philosophers, as the height of human wisdom and into whose mould of sceptical indifference he had poured his unimpassioned adolescence. Against the pyrrhonian suspense of judgment and the stoical imperturbability he had often rebelled. But had the rebellion ever been really serious? Pascal had made him a Catholic – but only so long as the volume of *Pensées* was open before him. There were moments when, in the company of Carlyle or Whitman or bouncing Browning, he had believed in strenuousness for strenuousness' sake. And then there was Mark Rampion. After a few hours in Mark

Rampion's company he really believed in noble savagery; he felt convinced that the proudly conscious intellect ought to humble itself a little and admit the claims of the heart, aye and the bowels, the loins, the bones and skin and muscles, to a fair share of life.

This last sentence provides the clue to the book's central 'idea' – a variation on the spirit-flesh duality, but with the scales weighted this time towards 'the flesh' – not now in the name of an irresponsible hedonism but of a biological vitalism obviously borrowed, in large measure, from D. H. Lawrence, who is caricatured admiringly in the novel in the painter, Mark Rampion, who preaches, in part, as follows:

'This damned soul,' he went on, 'this damned abstract soul – it's like a kind of cancer, eating up the real, human, natural reality, spreading and spreading at its expense. Why can't he be content with reality, your stupid old Beethoven? Why should he find it necessary to replace the real, warm, natural thing by this abstract cancer of a soul? The cancer may have a beautiful shape; but, damn it all, the body's more beautiful. I don't want your spiritual cancer.'

The spirit-matter dualism has not been resolved, but instead of an orientation towards the spirit à la Calamy, we have, not indeed a despairing acceptance of the futility of sensual-human life, but an attempt at its justification in terms of nature, vitality, health. Thus, to take but one typical example:

John Bidlake [a sexagenarian philanderer] made no apologies for the kind of love he had to offer. So far as it went, it entirely justified itself. A healthy sensualist, he made his love straightforwardly, naturally, with the good animal gusto of a child of nature.

. . . It was a love without pretensions, but warm, natural, and, being natural, good so far as it went – a decent, good-humoured, happy sensuality.

This novel, however, shows Huxley at his most inept. Badly constructed, incoherent, puerile in conception and presentation, and written in shoddy journalese, it reveals the fatal juvenility which, beneath the sophisticated surface, vitiates his understanding of life. The attempt to extend an inherently limited scope results in the crowding of the pages with flat caricatures of living personages, their characters and activities interpreted in terms no more searching than their relationship, 'wholesome' or 'perverted', to sex and physical life. With the conclusion of the novelette called *Brave New World* (1932) – a satirical projection into the future of the way of life implicit in a deliberate hedonism, which need not concern us here – the shadow of D. H. Lawrence lifts from Huxley's pages, and with his next work we are back to the main line of his development – to the haunting preoccupation with the futility of life and the possibility of finding a way of escape from its pointlessness and tedium.

III

FOUR years after *Brave New World* and eight after *Point Counter Point* there appeared Huxley's crucial novel, *Eyeless in Gaza* (1936); crucial, because it represents a direct attempt to deal with the problems raised by his earlier works, and because it stands at the mid-point of his career as a novelist. Here the characters, previously formalized to excess, gain in definition and humanity, and genuine drama begins to emerge, centring around the autobiographical figure of the writer, Anthony Beavis, and his movement from a self-indulgent, cynical detachment towards personal regeneration and the acceptance of human responsibility.

The autobiographical novelist-character in *Point Counter Point*, we have seen, was signally isolated from the world, from other persons. The following extract from his notebook links him indubitably with Anthony Beavis, who has come to precisely the same realization, and who, moreover, takes at last the hazardous step of implementing it in action:

> Till quite recently, I must confess [Philip Quarles writes] I took learning and philosophy and science – all the activities that are magniloquently lumped under the title of 'The Search for Truth' – very seriously. I regarded the Search for Truth as the highest of human tasks and the Searchers as the noblest of men. But in the last year or so I have begun to see that this famous Search for Truth is just an amusement, a distraction like any other, a rather refined and elaborate substitute for genuine living; and that Truth-Searchers become just as silly, infantile and corrupt

in their way as the boozers, the pure aesthetes, the business men, the Good-Timers, in theirs. . . . Shall I ever have the strength of mind to break myself of these indolent habits of intellectualism and devote my energies to the more serious and difficult task of living integrally?

The personal theme of *Eyeless in Gaza* is Anthony's realization of the fatal error which has distorted and vitiated his life as a human being; but there is also an impersonal theme – that of the process of time. Once more the opening paragraph sets the key:

> The snapshots had become almost as dim as memories. This young woman who had stood in a garden at the turn of the century was like a ghost at cock-crow. His mother, Anthony Beavis recognized. A year or two, perhaps only a month or two, before she died. . . .

And the structure of the novel, the erratic alternation of pages from the remote past, the near past and the present of Anthony's history, while it reveals the temporal preoccupation, at the same time perfectly expresses the essential discontinuity of Anthony's existence as a result of his crucial, though always unacknowledged, refusal to go forward to claim his personal destiny as a human being, to 'become himself'.

Anthony has chosen not to be humanly responsible, chosen not only 'the part of the detached philosopher' but of the detached sensualist, desiring neither to love nor to be loved. The crisis in his life occurs on his forty-second birthday when with his mistress of the moment, Helen – who happens to be the daughter of a former mistress, Mary Amberley – he is lying on the roof of his retreat in southern France, 'in a golden stupor of sunlight and fulfilled desire'. Despite his volition, his wish to sever himself from his past and to live only in the immediate enjoyment of the present, perspectives of memory, invoked by this and that apparently trivial sense-association, persistently open up before him:

> Even the seemingly solid fragments of present reality are riddled with pitfalls. What could be more uncompromisingly *there*, in the present, than a woman's body in the sunshine? And yet it had betrayed him. The firm ground of its sensual immediacy and of

his own physical tenderness had opened beneath his feet and precipitated him into another time and place. Nothing was safe. Even this skin had the scent of smoke under the sea. This living skin, this present skin; but it was nearly twenty years since Brian's death. . . . What if that picture gallery had been recorded and stored away in the cellars of his mind for the sole and express purpose of being brought up into consciousness at this present moment? Brought up, today, when he was forty-two and secure, forty-two and fixed, unchangeably himself, brought up along with those critical years of his adolescence, along with the woman who had been his teacher, his first mistress, and was now a hardly human creature festering to death, alone, in a dirty burrow? And what if that absurd childish game with the flints had had a point, a profound purpose, which was simply to be recollected here on this blazing roof, now as his lips made contact with Helen's sun-warmed flesh? In order that he might be forced, in the midst of this act of detached and irresponsible sensuality, to think of Brian and of the things that Brian had lived for; yes, and had died for — died for, another image suddenly reminded him, at the foot of just such a cliff as that beneath which they had played as children in the chalk pit. Yes, even Brian's suicide, he now realized with horror, even the poor huddled body on the rocks, was mysteriously implicit in this hot skin.

Anthony's spiritual crisis, its antecedents and outcome, has been subterraneously prepared out of his unwilling but inescapable realization of the treacherous quality of time, with its accompaniments, age and death; and this is reproduced in the narrative, which takes us consecutively through various stages of Anthony's history, always returning to the point of departure — the sunlit roof. It is precipitated by the shock of an unexpected and startling incident. Out of an aeroplane flying immediately above there falls a yelping dog, to drop like a missile on to the roof, spattering the reclining lovers with its blood. Recovering from the shock, Anthony feebly passes it off as a joke, but 'for all answer, Helen covered her face with her hands and began to sob'.

For a moment Anthony stood quite still, looking at her crouched there, in the hopeless abjection of her blood-stained nakedness, listening to the painful sound of her weeping. 'Like seccotine': his own words re-echoed disgracefully in his ears. Pity stirred within him, and then an almost violent movement of love for this hurt and suffering woman, this *person*, yes, this person whom he had ignored, deliberately, as though she had no existence except in the context of pleasure. Now, as she knelt there sobbing, all the tenderness he had ever felt for her body, all the affection implicit in their sensualities and never expressed, seemed suddenly to discharge themselves, in a kind of lightning flash of accumulated feeling, upon this person, this embodied spirit, weeping in solitude behind concealing hands.

He knelt down beside her on the mattress, and, with a gesture that was meant to express all that he now felt, put an arm round her shoulder.

But at his touch she winced away as if from a defilement. With a violent, shuddering movement she shook her head.

This is the crisis which jerks Anthony into an abrupt awareness of his mistaken path. The rest of the novel conducts us through the corridors of Anthony's past history, his long, mistaken path being traced to its primal root in his early liaison with Mary Amberley, by whom he is idly prompted to betray his friend's trust and ultimately to cause Brian's suicide, by wantonly seducing the girl to whom he is betrothed, while concurrently, we are shown his later progress towards responsible participation in human affairs and the eventual acceptance of an ascetic, neo-Buddhist 'spirituality'.

The story, written with manifest sincerity, is a serious attempt to state a genuine human predicament and to find a way around it. Yet the statement, and the solution, when all is allowed, leave one with a disturbed feeling that all is not well, that somewhere there is a hiatus, a dislocation and a spiritual failure.

Anthony's conversion takes place at the point where he is made abruptly to realize that he has denied the inwardness of another person; that he has denied love for the sake of a detached sensuality. But as the narrative proceeds, we become aware that his personal discovery of love is turning from its proper object and becoming generalized, at first into hypothetical beneficence for humanity and at last into a cold moralism which derives its sanctions from a peculiarly impersonal metaphysic.

K

Returning to the antecedents of his conversion, we find that the tentative emotion of love (for Helen) becomes confused and finally submerged in the emotion of disgust (for Helen's mother, his once charming mistress, now a drunkard, a dope-addict, a squalid wreck). Simultaneously, this disgust fuses with the horror of time, of the accumulation of moments which leads inexorably to decay and death. The horror of time, as it accumulates in human life as age, is in turn associated with disgust for the physical body which experiences and expresses this accumulation. So that we are back at the position stated so clearly, eleven years before, in *Those Barren Leaves*. When, in his thirties, Anthony re-encounters Mary Amberley after an estrangement of more than ten years' duration, his predominant emotion is not pity but horror:

> 'Doing what one doesn't want,' she repeated, as though to herself. 'Always doing what one doesn't want.' She released his hand, and, clasping her own behind her head, leaned back against the pillows in the attitude, the known and familiar attitude, that in the Hôtel des Saints-Pères had been so delicious in its graceful indolence, so wildly exciting because of that white round throat stretched back like a victim's, those proffered breasts, lifted and taut beneath the lace. But today the lace was soiled and torn, the breasts hung tired under their own weight, the victim throat was no more a smooth column of white flesh, but withered, wrinkled, hollow between starting tendons.
>
> She opened her eyes, and, with a start, he recognized the look she gave him as the same, identically the same look, at once swooning and cynical, humorous and languidly abandoned, as had invited him, irresistibly then, in Paris fifteen years ago. It was the look of 1913 in the face of 1928 – painfully out of its context. He stared at her for a second or two, appalled; then managed to break the silence.

It becomes clear that Anthony's conversion is merely negatively and passively motivated. He has not sought reality and truth, but evaded them, until at last reality has found him and chased him – the analogy is his own – from his bolt-hole:

> Even in the deepest sensual burrow, Anthony reflected as he walked back to his rooms, even in the snuggest of intellectual other-worlds, fate could find one out. And suddenly he perceived that, having spent all his life trying to react away from the stan-

dards of his father's universe, he had succeeded only in becoming precisely what his father was – a man in a burrow. With this small difference, that in his case the burrow happened to be intermittently adulterous instead of connubial all the time; and that the ideas were about societies and not words. For the moment, he was out of his burrow – had been chased out, as though by ferrets. But it would be easy and was already a temptation to return.

Anthony is in fact seeking some way of *escape* from the conditions of human life rather than some way of positively transforming those conditions. And the spirituality which he is indicated as making his own towards the end of the book does actually fortify him, though with a shift of emphasis, in that very detachment and impersonality from which the incident of the dog and his emotional crisis has momentarily jolted him.

'God may or may not exist,' he writes in his diary. 'But there is the empirical fact that contemplation of the divinity – of goodness in its most unqualified form – is a method of realizing that goodness to some slight degree in one's life. . . .' His form of belief seems quite unashamedly chosen to conform to his own ingrained life-attitude:

God – a person or not a person? *Quien sabe?* Only revelation can decide such metaphysical questions. And revelation isn't playing the game – is equivalent to pulling three aces of trumps from up your sleeve.

Of more significance is the practical question. Which gives a man more power to realize goodness – belief in a personal or an impersonal God? Answer: it depends. Some minds work one way, some another. Mine, as it happens, finds no need, indeed, finds it impossible to think of the world in terms of personality.

And, appropriate to this central laxity, his new-found 'spirituality', so far from attending upon the wind that blows where it lists, resolves into the cataloguing of technicalities:

The fundamental problem is practical – to work out systems of psychological exercises for all types of men and women. Catholicism has many systems of mental power – Ignatian, Franciscan, Liguorian, Carmelite and so on. Hinduism, Northern, Southern and Zen Buddhism also have a variety of practices. There is a great work to be done here. Collecting and collating information from all these sources. Consulting books and, more important, people who have actually practised what is in the books, have had the experience of teaching novices. In time it might be possible to establish a complete and definite *Ars Contemplativa*. A series of techniques, adapted to every type of mind. Techniques for meditating on, communicating with and contemplating goodness. Ends in themselves and at the same time means for realizing some of that goodness in practice. . . .

What better comment could be made on this than that which Anthony himself commits to his diary at one candid stage of his reflections:

Reflect that we all have our Poonas, bolt-holes from unpleasant reality. The danger, as Miller is always insisting, of meditation becoming such a bolt-hole. Quietism can be mere self-indulgence. Charismata like masturbations. Masturbations, however, that are dignified, by the amateur mystics who practise them, with all the most sacred names of religion and philosophy. 'The contemplative life.' It can be made a kind of high-brow substitute for Marlene Dietrich: a subject for erotic musings in the twilight.

IV

'MAN', wrote Søren Kierkegaard in a famous definition, 'is spirit. But what is spirit? Spirit is the self"; and, further, 'eternity is essential continuity'. 'Selfness or personality,' according to Aldous Huxley in his last, mystical-didactic phase, is a ' "stinking lump" . . . which has to be passionately repented of and completely died to before there can be any "true knowing of God in purity of spirit." '

The mind-body carries with it the ineradicable smell of all that has been thought and done, desired and felt, throughout its radical and personal past. . . . The world is what (in our eyes) it is, because of all the consciously or unconsciously and physiologically remembered habits formed by our ancestors or by ourselves, either in our present life or in previous existences. These remembered bad habits cause us to believe that multiplicity is the sole reality and that the idea of 'I', 'me', 'mine', represents the ultimate truth. *Nirvàna* consists in 'seeing into the abode of reality as it is', and not reality *quoad nos*, as it seems to us. Obviously, this cannot be achieved so long as there is an 'us', to which reality can be relative. Hence the need, stressed by every exponent of the Perennial Philosophy, for mortification, for dying to self. And this must be a mortification not only of the appetites, the feelings and the will, but also of the reasoning powers, of consciousness itself and of that which makes our consciousness what it is – our personal memory and our inherited habit-energies. To achieve complete deliverance, conversion from sin is not enough; there must must also be a conversion of the mind, a *paravritti*, as the Mahayanists call it, or revulsion in the very depths of consciousness. As the result of this revulsion, the habit-energies of accumulated memory are destroyed, and, along with them, the sense of being a separate ego. Reality is no longer perceived *quoad nos* (for the good reason that there is no longer a *nos* to perceive it), but as it is in itself.

Sin, for Huxley, is selfness. For Kierkegaard, as a Christian believer, sin is despair, and despair is precisely the dissociation, the dislocation of the self in its refusal to 'choose itself' – to put itself into inward motion and go forward to claim its unique destiny as a messenger of meaning to the world.

'When did the ego begin to stink?' asks a recent aesthetic sage, in a phrase which seems to have captured the public ear. Answer: *When it began to decompose.*

The later work of Aldous Huxley must be interpreted as a bitter diatribe against personality, which he sees as synonymous with selfness – selfness *when it begins to decompose.*

The word 'personality' is derived from the Latin, and its upper partials are in the highest degree respectable. For some odd philological reason, the Saxon equivalent of 'personality' is hardly ever used. Which is a pity. For if it were used – used as currently as 'belch' is used for 'eructation' – would people make such a reverential fuss about the thing connoted as certain English-speaking philosophers, moralists and theologians have recently done? For 'selfness', though it means precisely the same, carries none of the high-class overtones that go with 'personality'. On the contrary, its primary meaning comes to us embedded, as it were, in discords, like the note of a cracked bell. For, as all exponents of the Perennial Philosophy have constantly insisted, man's obsessive consciousness of, and insistence of being, a separate self is the final and most formidable obstacle to the unitive knowledge of God. To be a self is, for them, the original sin, and to die to self, in feeling, will and intellect, is the final and all-inclusive virtue. . . .

That this God-eclipsing and anti-spiritual selfness should have been given the same name as is applied to the God who is a

Spirit, is, to say the least of it, unfortunate. Like all such mistakes, it is probably, in some obscure and subconscious way, voluntary and purposeful. We love our selfness; we want to be justified in our love; therefore we christen it with the same name as is applied by theologians to Father, Son and Holy Spirit.

A man who has never gone forward to claim his self, and achieve personality, can obviously never comprehend the meaning of personality, just as he can never understand the nature of communion and love. For him, personality *is* selfness, that dissolute conglomeration of appetites, volitions and perceptions which are functions of the body he is given by nature. And when the natural ego begins to disintegrate and to 'stink' beyond endurance there is only one course left – to get rid of it.

Not only must the sufferer withdraw from his offending self – he must withdraw from the world, from other persons, and finally from God. Huxley's mysticism is therefore a-historical, anti-personal and atheistic. The whole cosmic order is, in its eyes, a pointless and inexplicable escapade of an inert and irresponsible deity, or non-deity – an escapade from which we are called to 'liberate' ourselves with all possible speed, in order to turn to 'the pure One, the absolute not-God in whom we must sink from nothingness to nothingness [and who] is called in Mahayana Buddhism the Clear Light of the Void'. (*The Perennial Philosophy*.)

How is the novelist, the portraitist of human life and character, to work within this scheme? ' . . . On the strictly human level, there was nothing that deserved to be taken seriously except the suffering men inflicted upon themselves by their crimes and follies . . .' reflects Huxley's Mr. Propter in the next novel, *After Many a Summer* (1939). 'No, a good satire was much more deeply truthful and, of course, much more profitable than a good tragedy. The trouble was that so few good satires existed, because so few satirists were prepared to carry their criticism of human values far enough.' A defect Huxley undertakes to remedy, for here criticism of human values is carried to the point of their complete abolition.

Huxley's basic dualism is here made unconditional. As a result we have on the one hand the group of puppet-characters – Jo Stoyte, the millionaire, whose palatial Californian residence is the scene of the novel, Dr. Obispo, the ruthless, scientific-minded sensualist, Jeremy Pordage, the ineffectual, flute-voiced litterateur from Oxford, Virginia Maunciple, the innocent-depraved little chorus-girl – puppets whose thoughts and actions bespeak their utter worthlessness and futility – and on the other the more than human, withdrawn, contemplative-practical sage, Mr. Propter, the essentially static mouthpiece of Huxley's teachings on the futility of life on the 'strictly human level' and the necessity for a withdrawal from human life to 'the level of eternity'. Between the two poles significant movement is quite precluded. Life is a dance of puppets, grimly, savagely pointless.

The anti-personal bias of the novel is pronounced; thus Mr. Propter:

> Bondage is the life of personality, and for bondage the personal self will fight with tireless resourcefulness and the most stubborn cunning. . . . The spirit is always willing; but the person, who is a mind as well as a body, is always unwilling – and the person, incidentally, is not weak but extremely strong.

This strange hatred of 'the stinking slough of our personality' is carried to the point of absurdity –

> 'Turn round, please.'
> Mr. Stoyte obeyed. The back, Dr. Obispo reflected, was perceptibly less revolting than the front. Perhaps because it was less personal.

The dislocation of being is expressed in the counterposing of a neutral, arid and abstract 'mysticism' on the one hand by a grossly material sensualism: life is separated into two mutually exclusive compartments. On the one hand –

> 'What is man?' he whispered to himself. . . . 'A nothingness surrounded by God, indigent and capable of God, filled by God if he so desires.' And what is this God of which men are capable? Mr. Propter answered with the definition given by John Tauler in the first paragraph of his *Following of Christ*. 'God is a being withdrawn from creatures, a free power, a pure working.' Man, then, is a nothingness surrounded by, and indigent of, a being withdrawn from creatures, a nothingness capable of free power, filled with a pure working if he so desires.

And on the other:

> Through his dark glasses, Mr. Stoyte looked up at her with an

expression of possessiveness at once gluttonous and paternal. Virginia was his baby, not only figuratively and colloquially, but also in the literal sense of the word. His sentiments were simultaneously those of the purest father-love and the most violent eroticism. . . .

Delicious creature! The hand that had lain inert, hitherto, upon her knee, slowly contracted. Between the broad spatulate thumb and the strong fingers, what smoothness, what a sumptuous and substantial resilience!

'Jinny,' he said. 'My Baby!' . . .

Mr. Propter's peculiarly arid and abstract mysticism has its end in 'a non-personal experience of timeless peace. Accordingly, non-personality, timelessness and peace are what it means. . . .' And it involves, centrally, a repudiation of, and an escape from, time:

> ' . . . potential evil is *in* time; potential good isn't. The longer you live, the more evil you automatically come into contact with. Nobody comes automatically into contact with good. Men don't find more good merely by existing longer. . . . The solution is very simple and profoundly unacceptable. Actual good is outside time. . . . Time is potential evil, and craving converts the potentiality into actual evil. Whereas a temporal act can never be more than potentially good, with a potentiality, what's more, that can't be actualized except out of time.'

Time as evil, once more, manifests in human life as age, physical decreptitude, death. Thus the thread of narrative depends primarily from Jo Stoyte's haunting fear of the grave, which causes him to employ Dr. Obispo upon researches into the possibilities of artificial longevity. Wound with this principal thread is the intermittent commentary on the human characters provided by the baboons in their enclosure outside the Stoyte mansion:

> To the right, on another shelf of rock, a formidable old male, leather-snouted, with the grey bobbed hair of a seventeenth-century Anglican divine, stood guard over his submissive female. . . . The coast was clear. The young male who had been looking for dandruff suddenly saw his opportunity. Chattering with excitement, he bounded down to the shelf on which, too frightened to follow her master, the little female was still squatting. Within ten seconds they had begun to copulate.

Virginia clapped her hands with pleasure. 'Aren't they cute?' she cried. 'Aren't they *human*!'

These threads wind together as the researches of Dr. Obispo coincide with Jeremy Pordage's discovery, among the ancient papers he is cataloguing for Jo Stoyte, that the eighteenth-century fifth earl of the all but extinct line of Gonister has in his old age been similarly experimenting with a diet of raw carps' guts, and has mysteriously arranged for his own counterfeit funeral. On the insistence of the millionaire in his terror of death, the fifth Earl is eventually located in his stinking underground cave:

Beyond the bars, the light of the lanterns had scooped out of the darkness a narrow world of forms and colours. On the edge of a low bed, at the centre of this world, a man was sitting, staring, as though fascinated, into the light. His legs, thickly covered with coarse reddish hair, were bare. The shirt, which was his only garment, was torn and filthy. Knotted diagonally across the powerful chest was a broad silk ribbon that had evidently once been blue. From a piece of string tied round his neck was suspended a little image of St. George and the Dragon in gold and enamel. He sat hunched up, his head thrust forward and at the same time sunk between his shoulders. With one of his huge and strangely clumsy hands he was scratching a sore place that showed red between the hairs of his left leg.

'A foetal ape that's had time to grow up,' Dr. Obispo managed to say at last. 'It's *too* good!' Laughter overtook him again. 'Just look at his face!' he gasped, and pointed through the bars. Above the matted hair that concealed the jaws and cheeks, blue eyes stared out of cavernous sockets. There were no eyebrows; but under the dirty, wrinkled skin of the forehead a great ridge of bone projected like a shelf.

. . . 'But what's happened to them?'

'Just time,' said Dr. Obispo airily.

'Time?'

'I don't know how old the female is,' Dr. Obispo went on. 'But the Earl there – let me see, he was two hundred and one last January.'

The novel closes, bitingly acidulous, with Jo Stoyte's mentally preparing himself to accept the identical regime undergone by the fifth Earl.

That Huxley, driven by self-hatred and disgust with life, has reached a dead-end is finally demonstrated by his last, most tasteless production, *Time Must Have a Stop* (1945). Here the puppets, fixed in their unbreakable abstracts of human qualities, and offset by the static and detached figure of a pharisaical 'saint', exist at a remove from reality which gives the novel an air of complete futility to human experience. The 'saved' Bruno Rontini, like Mr. Propter a mere mouthpiece for Huxley's renunciatory gospel, is deprived of inward movement no less than the 'damned' puppet-characters immobilized in their habit of selfhood. In the previous novel, the only character not quite immune from 'the contagion of goodness' is the naïve and inarticulate Pete. It is no accident that for his hero this time Huxley should have chosen an adolescent (Sebastian Barnack is seventeen), that he should have involved him to his undoing for twenty-nine chapters in the depraved realm of 'the flesh' and then, by means of an abrupt hiatus, presented us, with the briefest of explanations, in the final chapter with a reformed and 'saintly' character, complete with copious extracts from those now all-too-familiar notebooks. For Huxley, as we have seen before, is for some reason at which one can only guess – we might label it 'arrested development' – at ease only with the immature. Incapable as he is of revealing the inner processes by which human beings come to inward maturity, even his supposedly adult characters remain adolescents upon whose juvenile responses has been superimposed arbitrarily the veneer of a quasi-adult sophistication and intellectuality.

Sensual depravity or an unreal 'spirituality' – down goes one scale heavily weighted with 'the flesh', and up goes the other with its insubstantial featherweight of spirit. The falsity to human experience of his naïve dislocation of being is paralleled in the novel both by the failure of its action to carry conviction and the air of unreality in which that action takes place. We can believe in the authenticity of Uncle Eustace's Italian villa, located, in accordance with Huxley's now pronounced retreat from history, in a dream-like nineteen-twenties, no more than we can accept the authenticity of Uncle Eustace himself or for that matter any of the book's characters. The vision, distorted for the satire of *After Many a Summer*, is here quite out of focus.

The adult reader is utterly unable to make the required connection between Uncle Eustace's trivial sensualities – his cheerful over-indulgence in wine, women and cigars – and the bathetic solemnities of his post-mortem experiences in the spirit world when, after an evening of luxury, he dies on the seat of the toilet. And the anti-climax of the disembodied Uncle Eustace's eventual choice of reincarnation out of the 'living uterine darkness', the 'vegetative heaven' of Mme. Weyle, should serve, at least, in the mind of no uncommonly penetrating reader, to put Huxley's 'mysticism' in its proper, very humble place.

With this final novel, we may safely conclude, Huxley's career as a significant novelist of the modern plight has come to an end. It is an end implicit, like so many, in its beginning. The novelist of futility, undergoing in mid-career a period in which the potentiality of meaning seemed for a time to offer itself – a potentiality accompanied by a realization of love and the value of human personality – has crossed over into a positive accentuation of futility accompanied by a positive doctrine of non-attachment and impersonality. No hope of development here! And, necessarily, this positive acceptance of the meaninglessness of human life, the worthlessness of personality, has its implications for art. When human life is seen as intrinsically meaningless and evil, then the work of the novelist, whose task is to present a picture of that life in terms of its significance and value, is deprived of all justification. Art and life must be thrown overboard together.

JAMES JOYCE

For many years understanding of Joyce has been obscured by an approach concentrating upon the technical aspect of his work without relating the technical innovations to the inward necessity which has determined them. This is as much as to say that, more than a quarter-century after the first appearance of *Ulysses*, we are still without a thoroughgoing and fully satisfactory account of the significance of Joyce's work. Now, it is obvious that only charlatans indulge in technical experiment for its own sake, and equally obvious that Joyce was not a charlatan. The form of his work cannot be considered and fully understood without its proper relation to the content. And it is precisely the content of Joyce's work which critics have shrunk from dealing with. They have taken it curiously for granted. As a result, their dealings with its form have been, inevitably, inconsequent and superficial. Yet such a book as *Ulysses* does not obtain its powerful hold upon men's minds by virtue of its technical excellence alone, and one is forced to conclude that the technical approach is a mental sleight adopted in order to maintain a show of capability in the face of a fundamentally unmanageable situation. There is more, a great deal more, in *Ulysses* than meets the eye; it has an exoteric and an esoteric significance, and it is disturbing to think that while its hundreds of thousands of readers are concerned with its overt structure, its inward presuppositions are being quietly assimilated into their consciousness.

Three main strands run through all of Joyce's work; these are: Solitude ('the soul's incurable loneliness'), Religion (in reverse – the repudiation of a Roman Catholic upbringing) and Art (the artist's lonely vocation). These are closely linked. Joyce's work has both an inherent and a representative significance. The biggest question raised by Joyce is that of the entirely self-subsistent work of art. The repudiation of belief implies the surrender of an active, personal task in the realm of existence. The question then arises, can there be a uniquely artistic vocation in separation from and in independence of a primary, existential orientation towards purpose? Joyce's entire work was an attempt to answer this question in the affirmative. It was, in other words, the work of an aesthete, and in Joyce aestheticism itself is under trial.

It will be agreed that Joyce's history is quintessentially that of the artist; and of the artist as aesthete. That is to say, he is an artist *in vacuo*, an artist for the sake of art. But to say this raises once more the whole angry question of the relation of art to life. Aestheticism I interpret as a malady of the spirit in which the poverty of a meaningless and static life is compensated by the transposition into living of properties borrowed from the artistic sphere. When the aesthete is also a practising artist, his work re-echoes the echo made by art in his life – thus Joyce's first book, *Chamber Music*. But the artist-aesthete who is not content to make his work the echo of an echo is faced with a dilemma. Despite all efforts, art cannot be severed from its relation to experience, and the material of the artist-aesthete who rejects the echo and the dream cannot be other than his own intrinsically meaningless and impoverished experience. Joyce accepted this position, and, transferring the meaning and purpose which he repudiated in life to the realm of art, he brought art and life together in a relationship of unparalleled immediacy: it was, so to speak, a symbiotic relationship, in which art fed upon and incorporated life into itself.

There is a story by Edgar Poe in which an artist transfers to canvas the life, health and beauty of his sitter, so that as the painting comes to life the subject undergoes a corresponding depletion of vitality. This parable of the morbid transposition of intrinsic meaning and value from life to art is echoed in *The Picture of Dorian Gray* of Oscar Wilde – another Irishman and aesthete. In Joyce we are able to see such transposition, of which there is an element in all artistic creation, carried to an extreme. Ultimately, such a procedure is a magical one: another aesthete, also an Irishman, W. B. Yeats, was a conscious dabbler in magical practices. The mastery which cannot be exercised in the face of existence is exercised over the material of art, and, by transposing raw life immediately into art, the artist becomes the creator of a magical super-life the validity of which lies in its own self-subsistent structure. *Ulysses* is nothing less than a paradigm of human existence, a microcosmical transliteration of typical experience into magical, verbal form. In the process of transubstantiating life into art, Joyce was forced to make unprecedented artistic inroads into the sordid, the insipid and the obscene, and as a result *Ulysses* has a proto-philosophical character which is not usually associated with aesthetical works. Joyce was not a philosopher, of course, but *Ulysses* contains in concrete, non-conceptual form the raw material of a philosophical system. In reality, no work of art is self-subsistent: every poem draws its meaning from a relation to the truth which is a reality beyond itself. What we witness in *Ulysses*, then, is not the creation of an artistic structure arising out of an orientation towards truth, nor yet a structure unrelated to truth (which would be an impossibility) but an account of the relinquishment of meaning through the abandonment of truth. Meaning implies selectivity, discrimination, which in turn are dependent upon an initial act of faith. By the abandonment of faith, discrimination is rendered impossible, and there must ensure a surrender to the indifferentiated flux of being: it is this which is presented in *Ulysses*. In *Finnegans Wake*, the abandonment of discrimination is carried from the objective world to the realm where object and subject are primitively confused: from the particular and microcosmic, Joyce moves to the macrocosmical, the universal, and corrupt mythological archetypes lumber through his pages. In this last work we see the autotelic work of art beginning to crumble from within: we see consciousness claimed by the aboriginal unconscious and the word inwardly disintegrated by the pressure of contradictory meanings let loose by the relapse from all discriminations of values.

The most imperceptive comment ever made on Joyce was perpetrated by T. S. Eliot, when in his book on literary heresy he wrote that of the eminent writers of his time Joyce was the most orthodox. Joyce's orthodoxy was limited to the Catholic indoctrination which he suffered in his youth, and from which all his subsequent life was an effort to free himself. Actually, the psychic quality of Joyce's work is astonishingly primitive; it shows marked leanings towards plain animism. This is clearly connected with the magical conception of art which Joyce shared with all aesthetes; *Finnegans Wake* is the most magical of Joyce's works and the most primitive. All the innovations which Joyce made resulted from the magical need to overcome the disparity between life and art: all were in the direction of the greater immediacy, concreteness and self-subsistence of the thing said. As his biographer, Herbert Gorman, truly says of the writing of the final work – 'An attempt would be made to break the bounds of formal speech and achieve that plane where the word, no longer a much-handled and partially-defaced token to arouse in the reader's mind an approximation of the thing meant, became the thing meant itself.' Where, in other words, life became transubstantiated magically into art.

Elsewhere in his biography, Gorman describes Joyce's superstitious awe when confronted with extraordinary natural phenomena. This is what Frazer has to say on the subject:

> Unable to discriminate clearly between words and things, the savage commonly fancies that the link between a name and the person or thing denominated by it is not a mere arbitrary and ideal association, but a real and substantial bond which unites the two in such a way that magic may be wrought on a man as easily through his name as through his hair, his nails, or any other material part of his person. In fact, primitive man regards his name as a vital portion of himself and takes care of it accordingly.

Many readers, I have no doubt, will regard this as a most unwarranted imputation to level at the foremost representative of modern literary culture. I wish it were. But consider: the modern man shares with the primitive all the fundamental traits of human nature; inasmuch as he had emancipated himself from the primitive bondage it is through the spiritual movements hypostasized in the forms of religious cult and dogma. With the abandonment of his religion, and all that it represents, there is nothing to prevent his relapse into psychic domination by cosmic forces. In Joyce we see precisely such an abandonment and precisely such a relapse, preserved for us only by the operation of the civilized techniques of detached and devoted artistic conscience.

I

'BY revising his own account of his early attitudes toward life and art,' writes Harry Levin in his critical monograph, 'Joyce has obscured the fact that they stem naïvely out of the naturalist movement.' The observation is just. The first prose work, *Dubliners*, is entirely naturalist in conception.

This naturalism is artistic passivity: the artist's mind is a sensitive film merely, carefully and impersonally recording the impressions of the external world. As with the photographer, the art consists in arrangement and selection. Nevertheless, the subjective element cannot be entirely overlooked, and this particular camera clicked its shutter only when the external setting synchronized with a fixed internal pattern. The passivity of technique has its counterpart in the mood of passivity and defeat in the face of external necessity which permeates the stories and determines the method of composition. The concluding lines of *Araby* are typical:

> Gazing up into the darkness I saw myself as a creature driven and derided by vanity; and my eyes burned with anguish and anger.

And so are those of *Eveline*:

> She set her white face to him, passive, like a helpless animal. Her eyes gave him no sign of love or farewell or recognition.

The purely aesthetic qualities of *A Portrait of the Artist as a Young Man* – its aromatic evocation of the moods and impressions of childhood, adolescence and immaturity – have tended to obscure the psychological pattern which underlies it. As the portrayal of the making of an artist it has features curious enough to incite comment. An inward passivity and recessiveness distinguish Stephen Dedalus's character from the beginning: passively he takes the impress of his environment, and passively he suffers the temporal necessity which estranges him first from childhood and then from boyhood and leaves him, at the last, a self-aware and self-willed aesthete on the threshold of maturity. It is never explicitly stated what is the force which urges him so irresistibly to the artist's destiny. But the recognition of it as something fatal and immutable follows immediately upon his explicit rejection of the Jesuit director's call to ordination and the religious life. 'The voice of the director . . . repeated itself idly in his memory. . . . His destiny was to be elusive of social or religious orders.' And to reject the life of sacerdotal sanctity is, for Stephen – there is no middle course – to embrace the profane. 'He was destined to learn his own wisdom apart from others or to learn the wisdom of others himself wandering among the snares of the world. . . . The snares of the world were its ways of sin. He would fall.' It is hard on the heels of this rejection that his call to the artistic vocation is imperatively sounded, during the seaside walk in which the exalting banter of some schoolfellows concerning his strange name, which 'seemed to him a prophecy . . . of the end he had been born to serve and had been following through the mists of childhood and boyhood', leads on to the ecstatic vision of the paddling girl, which provokes his soul to an 'outburst of profane joy'. The vision is recorded at the close of the fourth chapter. In the fifth and last Stephen the artist emerges, composing a villanelle, formulating a static, non-kinetic theory of art, and preparing himself for the artistic life of 'silence, exile and cunning' in exotic Paris.

To ask what sort of an artist Stephen-Joyce developed into is to find the answer ready-made. He ventured into literature with the ebb-tide of the 'decadent' movement of the *fin de siècle*, when the naturalist and the symbolist movements held joint hegemony over the advance guard of the arts: at a time when *The Yellow Book* was a vivid memory and a still potent influence. On his first visit to England Joyce was taken under the wing of Arthur Symons, who arranged the publication of *Chamber Music* with the decadents' publisher, Elkin Matthews. Returning from Paris (in *Ulysses*) Stephen is made to wear, appropriately, a Latin Quarter hat. As Eliot has pointed out, Joyce's early prose shows the deep impression of Pater and Newman. The association of these two names should give us pause. For they serve to bring potently to mind the odd relationship which then existed between the aestheticism of the decadents and the Roman Catholic religion.

This relationship has only to be stated to be recognized. It is a simple fact that both in France and England a dispropor-

L

tionately large number of decadents were pilgrims either from or towards the Roman Church. Curiously, there is a definite link in this respect even between Pater and Newman, for in his youth Pater had come profoundly under the influence of Keble, and had seriously considered taking holy orders – Keble himself being, of course, Newman's closest associate, prior to the latter's secession, in the Oxford movement. There would seem to be a close kinship between the static structure of the Roman Church, its ritual and theology, and the static quality of aestheticism. 'One of Stephen's central ideas', writes Theodore Spencer in his Introduction to the early manuscript, *Stephen Hero*, 'is that only improper art is "kinetic"; it moves us to do something, which true art should not do; on the contrary, the true "aesthetic emotion" is static, and the true artist is essentially impersonal.' That the impersonal element is strong in Roman Catholicism is also a possibly significant fact. It is certainly not accidental that the aesthetic movement was strongly tinged with a temper of diablerie, that it dabbled in strange sins and elaborate vices, in yellow prose and purple passion. It was, self-consciously, a profane literature, and it gloried, rather naïvely, in its daring paganism.

Stephen-Joyce was just such an aesthete. The poem which Stephen composes in the fifth chapter of the *Portrait*, the *Villanelle of the Temptress*, bears all the marks of this sort of yellow decadence. It has the authentic note of aesthetic world-weariness ('Are you not weary of ardent ways') and of abandon ('Lure of the fallen seraphim'). The young poet's 'broken cries and mournful lays rise in one *eucharistic* hymn', thus characteristically confusing the profane Eros with the sacred and Catholic Agape: and the lines of the final stanza:

> And still you hold our longing gaze
> With languorous look and lavish limb,

have the effect almost of parody: which they assuredly are not. In fact, in the book's fifth chapter, subject and treatment combine to reveal the aesthetic at its most lavish and languorous. Stephen's mind, 'when wearied of its search for the essence of beauty amid the spectral words of Aristotle or Aquinas turned often for its pleasures to the dainty songs of the Elizabethans'.

His thinking was 'lit up at moments by . . . lightings of so
clear a splendour that in those moments the world perished
about his feet as if it had been fire consumed: and thereafter his
tongue grew heavy and he met the eyes of others with unanswer-
ing eyes for he felt that the spirit of beauty had folded him round
like a mantle and that in reverie at least he had been acquainted
with nobility.' Waking one morning to compose his villanelle,
'His soul was all dewy wet. Over his limbs in sleep pale cool
waves of light had passed. . . . The night had been enchanted.
In a dream or vision he had known the ecstasy of seraphic life.'
And the initial stages of composition are described in terms
appropriate to a Hollywood producer's notion of the Vision
Beautiful:

> The instant flashed forth like a point of light and now from
> cloud on cloud of vague circumstance confused form was veiling
> softly its afterglow. Oh! In the virgin womb of the imagination
> the word was made flesh. Gabriel the seraph had come to the
> virgin's chamber. An afterglow deepened within his spirit, whence
> the white flame had passed, deepening to a rose and ardent light.
> That rose and ardent light was her strange wilful heart, strange
> that no man had known or would know, wilful from before the
> beginning of the world: and lured by that ardent roselike glow the
> choirs of the seraphim were falling from heaven.

Stephen the embryo artist, however, appears only towards
the end of the fourth chapter. Before that there is nothing to
indicate a specifically artistic destiny – or so it would super-
ficially appear. And it is only when we come to understand that
for Joyce the artistic vocation stands in antithetical relationship
to the religious, and that it is directly connected with 'the snares
of the world [which] were its ways of sin', that we can apprehend the relevance of the autobiographical material of the
first four chapters. For the substance of those chapters is the
conflict in Stephen's lonely, immature and over-indoctrinated
soul between his Catholic religiosity and his implication in the
realm of natural necessity which comes to an agonizing crisis
with the onset of adolescent sexuality.

The Stephen of Chapter Two is 'a boy . . . proud and sensitive and suspicious, battling against the squalor of his life and
against the riot of his mind'. With the money gained by an

exhibition and essay prize he attempts vainly to stem the squalid tide which threatens to submerge the socially declining family.

> How foolish his aim had been! . . . He saw clearly . . . his own futile isolation. He had not gone one step nearer the lives he had sought to approach nor bridged the restless shame and rancour that had divided him from mother and brother and sister.

Baulked, he 'turned to appease the fierce longings of his heart before which everything else was idle and alien'. And his sexual fantasies and solitary orgies have their culmination in his initiation into the mysteries of profane love.

The phrase is appropriate: for although Joyce describes with realism how in the throes of his lust, wandering the mean streets, Stephen 'moaned to himself like some baffled prowling beast', and writes of his 'wail of despair' as 'a wail of furious entreaty, a cry for an iniquitous abandonment, a cry which was but the echo of an obscene scrawl which he had read on the oozing wall of a urinal', the encounter with the prostitute to which these prowlings eventually lead reveals itself as an initial phase in the discovery of a veritable profane mystery, of which the life of the artist and the practice of art are stages of continuation. But let the narrative – with my italics – speak for itself:

> He had wandered into a maze of narrow and dirty streets. From the foul laneway he heard bursts of hoarse riot and wrangling and the drawling of drunken singers. He walked onward, undismayed, wondering *whether he had strayed into the quarter of the Jews*. Women and girls dressed in long vivid gowns traversed the streets from house to house. They were leisurely and perfumed. A trembling seized him and his eyes grew dim. The yellow gasflames arose before his troubled vision against the vapoury sky, *burning as if before an altar*. Before the doors and in the lighted halls groups were gathered *arrayed as for some rite*. He was in another world: he had awakened from a slumber of centuries.

There follows the description of Stephen's encounter with the harlot, his entry to her room and his ecstatic abandonment to her embraces. Her room 'was warm and lightsome'; as she disrobes he notes 'the proud conscious movements' of her 'perfumed head': she embraces him 'gaily and gravely . . . her face lifted to him in serious calm' while her lips 'pressed upon his brain as upon his lips as though they were the vehicle of a vague speech'.

It is of great interest to discern that Stephen's initiation has a cosmic significance of which he is but half aware, but which Joyce subtly delineates. He has, indeed, entered into the mystery of whoredom, which is the mystery of impersonal cosmic continuance – the procession of natural, physical necessity divorced from the integrating power of spirit. So that the third chapter begins with an account of Stephen's haunting of the brothel quarter, 'calmly waiting for a sudden movement of his own will or a sudden call from his sin-loving soul from their [the whores'] soft perfumed flesh', and passes straightway to the reflections which occupy his brooding mind during his hours of study.

> The equation on the page of his scribbler began to spread out a widening tail, eyed and starred like a peacock's; and, when the eyes and stars of its indices had been eliminated, began slowly to fold itself together again. The indices appearing and disappearing were eyes opening and closing; the eyes opening and closing were stars being born and being quenched. The vast cycle of starry life bore his weary mind onward to its verge and inward to its centre, a distant music accompanying him outward and inward. What music? The music came nearer, and he recalled the words, the words of Shelley's fragment upon the moon wandering companionless, pale for weariness. The stars began to crumble and a cloud of fine stardust fell through space.
>
> The dull light fell more faintly upon the page whereon another equation began to unfold itself slowly and to spread abroad its widening tail. It was his own soul going forth to experience, unfolding itself sin by sin, spreading abroad the balefire of its burning stars and folding back upon itself, fading slowly, quenching its own lights and fires. They were quenched, and the cold darkness filled chaos.

The significance of this frightening passage must not be minimized. It reveals an objective understanding of the process of depersonalization to which Stephen has submitted himself: the simile of the peacock's tail is a covert reference to the isolated, self-regarding ego, which moves with one step from isolation to universality – 'The chaos in which his ardour

extinguished itself was a cold indifferent knowledge of himself.'
His isolate and frigid condition, permeated with the consciousness of sin which, with his Jesuitical upbringing, he cannot
evade, is broken into by the rector's announcement of the
retreat. It is this retreat, with the preacher's elaborate and
harrowing sermon on the pains of eternal damnation awaiting
the confirmed and unrepentant sinner, which composes the
entire third chapter, the sermon itself being the largest single
block of consecutive prose in the entire book. Stephen's indifference is annihilated, and in agony of contrition he is driven to
make his confession and resolution of amendment.

There follows the account of Stephen's subsequent phase of
religiosity, which has at once an aesthetic and a pantheistic or
pancosmic character.

> Every part of his day, divided by what he regarded now as the
> duties of his station in life, circled about its own centre of spiritual
> energy. His life seemed to have drawn near to eternity; every
> thought, word and deed, every instance of consciousness could be
> made to revibrate radiantly in heaven: and at times his sense of
> such immediate repercussion was so lively that he seemed to feel
> his soul in devotion pressing like fingers on the keyboard of a great
> cash register and to see the amount of his purchase start forth
> immediately in heaven, not as a number but as a frail column of
> incense or as a slender flower.

Although his soul (the *Portrait* is an exceedingly soulful book)
is still unable to comprehend the passions of love and hate—'the
only love and . . . the only hate his soul would harbour' being
'a subtle, dark and murmurous presence' which would 'penetrate his being and fire him with a brief iniquitous lust',
nevertheless –

> . . . he could no longer disbelieve in the reality of love since
> God himself had loved his individual soul with divine love from
> all eternity. Gradually, as his soul was enriched with spiritual
> knowledge, he saw the whole world forming one vast symmetrical
> expression of God's power and love. Life became a divine gift for
> every moment and sensation of which, were it even the sight of a
> leaf hanging on the twig of a tree, his soul should praise and thank
> the giver. The world for all its solid substance and complexity no
> longer existed for his soul save as a theorem of divine power and
> love and universality. So entire and unquestionable was this sense

of the divine meaning in all nature granted to his soul that he could scarcely understand why it was in any way necessary that he should continue to live.

His devotion leads him to the practice of continual mortification of all five senses – to mortify his sense of smell, for instance, he seeks out and subjects himself to 'the only odour against which his sense of smell revolted [which] was a certain stale stink like that of longstanding urine'. With all this, however, he finds no inner power to surmount the petty trials of daily living. 'His prayers and fasts availed him little for the suppression of anger at hearing his mother sneeze or at being disturbed at his devotions.' At last, a 'sensation of spiritual dryness together with a growth of doubts and scruples' results from his inability 'to merge his life in the common tide of other lives'. His devotional phase concludes with the reflection that 'perhaps that first hasty confession wrung from him by the fear of hell had not been good?' and he asks himself, dubiously; 'I have amended my life, have I not?'

.   .   .

It is at this point that there occurs the interview at which Stephen's vocation for the priesthood is deliberated. And it is subsequent to this that Stephen takes his momentous seaside walk culminating in the vision of the bird-girl. Two threads may here be drawn together – Stephen's static and aesthetic religiosity and the association of art with the plunge into profane life. They are united in his priest-like devotion to the artist's work and his essential solitariness. The 'instinct, subtle and hostile', which 'armed him against acquiescence' to the director's proposal, is that of solitude.

He saw himself sitting at dinner with the community of a college. What, then, had become of that deep-rooted shyness of his which had made him loth to eat or drink under a strange roof? What had come of the pride of his spirit which had always made him conceive himself as a being apart in every order?

It is precisely the aesthetic aspect of the priest's life which attracts Stephen, and which Joyce puts into words which might have come from the pen of Baron Corvo:

He longed for the minor sacred offices, to be vested with the tunicle of subdeacon at high mass, to stand aloof from the altar, forgotten by the people, his shoulders covered with a humeral veil, holding the paten within its folds or, when the sacrifice had been accomplished, to stand as deacon in a dalmatic cloth of gold on the step below the celebrant, his hands joined and his face towards the people, and sing the chant, *Ite missa est*. If ever he had seen himself celebrant it was as in the pictures of the mass in his child's massbook, in a church without worshippers, save for the angel of the sacrifice, at a bare altar and served by an acolyte scarcely more boyish than himself.

And now, in his portentous walk, his profane experience combines in his solitary soul with his aesthetic religiosity, to bring forth the nascent artist. 'Now, as never before, his strange name seemed to him a prophecy. . . . This was the call of life to his soul . . . not the inhuman voice that had called him to the pale service of the altar. . . . He would create proudly out of the freedom and power of his soul, as the great artificer whose name he bore, a living thing, new and soaring and beautiful, impalpable, imperishable.' It is then that he encounters the girl who 'seemed like one whom magic had changed into the likeness of a strange and beautiful sea-bird', and their wordless communion sets Stephen 'singing wildly to the sea, crying to greet the advent of the life that had cried to him.'

> Her image had passed into his soul for ever and no word had broken the holy silence of his ecstasy. Her eyes had called him and his soul had leaped at the call. To live, to err, to fall, to triumph, to recreate life out of life! A wild angel had appeared to him, the angel of mortal youth and beauty, an envoy from the fair courts of life, to throw open before him in an instant of ecstasy the gates of all the ways of error and glory. On and on and on and on!

It is interesting to observe that this revelation, again, has cosmic overtones:

> He felt above him the vast indifferent dome and the calm processes of the heavenly bodies: and the earth beneath him, the earth that had borne him, had taken him to her breast. . . . His eyelids trembled as if they felt the vast cyclic movement of the earth and her watchers, trembled as if they felt the strange light of some new world. His soul was swooning into some new world, fantastic, dim, uncertain as under sea, traversed by cloudy shapes and beings.

That passage looks forward to *Ulysses*: and the final sentence might be an anticipation of *Finnegans Wake*.

II

BETWEEN the *Portrait* and *Ulysses* there is a vast difference in scope, mood and style. From the new epical work the strain of ninetyish decadence is eliminated, while the 'soulful' sentimentality has been replaced by a determined physicality indicated by the attribution to each part of *Ulysses*, not only of its Homeric parallel but also its physiological keynote. In method, *Ulysses* is a compound of photographic, statistical realism and of poetic allegory. From its pages emerges a factual picture of Dublin life and a paradigm of human existence.

The isolation which was characteristic both of Joyce as a man and of his view of existence presented him with certain problems as a writer. In *Dubliners* he had overcome his difficulties by writing objectively about the people he saw around him. In the *Portrait* he had evaded them by turning his artist's eye towards his reflection in the mirror. Now a casual scrutiny of *Ulysses* reveals that nearly half of its supernumerary characters have been lifted bodily from *Dubliners*, while Stephen Dedalus, who shares the principal role with Leopold Bloom, steps straight from the final page of the *Portrait*. In fact, *Ulysses* is a synthesis, as it were, of the two earlier books. It is both externally realistic and inwardly autobiographical, and furthermore, it is a parable. A parable of solipsism.

There is a sentimental element in nearly all aestheticism, which may be attributed to the aesthetic attempt to enjoy beauty in separation from truth. It is exactly this false striving after an isolated beauty which is responsible for the many tasteless passages in the *Portrait*. Since *Ulysses* is patently not without its direct relation to the *Portrait*, one may pertinently enquire what has happened to the sentimentality of the earlier book.

Sentimentality carries with it its own penality: brutality. Consider Joyce's first work, the slight, wistful lyrics contained in the volume entitled *Chamber Music*. We have Herbert Gorman's assurance that this book's title does in fact carry the lubricious *double entente* which might be expected. That is entirely comprehensible and fitting. A sentimental devotion to beauty leads the mind unavoidably into a compensatory movement towards the brutality of the squalid.

Ulysses itself represents just such a movement: it is among other things a rubbing of the aesthetic nose in the mean, the banal, the sordid. The sentimentality is still there, but Joyce has disowned it. It is now a part of the external human world which he describes. The nearest he allows himself to approach it is through parody.

So far as Joyce may be said to have had a personal style, it was a compound of the scrupulously commonplace and the pompous affectation of the decadent aesthete. The stilted, priggish quality in the prose of *Stephen Hero* is retained right through to the period just preceding *Ulysses*. Despite the verbal craftsmanship which it everywhere displays, it cannot be said that even in *Ulysses* Joyce had found a distinctively personal style. He was essentially an imitator. With consummate skill he mimics the speech and mannerisms of the Dublin citizens under his observation, and with the same skill, lacking the provocation of the outward scene, he turns his talent for mimicry upon literature in order to produce the great blocks of parody with which *Ulysses* is intercalated.

Turning from the soulfulness which marks the *Portrait*, Joyce plunged into the densely physical world of the banal and commonplace. The themes which dominate *Ulysses* are Unbelief, Nature and Necessity, Physicality, Promiscuity, the Commonplace and the Universal, or General, all of which, needless to say, relate to a common centre. 16th June 1904, the date on which the action takes place, is, as Gorman says, 'a day like all others and yet . . . all days in one'.

It cannot be denied that the spiritless universe depicted in *Ulysses* does exist – that multitudes of human lives are plunged miserably into its meaningless banality. Yet, as Joyce well shows, even this banal world has its relation to spirituality, and he is consummately successful in diverting his aesthetic sentimentality to the realm of the commonplace and in mimicking the mediocre life-style of his Dubliners.

The curious rancid sweetness of debased popular 'art' derives directly from this very sentimentality which is the inevitable result of the attempt to separate beauty from truth and to utilize its cosmetic qualities to cover the grossness of the life of appetite. The art of the Dublin citizens is, characteristically, singing – a physical art connected, as Joyce makes clear, with sexuality. *Ulysses* is saturated – it is part of the book's achievement – with this special quality, the mushy, sickly-sweet art of the 'bad infinity', a temporal effusion containing no eternal element. The mawkish, hypocritical quality it produces is represented in speech by the cant religious phrase never far from the Dubliner's lips, while in art it is the insipid charm of the nymph from *Photo Bits* which hangs over Molly Bloom's bed, of 'Love's Old Sweet Song' which Molly is preparing to sing for the adulterous Blazes Boylan, and the stylized lubricity of the pornographic novels which Bloom turns over on the bookstall. All this, however, is but an aspect of the total movement towards immersion in the undifferentiated realm of the general and universal which is portrayed in the course of *Ulysses*, and which I now proceed to delineate.

The interpretation of *Ulysses* which I am here proposing will be deprived of much of its apparent oddity by a citation of the words of a recognized authority. In his book, *James Joyce's Ulysses*, written in consultation with Joyce, Stuart Gilbert emphasizes the *mystical foundations* of the work.

'The fabric of *Ulysses*', bluntly announces Gilbert, 'is woven on strands of mystical religion, and, for readers who would explore the maze . . . and appreciate the subtleties of its pattern, some acquaintance with the cosmology on which it is based seems indispensable.' Gilbert then goes on to cite authorities on Buddhist mysticism. From Sinnett's *The Growth of the Soul* he quotes the following passage.

'There is no line to be drawn in Nature between important things that it is worth while for her laws to pay attention to, and others which are insignificant and fit to be left to chance. The earth's attraction operates equally on a microbe and a mastodon, and the chemical affinity that holds together the elements of the ocean is not permitted to neglect those of the smallest drop of dew.' 'Human affairs are so intensely entangled that it looks as if we must say – all or nothing; either every act, to the smallest, must be automatic and inevitable, or there is no prearranged course of events and no regular working out of Karma at all.'

Gilbert elaborates the implications of that in his own words as follows:

> The law of destiny, an application of the law of causation, is an axiom of esoteric doctrine. Similarly the associated law of the conservation of energy on the physical plane has its counterpart in a law of the conservation of spiritual forces or personalities. For soul, like matter, is indestructible. All that exists has already existed and will always exist; creation and destruction are both impossible; a flux of transformation pervades the universe but nothing can ever be added to it or taken away from it. Admitting, then, that human personality, the soul, exists, since *ex nihilo nihil fit*, it must have always existed, it can never cease to exist. As Stephen Dedalus remarks . . . 'From before the ages He willed me and now may not will me away for ever. A *lex eterna* stays about Him.' This *lex eterna* is, for esoteric thinkers, the law of Karma.

'The structure of *Ulysses*', Gilbert further remarks, 'indicates that Joyce aspires to outsoar the category of time and see a simultaneous universe – to take, so to speak, a God's eye view of the cosmos' – of a necessitarian cosmos, that is, into the mechanism of which every moment, word, action, is 'ineluctably' integrated.

> Nothing in creation [*sic*] is irrelevant – our 'errors' are more than the automatic gestures of some instinctive desire; they are part of the scheme of things, incidents on the long way round which we must travel to meet ourselves; they are – to use one of Stephen's favourite words – ineluctable. . . . For no passage, no phrase in *Ulysses* is irrelevant; in this grain of sand, this banal day in the life of an inglorious Dubliner, we may discover an entire synthesis of the macrocosm and a compelling symbol of the history of the race.

In this system, it is clear, there is no room for freedom: it has been ousted by necessity, as spirit has been ousted by the flesh, as love by sexuality, faith by promiscuity. There remains, at most, chance; chance being, for Bloom in the brothel, what moly – 'a white flower springing from a dark root' – is for Odysseus in the hall of Circe; even so –

> To omniscience and to such mortal men as are good delvers both the flower and its hidden roots are apprehensible. Even the

winning number at the roulette table could be predicted by one who could discern all the dark roots of the event.

Now, when Gilbert asserts that *Ulysses* is woven on strands of mystical religion, we can accept this only in the negative sense that through his repudiation of the Catholicism of his early years, Joyce was being drawn compulsively towards that view of the world which is prior and basic to the monistic and pantheistic religio-philosophical systems of the East, and which is the outcome of the primal immersion of the soul in the undifferentiated phenomenal flux. The view that 'all that exists has already existed and will always exist', that 'a flux of transformation pervades the universe but nothing can ever be added to it or taken away from it', is clearly the result of an immersion in the world-whirlpool which obviates the possibility of the concept of Creation, and which, therefore, when the concept of spirit is introduced, can make no distinction between God and the world, seeing the world as itself immanently permeated with the divine essence. Since according to this view the temporal flux is an endless cycle of indestructible substances, the freedom of the spirit must consist in liberation from the cosmic chains. The law of Karma is not educed from the mere contemplation of the cycle, but is the result of an attempt to introduce rational and ethical considerations into the contemplation of the otherwise meaningless and evil vital process. According to Buddhist teachings, it is the force of desire which binds together and perpetuates physical existence and liberation must come from the negation of its compulsive action. Since, however, Joyce is not a philosopher or ethical teacher but an aesthete, we find Hindu and Buddhist terms employed in his work not for their doctrinal significance but merely because of their evocation of the fundamental perception of the undifferentiated phenomenal flux towards which he is moving: the perception which wanders through the mind of the distracted Hamlet when, after despatching Polonius, he replied to the King's questions with the gnomic reflection that 'a man may fish with the worm that hath eat of a king, and eat of the fish that hath fed of that worm', meaning nothing by this but to show 'how a king may go a progress through the guts of a beggar'.

The 'strands of mystical religion', then, draw the possibility of their existence at the expense of the Catholic Christianity with the form of which Joyce's mind was penetrated. In order that the monistic, necessitarian cosmos may emerge, with its ineluctable laws, grinding remorselessly towards a final stasis, all those vestiges of spirit, love and freedom which still glimmer through the hypostasized forms of systematic Catholicism must be discredited and eliminated.

*   *   *   *

The Stephen Dedalus whom we meet in the first pages of *Ulysses*, 'wearily', 'quietly', 'gloomily', 'coldly', conversing with the blithe and blasphemous Buck Mulligan is a young man immersed in the melancholy of that despair which is, according to Kierkegaard, the obverse of *faith*. His position is defined in conversation with the philistine Englishman, Haines.

> Haines, who had been laughing guardedly, walked on beside Stephen and said:
> – We oughtn't to laugh, I suppose. He's rather blasphemous. I'm not a believer myself, that is to say. Still his gaiety takes the harm out of it somehow, doesn't it? What did he call it? Joseph the Joiner?
> – The ballad of Joking Jesus, Stephen answered.
> – O, Haines said, you have heard it before?
> – You're not a believer, are you? Haines asked. I mean, a believer in the narrow sense of the word. Creation from nothing and miracles and a personal God.
> – There's only one sense of the word, it seems to me, Stephen said. . . .
> – Yes, of course [Haines] said as they went on again. Either you believe or you don't, isn't it? Personally I couldn't stomach that idea of a personal God. You don't stand for that, I suppose?
> – You behold in me, Stephen said with grim displeasure, a horrible example of free thought.

To read these opening chapters of *Ulysses* is to experience the persistent, uneasy feeling that one has met this melancholy young man, clad in sombre mourning, before: and that it is not alone his inky cloak nor customary suits of solemn black, but that indeed he has that within which passes show. There is a death, certainly; and a question of guilt.

- The aunt thinks you killed your mother, he said. That's why she won't let me have anything to do with you.

- Someone killed her, Stephen said gloomily.

- You could have knelt down, damn it, Kinch, when your dying mother asked you, Buck Mulligan said. I'm hyperborean as much as you. But to think of your mother begging you with her last breath to kneel down and pray for her. And you refused. There is something sinister in you. . . .

That is on the third page. And on the same page there is a ghost.

Silently, in a dream she had come to him after her death, her wasted body within its loose brown graveclothes giving off an odour of wax and rosewood, her breath, that had bent upon him, mute, reproachful, a faint odour of wetted ashes. . . .

In Buck Mulligan, furthermore, we glimpse a more famous prototype, another usurper. There is a familiar ring to his sentiments on death.

- And what is death, he asked, your mother's or yours or my own? You saw only your mother die. I see them pop off every day in the Mater and Richmond and cut into tripes in the dissecting room. It's a beastly thing and nothing else. It simply doesn't matter. . . .

Indeed, we have to wait only a few pages for an open reference to that which is to be one of the dominating themes of the book, an integral component of Stephen's consciousness. 'Wait till you hear him on *Hamlet*, Haines,' jests Buck Mulligan on Stephen's pet theory: 'He proves by algebra that Hamlet's grandson is Shakespeare's grandfather and that he himself is the ghost of his own father.'

- I mean to say, Haines explained to Stephen as they followed, this tower and these cliffs here remind me somehow of Elsinore *That beetles o'er his base into the sea*, isn't it? . . .

- I read a theological interpretation of it somehow, he said bemused. The Father and the Son idea. The Son striving to be atoned with the Father.

In these brief passages we have set out the ingredients for the entire Hamlet motif which subterraneously pervades *Ulysses*. And it is at this point, significantly, that Mulligan begins to chant his scurrilous 'Ballad of Joking Jesus', at the close of which there occurs the discussion of belief already alluded to.

I have set out in another place the reasons, which seem to me overwhelming, for regarding *Hamlet* as pre-eminently a parable of unbelief. Like Hamlet Stephen is, in Arnold's words, 'wandering between two worlds, one dead – The other powerless to be born' – the dislocated worlds of nature and spirit. But Stephen's orientation differs from Hamlet's in that he has turned his face from the realities hypostasized in the dogmatic religion of his childhood and youth and is moving irresistibly towards undifferentiated nature. The article of belief which still exercised the greatest fascination over his mind is that of the consubstantiality of the Son with the Father, and this he associates curiously with the problem of Shakespeare and *Hamlet*. This train of thought culminates in the long disquisition which Stephen embarks upon in the ninth chapter, to the assembled literati in the Dublin public library, in which the two threads are woven into a single strand.

References to and quotations from the play litter the path of Stephen throughout *Ulysses*. There are seven casual and incidental *Hamlet* references in the short 'Proteus' section (Chap. III) in which Stephen walks alone across the strand towards the city. His Latin Quarter hat of the first chapter becomes 'my Hamlet hat'. And the sense of dread, powerfully suggested throughout the play, appears in the reiterated phrase about the beetling cliff. ('Jesus!' ejaculates Stephen on the beach, 'If I fell over a cliff that beetles o'er his base, fell through the nebeneinander ineluctably.') In the 'Wandering Rocks' episode, as he passes the power-station, there is a clear association of religious *dread*, with the Hamlet motif:

> The whirr of flapping leathern bands and hum of dynamos from the powerhouse urged Stephen to be on. Beingless beings. Stop! Throb always without you and the throb always within. Your heart you sing of. I between you. Where? Between two roaring worlds where they swirl. I. Shatter them, one and both. But stun myself too in the blow. Shatter me you who can. Bawd and butcher, were the words. I say! Not yet awhile. A look around.
>
> Yes, quite true. Very large and wonderful and keeps famous time. You say right, sir. A Monday morning, 'twas so, indeed.

Here the naked animistic power of the dynamos leads by direct transition to dread of the cosmic energies which threaten the divided being 'swirling . . . between two roaring worlds'. The exclamation 'Bawd and butcher' is a repetition of Stephen's words in the library, when he refers to 'The playwright who wrote the folio of this world and wrote it badly' as '*dio-boia*, hangman god'. The repetition of the blasphemy awakening a superstitious fear, however, the automatic response is a repetition of Hamlet's quick change of subject at the approach of Polonius, whom he has been ridiculing to Rosencranz in Act II, Scene ii, of the play.

It is difficult to believe that Joyce's employment of this theme was deliberate. It would seem that while consciously he paid minute attention to the intricate Homeric parallel, the Hamlet theme intruded itself semiconsciously, to work as an obscure leaven through the great mass of the novel. If this theme had been kept consciously in mind, nothing could have kept it from dominating the entire material and bringing about a greater inner unity and intensity of the whole book. As it is, no reader can have failed to remark that after the ninth of the eighteen episodes Joyce's creative impulsiveness seems to flag. The rest of the book is decidedly stiffer reading. In the 'Circe' episode interest quickens, but it is not until we reach the unpunctuated spate of Molly Bloom's bed-monologue which rounds off the book that we feel a full emotional pressure rising unmistakably through the surface of the prose.

Walking alone on the strand after leaving Mr. Deasy's school, ruffled by 'nipping and eager airs', Hamlet-Stephen reflects on his origins.

> Wombed in sin darkness I was too, made not begotten. By them, the man with my voice and my eyes and a ghostwoman with ashes on her breath. They clasped and sundered, did the coupler's will. From before the ages He willed me and now may not will me away or ever. A *lex eterna* stays about Him. Is that then the divine substance wherein Father and Son are consubstantial?
> . . .

Consubstantiality of Father and Son, the remnant of Catholic dogma which so nags at Stephen's mind, is queried here in terms of Necessity. It is by necessity (sexuality) that man is

M

born into the world, but behind the particular sexual act Stephen sees the operation of an eternal necessitarian principle, that of the *dio-boia*, hangman god. The *lex eterna* – we have Gilbert's word for it – is the law of Karma. So that what Stephen is asking is whether it is in the law of Karma, the irreversible process of cosmic necessity, that Father and Son, God and Man, are mutually subsumed. We must turn to the Hamlet disquisition in the library for the further pursuit of these threads.

This literary curiosity rests significantly upon an unquestioned identification of biographical with literary data, and in itself would justify a partially biographical approach to Joyce's own work. In fact, Joyce is clearly identifying himself with Shakespeare in the whole exposition. 'Elizabethan London', we are told, 'lay as far from Stratford as corrupt Paris lies from virgin Dublin.' Whether or not, as Stephen Dedalus asserts, Shakespeare's name was dear to him, that is abundantly true of Stephen himself. And likewise the note of banishment, 'banishment from the heart, banishment from home', which Stephen finds ubiquitous in Shakespeare, aptly characterizes his own work. And the Shakespeare whom, at last, Stephen sketches returning to that spot of earth where he was born, is 'Hamlet *père* and Hamlet *fils*. Dane or Dubliner'. More than that, to stray into the area of biography, Joyce was, at the time of the writing of *Ulysses*, like the author of *Hamlet*, 'a greying man . . . with thirty-five years of life, *nel mezzo del cammin di nostra vita*.'

In brief, Stephen's thesis runs as follows. At an early age Shakespeare had been seduced by Anne Hathaway, 'a bold-faced Stratford wench who tumbles in a cornfield a lover younger than herself'. Belief in himself has been untimely killed; Shakespeare is the fated cuckold. In London he lives loosely, but meanwhile Anne is betraying him with his brother. The theme of the false brother continually recurs in the plays, where also the names of two of the poet's brothers, Edmund and Richard, appear with villainous connotation, and where, furthermore, Shakespeare has hidden here and there his own name, 'as a painter in old Italy set his face in a dark corner of the canvas'. In the play of *Hamlet*, then, Shakespeare is not to be identified with the Prince, but with the betrayed and cuckolded

ghost of the King, whose role he is popularly credited with
having taken himself upon the stage.

> Is it possible that that player Shakespeare, a ghost by absence,
> and in the vesture of buried Denmark, a ghost by death, speaking
> his own words to his own son's name (had Hamlet Shakespeare
> lived he would have been prince Hamlet's twin) is it possible, I
> want to know, or probable that he did not draw or foresee the
> logical conclusion of those premises: you are the dispossessed son;
> I am the murdered father; your mother is the guilty queen, Ann
> Shakespeare, born Hathaway?

A father, says Stephen, is a necessary evil. Shakespeare wrote
Hamlet hard upon the death of his own father, and if you hold
that he, a greying man with two marriageable daughters, is the
youthful Hamlet, then you must hold that his ancient mother is
the lustful queen. 'No. The corpse of John Shakespeare does
not walk the night. . . . He rests, disarmed of fatherhood,
having devised that mystical estate upon his son.' Fatherhood,
Stephen continues, is not a biological but 'a mystical estate, an
apostolic succession, from only begetter to only begotten'.

> – Sabellius, the African, subtlest heresiarch of all the beasts of
> the field, held that the Father was Himself His own Son. . . .
> Well: if the father who has not a son be not a father can the son
> who has not a father be a son? When Rutlandbaconsouthampton-
> shakespeare . . . wrote *Hamlet* he was not the father of his own
> son merely but, being no more a son, he was and felt himself the
> father of all his race, the father of his own grandfather, the father
> of his unborn grandson. . . . [He is the ghost and the prince
> . . . He is all in all.]
> . . . The boy of act one is the mature man of act five. All in all.
> In Cymbeline, in Othello he is bawd and cuckold. He acts and is
> acted on. Lover of an ideal or a perversion, like Jose he kills the
> real Carmen. His unremitting intellect is the hornmad Iago
> ceaselessly willing that the moor in him shall suffer.

Since Stephen Dedalus is in the Hamlet role, his interpretation of the play cannot be other than that of his own situation.
He interprets it, accordingly, not in the appropriate terms of
the disparity between nature and spirit but in the light of his
obsession with the problem of consubstantiality. His interpretation is in effect an affirmative answer to the question which he

has already raised as to whether natural necessity, the *lex eterna*, is the 'divine substance wherein Father and Son are consubstantial'.

At the beginning of his disquisition, Stephen interjects this reflection:

> – As we, or mother Dana, weave and unweave our bodies . . . from day to day, their molecules shuttled to and fro, so does the artist weave and unweave his image. And as the mole on my right breast is where it was when I was born, though all my body has been woven of new stuff time after time, so through the ghost of the unquiet father the image of the unliving son looks forth. In the intense instant of imagination, when the mind, Shelley says, is a fading coal that which I was is that which I am and that which in possibility I may come to be. So in the future, the sister of the past, I may see myself as I sit here now but by reflection from that which then I shall be.

And he continues a little later:

> – His own image to a man with that queer thing genius is the standard of all experience, material and moral. . . . The image of other males of his blood will repel him. He will see in them grotesque attempts of nature to foretell or repeat himself.

In the course of the exposition, Stephen refers to incest as 'an avarice of the emotions', in which 'the love so given to one near in blood is covetously withheld from some stranger'. Father and son, however, are 'sundered by a bodily shame so steadfast that the criminal annals of the world, stained with all other incests and bestialities, hardly record its breach'.

Yet, 'Fatherhood, in the sense of conscious begetting, is unknown to man. It is a mystical estate, an apostolic succession, from only begetter to only begotten.' In these curious and obscure speculations Stephen is evidently indicating the possibility, or the necessity, of some kind of spiritual incest of son with father. Continuing this obsession, there runs through his mind a blasphemous parody of the Creed – 'He Who Himself begot, middler the Holy Ghost, and Himself sent Himself, Agenbuyer, between Himself and others, who, put upon by His fiends, stripped and whipped, was nailed like bat to barndoor, starved on crosstree, who let Him bury, stood up, harrowed hell, fared into heaven and there these nineteen hundred years sitteth on the right hand of His Own Self.'

It is plain that everything relates to solipsism. The man 'with that queer thing genius' relates everything to the perfection of his own image. More, he is himself, his own (spiritual) father. The image of himself as the unliving son (in the past) looks through the ghost of the unquiet father (the future): it is the process of time which unites father with son: so that time, cosmic necessity, is the *lex eterna* in which Father and Son are consubstantial. Spirit and freedom are eliminated, and only the monistic necessitarian cosmic mechanism remains. Stephen's entire disquisition on Hamlet-Shakespeare concludes as follows:

> – He found in the world without as actual what was in his world within as possible. Maeterlinck says: *If Socrates leave his house today he will find the sage seated on his doorsteps. If Judas go forth tonight it is to Judas his steps will tend.* Every life is many days, day after day. We walk through ourselves, meeting robbers, ghosts, giants, old men, young men, wives, widows, brothers-in-love. But always meeting ourselves. The playwright who wrote the folio of this world and wrote it badly (He gave us light first and the sun two days later), the lord of things as they are whom the most Roman of Catholics call *dio boia*, hangman god, is doubtless all in all in all of us, ostler and butcher, and would be bawd and cuckold too, but that in the economy of heaven, foretold by Hamlet, there are no more marriages, glorified man, an androgynous angel, being a wife unto himself.

Stephen is a self-portrait of Joyce in his immediately postgraduate days. Who then is Bloom? In the meeting of the rootless aesthete with the shrewd, resigned, middle-aged sensual man, Leopold Bloom – himself seeking a counterpart of his dead child, Rudy – there is presented a parable, Gilbert declares, of a universal quest.

> Human life is a process of adjustment, a striving after 'atonement' with a sublime father; achieved adjustment would involve personal extinction, yet it is the end to which all creation moves. There is a perpetual levelling in the universe, a crumbling of individualities, which, like mountains, are slowly eroded, silted down, towards the plain of uniformity, towards amalgamation in a 'perfect round'. 'But where are we going?' Novalis asks, and answers: 'Always home.' That return is symbolized in the tale of

Odysseus, in a thousand and one legends of all races, and its biblical paradigm is the homecoming of the prodigal son.

In the Hamlet digression, the overt Homeric theme sometimes overlaps the covert Shakespearian one. Anne Hathaway is referred to as 'poor Penelope in Stratford', while Shakespeare, projecting his image into the late play, *Pericles*, is a man tried 'like another Ulysses'. To follow further Joyce's example of indulgence in biographical criticism, we are justified in arranging a complex syllogism after this pattern. Joyce is Stephen Dedalus, and Stephen in turn is identified with Prince Hamlet. Hamlet in turn is a projection of Shakespeare (identified with Joyce), who also projects himself as the King; he is 'all in all' and therefore is also Pericles-Ulysses. Ulysses is, of course, Bloom, as Penelope is Marion Bloom. So that all are 'consubstantial' one with another. Bloom-Ulysses-Pericles-Shakespeare-Joyce meets at the centre with Joyce-Shakespeare-Hamlet-Telemachus-Stephen. Joyce is both Stephen Dedalus and Leopold Bloom, and the divine substance wherein Father and Son are consubstantial is the process of time which separates his youthful from his mature self. Throughout *Ulysses*, Bloom is the point towards which Stephen is moving. He is, in fact, Stephen's other self. In this day which is 'all days in one', sixteen years are annihilated, and Joyce's former image meets and is atoned with his future self; to repeat the phrase, *he is himself his own father*. Through union with Bloom, the solitary aesthete emerges into the realm of the banal, the commonplace, and the universal. Stephen's solution of the Hamlet problem disposes of the inner drama of doubt which it presents; spirit is theoretically eliminated, and he is prepared for the immersion in nature which is to follow; from the library to the brothel and from the brothel to Eccles Street and Marion Bloom.

Through the entire Hamlet sequence, the subconscious pressure is very great. The reference to Judas in the culminating passage of Stephen's discourse is especially revealing: it was Judas who betrayed his Lord – for thirty pieces of silver. A repudiation of spirit and a movement towards the total embracing of necessity cannot but be felt as a betrayal. 'Do you *believe* your own theory?' asks John Eglinton, and Stephen replies promptly, 'No.'

I believe, O Lord, help my unbelief. That is help me to believe or help me to unbelieve? Who helps to believe? *Egomen*. Who to unbelieve? Other chap.

So runs Stephen's inner monologue. It is again suggestive that precisely at this point John Eglinton remarks to Stephen, who will allow his theory to appear in print only if he is to be paid for it, 'You are the only contributor to *Dana* who asks for *pieces of silver*.' As if to hammer home the subterranean inferences, the episode closes with Buck Mulligan's trilling of a bawdy song concerning masturbation, 'the solitary vice', and his reading of a mock scenario on the subject, while Stephen, hardly aware of the passing presence of Bloom, who is just then leaving the library, reflects, ' . . . if Judas go forth tonight. Why? That lies in space which I in time must come to, ineluctably.' He is moving forward to his meeting with his paternal *alter ego*, foretold in his dream of the previous night, in the 'street of harlots'. Bloom and Stephen will be atoned in the realm of solitary and at the same time universal sexuality.

III

OMITTING the thirty-odd pages devoted to Stephen's discourse, there must be close upon half a hundred Hamlet references scattered throughout *Ulysses*. The greater number of these are associated with Stephen; Bloom, who is beyond the reach of the inner division which afflicts Stephen (he is too well adjusted to the world of mediocrity), has a motif of his own – that of Don Giovanni; an air from Mozart's opera haunts him intermittently throughout the day, while in the brothel he is referred to openly as 'a plebeian Don Juan'. Yet Joyce is not consistent in his attribution of the Hamlet motif to Stephen, and the unity of the two characters is underlined by Bloom's partial participation in the Hamlet theme. The burial episode, which cannot but offer itself as a parallel to Act V, scene 1, of *Hamlet*, is given not to Stephen but to Bloom, whose reflections assume a cast part clownish, part Hamletesque. ('Gravediggers in *Hamlet*,' Bloom reflects; 'shows the profound knowledge of the human heart,' and, snubbed by John Henry Menton at the cemetery gates,

Bloom, like Yorick, is 'chapfallen'.) Indeed, the fatuous, complacent indignity of Bloom's *weltanschauung* is well shown in his graveside meditations:

Mr. Kernan said with solemnity:
– *I am the resurrection and the life.* That touches a man's inmost heart.
– It does, Mr. Bloom said.
Your heart perhaps but what price the fellow in the six feet by two with his toes to the daisies? No touching that. Seat of the affections. Broken heart. A pump after all, pumping thousands of gallons of blood every day. One fine day it gets bunged up and there you are. Lots of them lying around here; lungs, hearts, livers. Old rusty pumps: damn the thing else. That last day idea. Knocking them all up out of their graves. Come forth, Lazarus! And he came fifth and lost the job. Get up! Last day! Then every fellow mousing around for his liver and his lights and the rest of his traps. Find damn all of himself that morning. Pennyweight of powder in a skull. Twelve grammes one pennyweight. Troy measure.

Don Juan is the embodiment of promiscuity, and promiscuity is the point of meeting for all the characteristic themes in *Ulysses*. Promiscuity at once presumes solitariness and impersonality, together with universality or generality. The universal-general is the undifferentiated commonplace, the sordid, the banal. Consequently it is towards all of these that Stephen is moving, and the final episodes are permeated with these qualities. Now Don Juan, ravisher of a thousand maidenheads, is, as we know from Coleridge and Kierkegaard, a daemonic personification of an elemental force, uncomplicated by the intrusion of spirit. In the Don Juan plays, as in Hamlet, there is indeed an intrusion of the supernatural – in the form of the statue which appears to conduct the libertine to the fires of hell; but Don Juan's attitude to the supernatural powers thus objectified is, unlike Hamlet's, undaunted and contemptuous throughout. In *Ulysses* the ghost is not masculine but feminine: it is that of Stephen's mother, for whose sake he would not, at her deathbed, kneel down to pray. The witches' sabbath in the brothel is brought to a conclusion by the final uprising of this apparition. In his desperate repudiation Stephen raises his ashplant and smashes the chandelier: and it is only after this that

Bloom decisively takes him under his protection, settles for the damage, and conducts him away to Eccles Street and Marion Bloom.

'Stephen's mother,' runs the text, 'emaciated, rises stark through the floor in leper grey with a wreath of faded orange blossoms and a torn bridal veil, her face worn and noseless, green with grave mould. . . .' To her uttered 'Beware' Stephen responds with an obscene word and the declaration, '*Non serviam!*'

THE MOTHER

(*Wrings her hands slowly, moaning desperately.*) O Sacred Heart of Jesus, have mercy on him! Save him from hell, O divine Sacred Heart!

STEPHEN

No! No! No! Break my spirit all of you if you can! I'll bring you all to heel.

THE MOTHER

(*In the agony of her deathrattle.*) Have mercy on Stephen, Lord, for my sake! Inexpressible was my anguish when expiring with love, grief and agony on Mount Calvary.

STEPHEN

Nothung! (*He lifts his ashplant high with both hands and smashes the chandelier. Time's livid final flame leaps and, in the following darkness, ruin of allspace, shattered glass and toppling masonry.*)

In that apocalyptic instant of denial Stephen's world has come to an end: his possibilities are exhausted, and he hands over the principal part to Bloom. So far as relations between the two are concerned, the world of Bloom begins, psychologically, at this point. It is the world which we have already encountered in the previous wanderings of Odysseus in which Stephen as Telemachus has no part, and it is characterized by a predominance of the sensual, the commonplace. The style of the two following episodes, 'Eumaeus' and 'Ithaca', is scrupulously banal, empirical, dispassionately impersonal. Only in the final episode, the 'Penelope', which is, however, substantially banal, is there the equable, physiological-erotic fervour of the All-Mother, nature personified, in whom all vestiges of spirit have been obliterated, and who is as free from conflict as from discrimination.

The negative spiritual core of *Ulysses* is the drama of unfaith. The inner process which the book reveals is the movement from meaning towards the meaningless. Supernatural faith is the total transcendent act which raises the self above the phenomenal flux in anticipation of the divine. Faith is the precondition of all discrimination: unfaith is indiscriminate, promiscuous: in the prophetic language of Ezekiel and *Revelation* it is 'fornication'. When the apparition of Stephen's mother arises in the brothel, it is in a wreath of faded orange blossoms and a torn bridal veil. Why? The mystery of whoredom is the desecration of marriage. The apparition symbolizes not only spirit, but faith, both in the divine and in the human aspects: that it is the apparition of a corpse reveals symbolically the inner spiritual condition of Stephen. Marriage is the sacrament of personal communion in which isolation is overcome and spirit and nature atoned through love; whoredom, which isolates the personality and then disintegrates it in the bad universal, is the profane rite of impersonal faithlessness.

Promiscuity is not merely taken for granted in *Ulysses*: it is fundamental to its psychic structure. Yet Joyce was raised a strict Roman Catholic, and the Roman teachings on marriage are hard and irrefragable. It is hardly possible for a Catholic to rid himself so easily of so basic an article of belief, reaching so intimately into the individual life as this. There is here, patently, some gap in Joyce's inner history; a gap which, if it could be filled, might help greatly to explain the disparity between the soulfulness of much of Joyce's earlier work and the brute materiality of *Ulysses*.

Fortunately, the gap can be filled. During the period between the completion of the *Portrait* and the commencement of *Ulysses*, Joyce wrote with unusual speed the little-considered three-act play, *Exiles*, which, in the words of Harry Levin, 'is an attempt to externalize the situation of domestic estrangement in "The Dead" ' – a story in *Dubliners*. In 'The Dead' there is a conflict between flesh and spirit, presented in terms of the contrast between the writer Gabriel Conroy's physical desire for his wife on their return from a Christmas party and the ideal, 'spiritual' devotion of a boy who had loved her in her youth, and who had died as a result of a romantic, clandestine visit to her window in a night of rain. Made aware of the comparison, Gabriel is deflated: 'He saw himself as a ludicrous figure . . . a nervous, well-meaning sentimentalist, orating to vulgarians and idealising his own clownish lusts.' *Exiles* presents the struggle in the mind of an isolated and self-absorbed writer, Richard Rowan, between faithfulness and promiscuity. Playing with resolution the role of the detached onlooker, he permits his wife Bertha to encourage the advances of an old friend, Robert Hand, journalist and man of the world, refusing despite her pleas to influence her one way or another. 'You are a stranger to me,' she cries. 'You do not understand anything in me – not one thing in my heart or soul. A stranger! I am living with a stranger!' When Robert Hand becomes aware of Richard's knowledge of his adulterous intentions, his initial discomfiture passes, when he grasps Richard's inner uncertainty, into challenge. 'I believe that on the last day,' he declares, '(if it ever comes), when we are all assembled together, that the Almighty will speak to us like this. We will say that we lived chastely with one other creature. . . .' – ('Lie to Him?' interjects Richard) – 'Or that we tried to. And he will say to us: Fools! Who told you that you were to give yourselves to one being only? You were made to give yourselves to many freely. I wrote that law with my finger on your hearts.' To this specious argument, Richard succumbs. 'Reach it [i.e. bodily union with Bertha] if you can,' he allows. 'I will use no arm against you that the world puts in my hand. If the law which God's finger has written on our hearts is the law you say I too am God's creature.' Richard then leaves wife and friend together, writes all night in his study, and refuses ever to know what has occurred between them.

That Richard's negative attitude towards his marriage is directly related to his inner isolation and his impotence in the central matter of faith is clear. The confusion between spirit and nature perpetrated in Robert Hand's argument of the divine law reflects Richard's own perplexity. In resigning himself to the cuckold's role, he is resigning himself nominally to divine law, but the divine law of the *dio boia*, or demiurge of

nature, whose realm is that of necessity. It is a drama of unbelief, as Richard's final words make abundantly plain. 'I am
wounded, Bertha . . . I have a deep, deep wound of doubt in
my soul . . . I have wounded my soul for you – a deep wound
of doubt which can never be healed. I can never know, never
in this world. I do not wish to know or to believe. I do not care.
It is not in the darkness of belief that I desire you. But in restless
living wounding doubt. To hold you by no bonds, even of love,
to be united with you in body and soul in utter nakedness. . . .'
It is a far remove from the highly-charged emotional crisis
which is presented in this play to the unconcerned acceptance
of promiscuity throughout *Ulysses*: but the one is a necessary
preliminary to the other. In *Ulysses*, Bloom is the cuckold who
acquiesces phlegmatically and even with a perverse satisfaction
in his wife's successive infidelities. It does not in the least
disturb him to think of her as a whore. 'Suppose he gave her
money,' he reflects of the adulterous Boylan. 'Why not? All a
prejudice. She's worth ten, fifteen, more a pound. What? I
think so. All that for nothing.'

From solitude to universality is but a single step; but in that
step the realm of personal communion represented by marriage is overpassed. There is no contradiction between the
structure of *Ulysses* as a parable of solipsism and its typical and
universal qualities. In terms of sexuality, Stephen's onanistic
isolation leads directly to the promiscuity, the profane universality, of the brothel. We find a parallel in those Eastern doctrines
which assume the complete isolation of the individual soul from
incarnation to incarnation, which can be overcome only by
liberation from the cycle of rebirth and reabsorption in the
universality of the divine oversoul.

As early as the second episode of *Ulysses* we find Stephen
asserting his pantheistic or pancosmical outlook to Mr. Deasy:

– History, Stephen said, is a nightmare from which I am trying
to awake.
   From the playfield the boys raised a shout. A whirring: goal.
What if that nightmare gave you a back kick?
   – The ways of the Creator are not our ways, Mr. Deasy said.
All history moves towards one great goal, the manifestation of
God.

Stephen jerked his thumb towards the window, saying:

– That is God.
Hooray! Ay! Whrrwhee!
– What? Mr. Deasy aske d.
– A shout in the street, Stephen answered, shrugging his shoulders.

And *Ulysses*, indeed, as it moves gradually from morning towards night, moves out of history into the cosmic embrace of nature. It begins with Stephen, continues with Bloom and terminates in the bed of Marion Bloom.

Everyone is aware of the meaning of Molly Bloom, whose long, unpunctuated monologue at the close of *Ulysses* in a sense sums up and includes all that had gone before, and whose erotic memories and ruminations end with a reiterated 'Yes' to the blind biological impulse which she transmits and embodies. To quote Gilbert:

> . . . Molly Bloom acts as the paradigm or *Massstab* of all the characters (or nearly all) in *Ulysses*. She sums them up in her monologue and in the light of her natural understanding we see their proportions reduced to a real scale of magnitudes. She takes their measure according to an ancient wisdom, the warmblooded yet unsentimental exigence of the life-force. . . . Gaea-Tellus is 'timeless' and 'artless'. . . . She begins small, a very ordinary woman, the *petite bourgeoise* of Eccles Street, a humbler Madame Bovary, to end as the Great Mother of gods, giants and mankind, a personification of the infinite variety of Nature as she had developed by gradual differentiation from the formless plasma of her beginning.

It is towards Molly as Gaea-Tellus that Stephen, through Bloom, is moving. It is she in whom Father and Son are resolved and identified – in the indiscriminate spate of vital being. And it is in relation to her that the note of reincarnation, or metempsychosis, is continuously sounded. Lying abed in the 'Calypso' episode, she connects it with the profane-erotic; the word 'metempsychosis' occurring in a novel by Paul de Kock ('Nice name he has'), she asks her cuckold-husband to explain it to her; and transmogrified to 'met him pike hoses' it echoes throughout Bloom's day with an erotic connotation – for instance, it recurs in connection with a passage from the novel Bloom inspects entitled *Sweets of Sin*.

Reincarnation signifies the relapse of the soul into the undifferentiated phenomenal flux: in another aspect, the relapse is signified by the prevalence of the commonplace. In the solid blocks of verbiage which constitute the last three sections of *Ulysses*, the sovereignty of the mediocre and the commonplace is established. Both matter and style in the fifty pages of the cabmen's shelter episode are designed to immerse the mind in the dreary minutiae of purposeless mundane existence. Boredom is the motif, and the pompous-facetious tone of the writing exactly conveys the desiccated being of the cultural proletarian.

This calculated drabness of submergence is carried further towards impersonality in the penultimate section – 'Ithaca' – by the treatment of the intimate details in Bloom's life, his domestic environment and his marital concerns in the distant and frigid tone of the courtroom and the laboratory. Bloom's simple, irrelevant action in turning on the tap occasions a detailed account of the Dublin municipal water supply; and after the tabulation of data which includes an exact catalogue of the kitchen utensils and a pointless calculation, on the assumption of a constant ratio, of the relative ages of Bloom and Stephen, Bloom's meditations move to the contemplation of interstellar space and the aeons of geological periods: he feels 'The cold of interstellar space, thousands of degrees below freezing point or the absolute zero of Fahrenheit, Centigrade or Reaumur.'

Bloom is resigned to his existence as a fragment of vital substance in a purposeless world motivated by crude appetite. Retiring, with the unavoidable reminder of his wife's marital defections, he composes his mind to equanimity.

Equanimity?
As natural as any and every natural act of a nature expressed or understood executed in natured nature by natural creatures in accordance with his, her and their natured natures, or dissimilar similarity. As not as calamitous as a cataclysmic annihilation of the planet in consequence of collision with a dark sun. As less reprehensible than theft, highway robbery. . . . As not more abnormal than all other altered processes of adaptation to altered

condition of existence, resulting in a reciprocal equilibrium between the bodily organism and its attendant circumstances, foods, beverages, acquired habits, indulged inclinations, significant disease. As more than inevitable, irreparable.

He justifies to himself his sentiments by 'The preordained frangibility of the hymen . . . the continued product of seminators by generation: the continual production of semen by distillation: the futility of triumph or protest or vindication: the inanity of extolled virtue: the lethargy of nescient matter: the apathy of the stars', while his antagonistic sentiments converge in a final mood of acquiescent satisfaction:

> . . . at the ubiquity in eastern and western terrestrial hemispheres . . . of adipose posterior female hemispheres, redolent of milk and honey and of excretory sanguine and seminal warmth, reminiscent of secular families of curves of amplitude, insusceptible of moods of impression or of contrarieties of expression, expressive of mute immutable mature animality.

Gaea-Tellus sustains the theme.

IV

THE dilemma in which the aesthete-artist finds himself is that which results from the inevitable discovery that ultimately every work of art, however refined or dreamlike or fantastic, necessarily draws its reality from its commerce with the world beyond itself. No artist has the power to create in an absolute vacuum an artistic entity which shall have about it no taint of lived experience. Aestheticism, in fact, is not logically or practically a tenable position: even the most extreme exponent of art for art's sake implicitly requires of the art-work the quality of formal meaning, and in no conceivable work of art is meaning an inherent, self-enclosed quality existing in independence of meaning beyond itself; and, by the same token, neither can meaning reside with magical intrinsicality in the word. The life which, despite his intention, still nourishes his art, the aesthete must perforce regard as a scandal, like the dollmaker's child in Yeats's poem. How to get rid of it?

Joyce's way of getting rid of life was by expanding the work of art so far that it provided, in intention in least, a verbal counterpart to experienced actuality which could be taken as a substitute for that experience. All of his work from the *Portrait* onwards draws its special quality of concreteness and intensity from the unprecedented attempt to obviate the conventional circumlocutions of fictional narrative and to transpose the raw stuff of experience into the magical immediacy of verbal expression. This explains the ventures into obscenity of this personally rather prudish writer. While this method led, in *Ulysses*, to the scrupulous cataloguing of the minutiae of daily living, in *Finnegans Wake* it resulted in the endeavour, which can only be regarded as magical, to create an all-inclusive cosmos in which the word was equivalent to the fact. Thus, paradoxically, it is the aesthete, who, in his retreat from life, effects the closest possible integration of literature with experience. Nevertheless, the misconception of the role of art remains, and is linked to the prior misconception of the task in relation to experience.

If life is inherently meaningless, how is that meaninglessness to be brought within the meaningful boundaries of art? We know how Joyce dealt with this in *Ulysses*: by an implicitly meaningful depiction of the process of the relinquishment of meaning. In *Finnegans Wake*, however, meaning has reached a further stage of dissolution, and there is nothing for it but to pack the cosmos into the work, entire. Only in relation to this endeavour can Joyce's multiple disruption and recombination of language be explained: language had to be packed so full that it contained everything possible, short of its total disruption into incoherence. In this respect, Joyce was not logical: he did not overstep the bounds of articulation. *Finnegans Wake* is a living contradiction of itself.

There can be no doubt that Joyce is a writer of outstanding quality, and that his work is of the greatest significance. At the same time, respect for his constructive achievement, and for his purely artistic integrity, must not be permitted to blind us to the inner meaning of his work, the self-contradiction which it embodies, and above all the direction to which it points. Joyce has received a great deal of uncomprehending adulation from the sort of culture-snob who is always found around the pedestal of the innovator, just as he has suffered equally the senseless

abuse of the philistine. *Finnegans Wake* still occupies an equivocal position in current esteem, receiving much ill-considered
lip-service from those who have not examined all the implications of the work. Now, either the prose in which *Finnegans
Wake* is composed represents an enormously potent advance in
the manipulation of language, an advance of which any subsequent literary work of a creative order must perforce take full
account, or it reveals a corruption of language which r equires
to be exposed and traced to its source. My own view should be
patent.

I regard aestheticism as itself fundamentally mistaken, and
persisted in, perverse and destructive in its effects. Language is
not isolate, is not magical. It is the vehicle of communication
and is related intrinsically to meaning, and through meaning, to
truth – which is a transcendent value. Language is healthy
when it is related directly to meaning, and it can be so related
only when the mind itself aspires vertically to truth as an
absolute centre. It is corrupt when divorced from meaning, or
when through the absence of primary orientation to truth the
relation is shifting and confused. This is so even with poetic
ambiguity, which must be a unification of multiple meanings
and never a dissipation of meaning. Yet, if my analysis is correct,
Joyce's entire work is founded upon an initial relinquishment of
the possibility of meaning.

A writer in *The Times Literary Supplement* has drawn attention to the disruption of language in *Finnegans Wake* under the
pressure of unrelated and contradictory references. Taking the
sentence, 'Not yet, though venissoon after, had a kidscad
buttended a bland old isaac', he correctly points out that the
word 'venissoon' suggests not only 'very soon' and 'venison'
but also Swift's Vanessa: this multiplication of reference,
characteristic of Joyce's method, being sometimes carried to
bewildering lengths.

> The intention of the word 'venissoon' is to provide a chord,
> three different literal meanings, three different complexes of
> association, striking harmoniously and simultaneously on the
> reader's mind. But the analogy is false and harmony is precisely
> the essential effect which is missed.

N

The associations of notes in a chord are mathematically explicable, but the associations of Jacob's venison and Swift's Vanessa are wholly arbitrary. . . . Unless we treat Joyce as God and believe that the whole subconscious mind of humanity is clearly visible to him, we must protest that there is no pre-existent connection in our minds between venison and Vanessa, still less between the venison of Esau and the Vanessa of Swift. Nor can Swift's elision create any such connection for us, since even in the text the connection is purely structural. Still more destructive of any harmonious effect are the unintended sound-associations which these portmanteau words may contain.

Even this writer, however, supposes that 'for all these ruinous faults a great and magnificent building lies somewhere concealed under the jungle of accretions, the fantastical surface of architectural superfluities', adding that 'perversely Joyce covered his structure with thick layers of loam'. But this was hardly the case. The distortion, the disintegration of language is a reflection of interior disintegration of a psychic world deprived of the possibility of meaning and of form.

Even the meaninglessness of *Finnegans Wake* (which is, of course, not total) stands in an oblique relationship to meaning. But the meaning is beyond the book. *Finnegans Wake* is not nonsense, or not much more so than *Alice in Wonderland*, which it curiously resembles, is nonsense: it is an articulation of meaninglessness. As such it is even a considerable work of art: with wonderful finesse it expresses a malady of the spirit through a corruption of language. It is like the utterance of a corpse. Although the morbid coalescence and distortion of language express the disrelation of meaning, the very imprecision of language by which Joyce gains his effects depends upon the tacit assumption of the existence elsewhere of a precise denotation.

What of the book's essential quality, of which the language is the expression? 'The concluding pages,' writes Stuart Gilbert of *Ulysses*, ' . . . are at once intensely personal and symbolic of the divine love of Nature for her children, a springsong of the Earth; it is significant for those who see in Joyce's philosophy nothing beyond a blank pessimism, an evangel of denial, that *Ulysses* ends on a triple paean of affirmation.' That is rather to sentimentalize the concupiscent meanderings of the blowsy trollop of Eccles Street, I fancy: but I forbear quotation. That *Ulysses* ends on an affirmative note is true enough, but affirmation of itself is not necessarily important or interesting: something depends on the quality of that which is affirmed. Molly Bloom certainly does not affirm beauty, goodness or truth. What she affirms is the indiscriminate and total acceptance of a world devoid of every trace of those values. Reduced to its central point, she affirms the ubiquity and all-importance of sexual excitation; she is the woman who says 'Yes' indeed – to the indiscriminate advances of everything in trousers. The description of her stream of muddy reflections as 'intensely personal' and symbolic of 'divine love' can hardly be regarded as other than an abuse of language. That she is intended to embody the diffuse flux of Nature, is, however, a point nobody could quarrel with. The bogey of affirmation or denial on Joyce's part arises to trouble the consciences of the enthusiastic and ingenious commentators, Joseph Campbell and Henry Morton Robinson. 'Here', they comment, half-way through their monumental *Skeleton Key to Finnegans Wake*, 'is Joyce's world-affirmation, for those who require to see it in so many words.' And the indicated passage runs as follows:

> . . . For as Anna was at the beginning lives yet and will return after great deap sleap rerising and a white night high with a cows of Drommhiem as shower as there's a wet enclouded in Westwicklow or a little black rose a truant in a thorntree. We drames our dreams tell Bappy returns. And Sein annews. We will not say it shall not be, this passing of order and order's coming, but in the herbest country and in the country around Blath as in that city self of legiends they look for its being ever yet. So shuttle the pipers done. Eric aboy! And it's time that all paid tribute to this massive mortiality, the pink of punk perfection as photography in mud. Some may seek to dodge the gobbet for its quantity of quality but who wants to cheat the choker's got to learn to chew the cud.

As a footnote to that passage, we find the following altogether typical sentence, in which a statement and its negation are simultaneously present: 'Gosem pher, gezumpher, greeze a jarry grim felon! Good bloke him!'

'We have to had them whether we'll like it or not,' writes Joyce, destroying the temporal sequence, of the aboriginal parent figures:

> They'll have to have us now then we're here on theirspot. Scant hope theirs or ours to escape life's high carnage of semperidentity by subsisting peasmeal upon variables. Bloody certainly have we got to see to it ere smellful demise surprends us on this concrete that down the gullies of the eras we may catch ourselves looking forward to what will in no time be staring you larrikins on the postface in that multimirror megaron of returningties, whirled without end to end.

On the quality of the 'affirmation' it seems hardly necessary to comment. 'Young man, you'd better,' said Carlyle grimly to the fledgeling who largely informed him: 'I accept the universe.' The affirmation is meaningless in itself, and the element of compulsion renders it valueless in any case.

Finnegans Wake begins in every respect where *Ulysses* left off. In location, it begins in bed: and further, it remains there. The immersion in undifferentiated being towards which the course of the earlier book was flowing is here almost complete. The solipsistical character of Joyce's universe is even more clearly brought out. In *Ulysses* the reader is plunged into the world of undifferentiated external phenomena: here, however, the border between the objective and the subjective is in dissolution and we peer through a murky and wavering twilight of looming, muttering figures which confuse with each other and re-emerge in the 'ineluctable' movement of the unending cosmic cycle. The characters from *Ulysses*, themselves figments of solipsism, are here present in universalized force. Bloom, who in the 'Ithaca' episode had already been dubbed 'Everyman or noman', is here blown up to monstrous dimensions as the mythological tavern-keeper of Chapelizod, Humphrey Chimpden Earwicker, who in turn merges indistinguishably into the earth-presence of the animistic father-figure, Here Comes Everybody, universal man. Marion Bloom becomes, in Anna Livia Plurabelle, incarnate femininity metamorphosed into the chattering stream, running towards dissolution in the sea. Stephen Dedalus and Buck Mulligan, antitypes even in *Ulysses*, are here, as Shem and Shaun, elevated to twin sons of the universal father.

The entire cycle is played out through the action and interaction of these type-figures drawn from the inchoate depths of isloated subjectivity and fixed in the endless motion of cosmic necessity. There is nothing here which is not potentially present in the earlier book. On examination, *Finnegans Wake* proves to be commonplace from end to end: despite its pretensions to mythological profundity, it is thoroughly banal; and despite the attempt, as in *Ulysses*, to impose an external structure (Viconian philosophy and the rest) it is formless and monotonous.

Like *Ulysses*, however, the book does rest upon a psychic pattern, and it is this which gives it what organic form it possesses. In *Ulysses* the pattern arises from the repudiation of meaning; here it is produced by the disintegration of being. The father-figure who looms large in the first part of the book, preyed upon by the agenbite of some obscure felony, gives place at length to his twin sons, each of whom represents an aspect of his divided self, aesthete-introvert and extrovert-libertine. In the third book, in which the extrovert-figure, Shaun, attempts to play the hero role in place of the superseded H.C.E., he appears first in character, delivering a masterful harangue to the people, then as Jaun (Don Juan) delivering a salacious sermon to a group of young girls, and finally as Yawn, in which condition he is himself the subject of a ruthless inquest in the course of which he dissolves murmurously back into the landscape from which all of the characters draw their origin. Having run her course, at the end of the book Anna Livia, universal mother, runs back into the parent ocean, and the final sentence turns to meet the first word on page one.

It had been widely recognized that *Finnegans Wake* is a comic conception. But what is the quality of its humour? Comedy is polar to tragedy, and can hardly be understood without reference to it. Now tragedy is bound up intrinsically with the concept of human dignity, of which indeed it is an assertion. And man's principal claim to dignity is precisely that he is spirit. Humour is the outcome of the ludicrous disparity between the possibility of spirit and its absence in actuality. Falstaff, for example, is (like Don Juan) a force of nature; he is also –

lecherous, bawdy, and oblivious of all except that pertaining to fleshly appetite – the epitome of human indignity. And *Finnegans Wake*, founded upon the raffish popular ballad of the hod-carrier Finnegan who dies by a fall from his ladder and revives at the wake when a drop of whiskey is splashed on his face, is unrelievedly Falstaffian throughout. It is no exaggeration to say that the book has a daemoniacal character. Just as it is erected upon utter spiritlessness and total immersion in the whirlpool of nature (the book is a great deal more obscene than *Ulysses*), the cosmic chuckle which is articulated through its pages is founded upon indignity – and desecration.

'Religion,' wrote Swift, 'supposes Heaven and Hell, the word of God and Sacraments and twenty other Circumstances, which taken seriously, are a wonderful check to Wit and Humour, and such as a true Poet cannot possibly give into with a saving to his Poetical License; but yet it is necessary for him, that others shou'd believe those things seriously, that his Wit may be exercised on their *Wisdom*, for so doing: For tho' a Wit need not have Religion, Religion is necessary to a Wit, as an Instrument is to the Hand that plays upon it.' In this case, however, wit has its say, not at the readers' expense, so much as at that of the residual catholicism still operative in Joyce's mind. This is particularly to be seen in its scurrilous treatment of symbols for the holy – for instance, the transformation of the Four Evangelists with their Gospel into the four old men leading their ass, and the reference to Jesus in the Church as 'the tout that pumped the stout'. Another psychotic compulsion is towards the transformation of the sacred into the erotic: e.g., 'Behose our handmades for the lured!' 'Let us pry,' and so forth. Joyce certainly worked hard to extirpate the Catholic in him, but the whole procedure, to the reader not involved in the situation, becomes excessively tedious when carried through seven hundred obsessed pages.

Not only *Finnegans Wake*, then, but the whole of Joyce's work is a symptom of the disintegration of the self-subsistent ego, turned in upon itself through the rejection of meaning consequent upon the initial failure of belief. Joyce puts this humorous self-accusation in the part of the book which concerns the activities of the autobiographical caricature, Shem the Penman:'You were bred, fed, fostered and fattened from holy childhood up in this two easter island on the piejaw of hilarious heaven and roaring the other place (plunders to night of you, blunders what's left of you, flash as flash can!) and now, forsooth, a nogger among the blankards of this dastard century, you have become of twosome twiminds forenenst gods, hidden and discovered, nay, condemned fool, anarch, egoarch, hiresiarch, you have reared your disunited kingdom on the vacuum of your own most intensely doubtful soul.' True enough, Joyce's history is that of the ingrowing, isolated ego, forced by the repudiation of faith and meaning into narrower circles of introversion and self-division, into further endeavours to overcome meaninglessness in terms of an impossible larger meaning which always receded. The disintegration of the isolated ego was countered by the devoted artistic labour of integration which itself was, nevertheless, inevitably subject to the same inner collapse. That Joyce was to some degree aware of the progress of the malady is shown in his account of the activities of Shem, in which the symbiotic character of his art-aestheticism is put into words more revealing than my comments could ever be:

Then, pious Eneas, conformant to the fulminant firman which enjoins on the tremylose terrian that, when the call comes, he shall produce nichthemerically from his unheavenly body a no uncertain quantity of obscene matter not protected by copriright in the United Stars of Ourania or bedeed and bedood and bedang and bedung to him, with this double dye, brought to blood heat, gallic acid on iron ore, through the bowels of his misery, flashly, faithly, nastily, appropriately, this Esuan Menschavik and the first till last alshemist wrote over every square inch of the only foolscap available, his own body, till by its corrosive sublimation one continuous present tense integument slowly unfolded all marryvoising moodmoulded cyclewheeling history (thereby, he said, reflecting from his own individual person life unlivable, transaccidentated through the slow fires of consciousness into a dividual chaos, perilous, potent, common to allflesh, human only, mortal) but with each word that would not pass away the squidself which he had squirtscreened from the crystalline world waned chagreenold and doriangrayer in its dudhud.

NOTES

P. 11. *Technique as Discovery* . . . by Mark Schorer. *The Hudson Review*, New York, Vol. 1, No. 1, Spring 1948. It is significant that Schorer arrives at the terms *form* and *content* by way of a descent from *beauty* and *truth*. 'Modern criticism, through its exacting scrutiny of literary texts, has demonstrated with finality that in art beauty and truth are indivisible and one,' he writes. 'The Keatsian overtones of these terms are mitigated and an old dilemma solved if for beauty we substitute form, and for truth, content. We may, without risk of loss, narrow them even more, and speak of technique and subject matter.' It is this inadmissible reduction of *truth* to *content* which is the root of Schorer's error.

Schorer's essay is selected for special commendation by Cleanth Brooks in his Foreword to the compendious collection, *Critiques and Essays in Criticism, 1920–1948*, edited by R. W. Stallman (New York, 1948), ' . . . a selection of the best critical writings of those who created, promoted, or followed in the development of the critical movement inaugurated by T. S. Eliot in *The Sacred Wood* (1920) and by I. A. Richards in *The Principles of Literary Criticism* (1924),' as the editor describes it. 'The purpose of this book,' Mr. Stallman also declares, 'is to consolidate and to make accessible the contemporary achievement in criticism.' Quoting Schorer's remarks on technique, Professor Brooks writes: 'I subscribe to all that is said here. It is an admirable summary of what modern criticism has achieved.' If that were so, one would have a serious quarrel with that amorphous entity, 'modern criticism'. But all that has in reality happened is that the academic mind has caught up with the earlier writings of Richards and Eliot and is engaged in consolidating and systematizing some of their ideas at second-hand, and with its customary bleak rigidity.

P. 32. *Heroic Ages of the Past* . . . Hemingway invites comparison with the Icelandic Sagas. Here is a characteristic passage from *The Story of Burnt Njal:*

Kol Egil's son said: 'Let me get at Kolskegg,' and turning to Kolskegg he said: 'This I have often said, that we two would be just about an even match in fight.'

'That we can soon prove,' says Kolskegg.

Kol thrust at him with his spear; Kolskegg had just slain a man and had his hands full, and so he could not throw his shield before the blow, and the thrust came upon his thigh, on the outside of the limb and went through it.

Kolskegg turned sharp round, and strode towards him, and smote him with his short sword on the thigh, and cut off his leg, and said: 'Did it touch thee or not?'

'Now,' says Kol, 'I pay for being bare of my shield.'

So he stood a while on his other leg and looked at the stump.

'Thou needest not to look at it,' said Kolskegg; ' 'tis even as thou seest, the leg is off.'

Then Kol fell down dead.

P. 33. *The Sun Also Rises*. In England, entitled *Fiesta*.

P. 38. *Transposition of emotional attitudes* . . . it must be remembered that in Italy Hemingway had been a serving soldier; in Spain he was that very different character, a war correspondent.

P. 41. *The primary emotional focal point of the novel.* . . . The strength of *For Whom the Bell Tolls* arises from the unconscious origin of its unifying symbols – exotic Spain, the filial Maria and the paternal Pablo, the war (conflict), the mountains, the bridged chasm. These identical symbols are employed by a lesser novelist, Victor Canning, in *The Chasm*, in exactly the same way. In this novel, however, it is a war-worn English architect instead of an American professor who is isolated in an Italian mountain village instead of a Spanish mountain cave, with a group of peasants; but he, too, falls intensely in love with the girl of the place, makes an enemy of his primitive rival in manhood, and, likewise in a tight corner, meets death in circumstances strikingly similar to Robert Jordan's – the breaking of a bridge across a chasm. This novel appeared in 1947, six years after Hemingway's book, but I do not suspect its author of plagiarism.

P. 52. *Sensitive and charming style.* . . . On this question of Forster's celebrated charm, I am reminded of Laura Riding's remarks concerning *A Room with a View*. 'Before reading this book I had met Mr. Forster and found him charming; the book was recommended to me by my friends as a charming book. I read it. I could not deny that it was charming. Yet it was to me unpleasantly painful to read. It was too charming. I do not mean to be flippant, or to disgust, or to alter my original conviction of Mr. Forster's personal charm. . . . But the truth is that it affected me in the same way as would the sight of a tenderly and exquisitely ripe pimple. I longed to squeeze it and have done with it.' – *Anarchism is not Enough* (1928).

P. 57. *Nature and Convention.* . . . An early story, 'The Machine Stops', is a Wellsian fantasy of the future, when the surface of the earth is derelict and mankind lives in luxurious subterranean cells 'serviced' by a perfected mechanical system. But at last the machine gradually breaks down, and two characters in revolt against its tyranny regain the earth's surface.

They wept for humanity, those two, not for themselves. They could not bear that this should be the end. Ere silence was completed their hearts were opened, and they knew what had been important on the earth. Man, the flower of all flesh, the noblest of all creatures visible, man who had once made god in his image, and had mirrored his strength on the constellations, beautiful naked man was dying, strangled in the garments that he had woven. Century after century had he toiled, and here was his reward. Truly the garment had seemed heavenly at first, shot with the colours of culture, sewn with the threads of self-denial. And heavenly it had been so long as it was a garment and no more, so long as man could shed it at will and live by the essence that is his soul, and the essence, equally divine, that is his body. The sin against the body – it was for that they wept in chief: the centuries of wrong against the muscles and the nerves, and those five portals by which we can alone apprehend – glozing it over with talk of evolution, until the body was white pap, the home of ideas as colourless, last sloshy stirrings of a spirit that had grasped the stars.

Bad writing, false feeling and loose thinking reinforce each other in this typical passage; it is, to borrow a word, sloshy. The early muddle between 'the essence that is soul' and 'the essence, equally divine, that is body' is a foreshadowing of the muddle in *Howards End* between culture and the practical life. Note the poetical bits about the stars.

P. 58. *The character of Leonard Bast.* . . . So mild a critic as Frank Swinnerton, in his *Georgian Literary Scene,* has precisely this objection to make. ' . . . I have been a clerk.' So has the present writer.

P. 87. *Sentimentality.* . . . That brilliant critic of the 'twenties, J. F. Holms, reviewing *Mrs. Dalloway* on its first appearance, in *The Calendar of Modern Letters* for July 1925, wrote that ' . . . most of the book, despite its pure and brilliant impressionism, is sentimental in conception and texture, and is accordingly æsthetically worthless. Such judgments, as is evident in this review, cannot be expressed in terms of purely literary criticism, which, indeed, is an instrument not applicable to the valuation of contemporary literature, as should be clear from experience and history.'

P. 101. *F. R. Leavis.* . . . Review of *Between the Acts* in *Scrutiny,* Vol. X, No. 3, January 1942.

P. 106. *Fullest enjoyment . . . irresponsibility of old age . . .* Quotations from *The Art of Growing Old,* 1944.

P. 107. *D. H. Lawrence.* . . . I elected to write on Margiad Evans rather than take the more obvious choice of subject, partly because I have already dealt in outline with Lawrence in a study which forms part of an earlier book of criticism.

P. 149. *A recent æsthetic sage* . . . none other than 'Palinurus', or Mr. Cyril Connolly, in *The Unquiet Grave*.

P. 155. *This final novel*. . . . Written in 1946. Since then Mr. Huxley has produced a further work, *Ape and Essence*, of which all I can say is that it abundantly confirms my analysis of his artistic decline. In this further projection of a Brave New World where a degraded human community is ruled by an 'enlightened' corps of eunuch priests enforcing an absolute repression of sexuality except at a periodic Saturnalia; where graves are desecrated and corpses systematically looted by seductive females with the words 'No, No' printed large on buttocks and breasts, and where all is in the power of a remote, inhuman, evil God whose hatred must be appeased by human sacrifice, one has an overwhelming sensation of encountering a strictly private universe. The book is a cruel self-parody.

P. 158. *Imperceptive comment on Joyce*. . . . The book is Mr. Eliot's *After Strange Gods* (1934).

P. 159. *His biographer, Herbert Gorman*. . . . In *James Joyce, a Definitive Biography* (1941).

P. 160. *Harry Levin*. . . . In *James Joyce* (1944).

P. 176. *Hamlet a parable of unbelief* . . . see my *Underground Man*.

P. 191. *The dollmaker's child*. . . . This poem, 'The Dolls', is in *Responsibilities* (1914). Afraid that her husband has heard the doll's outcry against the 'noisy and filthy thing' in the cradle, the doll-maker's wife –

> . . . murmurs into his ear,
> Head upon shoulder leant:
> 'My dear, my dear, oh dear,
> It was an accident.'

P. 196. *The quality of the affirmation*. . . . Compare with the 'Yea-saying' of Nietzsche's Zarathustra.

INDEX

AESTHETICISM, 20, 21, 71, 157, 161, 162, 191–3
After Many a Summer, 150–3, 154
Alice in Wonderland, 194
Anarchism is Not Enough, Notes
Antic Hay, 131, 133–4
Ape and Essence, Notes
Arnold, Matthew, 176
Art of Growing Old, The, Notes
Autobiography (Evans), 107–8, 123–8

BALZAC, 16
belief, 48, 73–6, 81, 82, 94, 147, 156, 174, 182–3, 186, 188
Berdyaev, 19
Bethink Yourselves, 9
Between the Acts, 96, 101–5
Bishop, John Peale, 14
Blake, 18
Brave New World, 142
Brooks, Cleanth, Notes
Buddhism, 171
Burra, Peter, 44, 45

CALENDAR *of Modern Letters, The*, Notes
Canning, Victor, Notes
Carlyle, 196
Chamber Music, 157, 161, 169
Christianity, 15, 97, 98, 106
Coleridge, 184
Connolly, Cyril, Notes
Corvo, Baron, 167
Country Dance, 107, 108–9
Creed, 115–23
Critiques and Essays in Criticism, 1920–1948, Notes
Crome Yellow, 131, 132–3, 137

DAICHES David, 73–5, 93
'Dead, The', 186
Death in the Afternoon, 28, 29
Defoe, 11
depersonalization, 19, 21, 24, 27, 31, 69, 97, 100, 104, 123, 125, 127, 130, 145, 149, 151, 155, 165, 188–91

Dickens, 11
Don Juan, 183, 197
Dos Passos, John, 39
Dostoevsky, 16
dualism, 132, 139, 141, 154
Dubliners, 160, 169, 186

EGOISM, 107, 112, 123, 149, 199
Eliot, T. S., 158, 161
Evans, Margiad, 19, 21, 106–28
Exiles, 186–8
Eyeless in Gaza, 142–8
Ezekiel, 186

FAREWELL *to Arms, A*, 23, 25, 32, 33, 40, 42
Fifth Column, The, 39
Finnegans Wake, 158, 169, 192–9
Flaubert, 30
Forster, E. M., 19, 21, 44–69, 89
For Whom the Bell Tolls, 23, 32, 36–43
Frazer, Sir J. G., 159

GORMAN, Herbert, 159, 169, 170
Gilbert, Stuart, 171–3, 178, 181, 194
Green Hills of Africa, 30, 39n.

HAMLET, 173, 174–84
hedonism, 21, 129, 131, 132, 135, 137, 142
Hemingway, Ernest, 19, 23–43, 80
Holms, J. F., Notes
Homer, 31
Howards End, 57–67, 68, 69
Hudson Review, The, Notes
Huxley, Aldous, 19, 129–55

ILIAD, *The*, 32
In Defence of Sensuality, 106
In Our Time, 24, 25

JACOB'S *Room*, 71, 79–80, 100
James, Henry, 16
James Joyce's Ulysses, 171
Jefferies, Richard, 125
Joyce, James, 19, 21, 156–99
Judas, 182–3

KEBLE, John, 162
Kierkegaard, 130, 148, 149, 174,
    176, 184
Kipling, 30

LAWRENCE, D. H., 11, 12, 21, 24,
    54, 107, 114, 141, 142
Leavis, F. R., 101
Levin, Harry, 160
Lewis, C. S., 31
liberalism, 46, 47
Longest Journey, The, 48, 50, 51-5,
    57

MACAULAY, Rose, 44
'Machine Stops, The', Notes
magic, 157-8
Marxism, 21, 40
Men Without Women, 26
Milton, 31
Moll Flanders, 11
Monday or Tuesday, 77
Mr. Bennett and Mrs. Brown, 79
Mrs. Dalloway, 71, 80-7, 88, 91,
    92, 95, 100, Notes

NEWMAN, 161-2
Nietzsche, Notes
Night and Day, 71-3, 76, 79, 81, 100
Nordic Twilight, 47

OXFORD Movement, The, 162

PANTHEISM, pancosmism, 69, 100,
    108, 123-27, 188-89, 195
Partisan Review, 39n.
Passage to India, A, 44, 45, 67-9
passion, 51, 122-3
Pater, Walter, 161-2
Perennial Philosophy, The, 130, 150
Philosophy of Solitude, A, 106
Picture of Dorian Gray, The, 157
Poe, Edgar Allen, 157
Point-Counter-Point, 140, 142
*Portrait of the Artist as a Young Man,
    A*, 160-8, 169, 192
Powys, J. C., 106, 107, 125
Powys, Llewelyn, 106
Preface to Paradise Lost, A, 31
primitivism, 23, 31, 102-5, 159
Principles of Literary Criticism, The,
    Notes

profanity, 119, 122, 164, 168, 174,
    180, 189, 198
promiscuity, 184, 186-7

RELIGION, 15, 20, 83-5, 156, 159,
    166, 198
Revelation, 186
Richards, I. A., Notes
Riding, Laura, Notes
Roman Catholicism, 156, 158,
    161-2, 163, 174, 177, 186
Room with a View, A, 48, 49, 50, 51,
    67

SACRED Wood, The, Notes
Schorer, Mark, 11, Notes
Scott, 16
Scrutiny, Notes
sensuality, 41, 104, 106-7, 141,
    143-4, 145, 187, 191
sentimentality, 53, 82, 169-70
Shakespeare, 178-9, 182
Skeleton Key to Finnegans Wake, 195
Slavery and Freedom, 91
solipsism, 181, 188, 196
solitude, 35, 39n., 107, 108, 111,
    113, 114, 124-5, 140, 147, 156,
    169, 183, 184, 199
Sons and Lovers, 11, 12
Stendhal, 16
Stephen Hero, 170
Story of Burnt Njal, The, Notes
Story of My Heart, The, 125, 127
Sun Also Rises, The, 33
Swift, 198
Swinnerton, Frank, Notes
Symons, Arthur, 161

THOSE Barren Leaves, 154-5
time, 71, 96, 97, 101-3, 143, 146,
    152, 153, 172, 181, 183
Time Must Have a Stop, 154-5
Times Literary Supplement, The, 193
To Have and Have Not, 27, 33, 39
Tolstoy, 9, 30
To the Lighthouse, 71, 87-94, 100,
    101
truth, 13, 14, 16, 17, 20, 158, Notes
Turf or Stone, 113-5, 122

ULYSSES, 134, 156, 158, 161, 169,
    170-91, 192, 194, 196, 197
Unquiet Grave, The, Notes

VIRGIL, 31
vitalism, 20, 21, 54, 57, 65, 82,
   103, 106–7, 124–28
Voyage Out, The, 71, 73, 75

WAR, 30, 32, 37–8, 47, 122
Waves, The, 96, 97, 98
What I Believe, 46, 47
Where Angels Fear to Tread, 48
whoredom, 34, 164–5, 186–7, 188
Wilde Oscar, 157

Wooden Doctor, The, 107, 109–12,
   115
Woolf, Virginia, 19, 21, 70–105
Writings of E. M. Forster, The, 44
Wuthering Heights, 107

YEARS, The, 96, 97–100, 101
Yeats, W. B., 21, 157, 191, Notes
Yellow Book, The, 161

ZARATHUSTRA, Notes

B4